Big Mouth St

Big Mouth Strikes Again

A Further Collection
of Two Fisted Journalism

Tony Parsons

André Deutsch

This paperback edition first published in 1999

First published in 1998 by André Deutsch
76 Dean Street
London
W1V 5HA
www.vci.co.uk

1 3 5 7 9 10 8 6 4 2

A catalogue record for this book is available
from the British Library

ISBN 0 233 99754 7

Typeset by Derek Doyle & Associates
Mold, Flintshire.
Printed in the UK by
Mackays of Chatham PLC, Kent.

Contents

This book is for David Morrison of Hong Kong.

One True Line:
Foreword and Acknowledgements

The mass media has never been as widespread as it is in the late nineties, and it has never been so widely despised. But perhaps the media is not quite as universally hated as we think it is – and it is certainly not as ubiquitous as it is cracked up to be.

There are still some parts of this planet that the information industry just can't reach. In the early evening on the last day of August, 1997, I arrived back in London on a flight from Beijing. It is a very strange feeling to enter a country reeling with grief when you are blissfully unaware that anything has happened.

From the Heathrow Hilton to Harrods, the flags were at half-mast. 'Well, the Queen Mother had a good innings,' I thought to myself, jet-lagged in the back of a black cab. But then I saw that people were crying in the street. It wasn't the Queen Mother who had died.

I slid back the glass panel and my cab driver filled me in. And I remember both of us choking back the tears as he told me how the Princess of Wales – which is what he called her, not 'Lady Di' or even 'Princess Diana' – had been hounded to her death by a pack of paparazzi. Like the rest of the nation, he was sad, shocked and incredibly angry. And for the first time in my life, I felt ashamed of my profession.

Later it turned out that apportioning blame was not quite so simple. The photographers who had been tailing Diana and Dodi Fayed were nowhere near their Mercedes at the time of the crash. The driver of the car was criminally rat-faced, racing at speeds that one security expert said would only be acceptable if he was trying to outrun the IRA while they were firing automatic weapons. And the only person in the car wearing a seatbelt was the bodyguard – although security experts maintained that a bodyguard was the only person who shouldn't be wearing a seatbelt.

And didn't the grieving public deserve some share of the blame? The media's interest in that star-crossed young woman was driven by the public's obsessive interest. No newspaper or magazine would ever have put Diana on their cover if her face made their sales go down.

The media may well have had blood on their hands over Diana's death. But they certainly weren't the only ones.

Yet, even when all the facts about the crash were known, the feeling persisted that the media, and especially the tabloid newspapers, were at least partly to blame for Diana's death.

When I went to Diana's funeral in Westminster Abbey, I was told by my newspaper, the *Mirror*, to be sympathetic and understanding if anyone came up to me and expressed a deep and bitter loathing for journalists. That's what was on my mind as I took my place in the congregation at Westminster Abbey – don't get into any fights.

And getting a punch in the pews wasn't an impossibility. Some meathead who looked as though he had played one too many rugby matches stared me down and only stopped his eyeballing when it became clear that the press pack was as moved by the proceedings as the guests. How could we fail to be? Republican or monarchist, beyond all the pomp and pageantry you were confronted by the heartbreaking fact of two young boys who had lost their mother.

Afterwards, as I walked through those strangely peaceable crowds in Whitehall, it occurred to me that this was the second major royal event that I had covered as a journalist.

In 1977 I was on the boat that the Sex Pistols took down the Thames on Jubilee Day and in 1997 I was in Westminster Abbey for Diana's funeral – the only hack who covered both. The world may hate my job but I still love it, not least because it is my ticket to the heart of the events that shape and reflect my nation.

The story I wrote for the *NME* about the Sex Pistols' boat trip was published in *Dispatches From The Front Line of Popular Culture*, my previous collection of journalism. The story I wrote about Diana's funeral for the *Mirror* is included in this new collection. The merits of both of those articles are for the reader to decide, but I am well aware of their faults.

On both the Pistols' boat trip and at Diana's funeral I was far too involved in what I was seeing, too much of a participant, too moved by what was going on around me. Both those pieces would have profited from at least a touch of calm, collected objectivity. But it wasn't possible.

I spent most of the Sex Pistols' boat trip sharing a gram of amphetamine sulphate with Johnny Rotten and I spent most of Diana's funeral fighting to control my emotions. At the former I had too much speed up my nose. At Westminster I had too many tears in my eyes. Both pieces would have been better if I had been a little more detached. But that's not the kind of stuff I write.

And how can you look at two young boys who have just lost their mother and not be moved? How can you share amphetamine with the spokesman of your generation and not feel a righteous anger when the police break up his party?

My stuff is all about gut reactions, expressing an opinion straight from the heart, mouthing off. And as the media deluge increases, I feel that it's the only way to go. If there's something lacking in my writing, it is the voice of reason and objectivity. But it's too late now. As Frank Sinatra once sang, 'Heavens rest us – I'm not asbestos.'

I have tried to follow Ernest Hemingway's dictum to the drowning writer – *write one true line*. For good or bad, every word in this book has been animated by that advice. And I still think that it is the best advice that any writer can be given – when you are stuck for something to say, just say something true.

Some of the things I wrote for *Arena* in the eighties look horribly cocky now (just as, in my last collection, the pieces that I wrote for the *NME* in the seventies look impossibly callow). My one and only defence is – that is how I honestly felt at the time, Your Honour.

Journalism may now be considered a venal profession, but when you don't write anything unless you can write one true line, it still feels as though it is capable of unlocking the secrets of the soul. I am grateful to this abused trade for giving me my life.

And I am also grateful to the following people, who are the brains behind the pieces collected here – Tim Rostron, Dylan Jones, Auberon Waugh, Peter Howarth, Will Ellsworth-Jones, Emma Soames, Nigel Reynolds, Jenny Tabakoff, Robert Posner, Lola Bubbosh, Max Hastings, Louise France, Michele Lavery, Ekow Eshun, Patrick Humphries, Christena Appleyard, Louise Chunn, Roger Alton, David Montgomery, Charles Wilson, Fiona Wyton, Tina Weaver, Jonathan Cooper, Mark Thomas, Brendon Parsons and the man who gave me my first job in the game, Nick Logan, publisher of *Arena, The Face*, *Arena Homme Plus* and *Frank*.

Thanks also to Mal Peachey, who got this great big beautiful ragbag of a book off the ground, and to Hannah MacDonald of André Deutsch for supporting us when we had lift-off.

My love and respect, as always, go to Caradoc King of A.P. Watt – the only agency a man will ever need.

And special thanks to Piers Morgan, who persuaded me to move from the *Daily Telegraph* to the *Mirror* with the magic words that every journalist dreams of hearing from their editor – *you can write what you like.*

I have made a career out of doing just that. The public widely – and sometimes rightly – despises the media. But I love my job too much to ever feel that way for very long.

Journalism's stock has never been lower but I have never loved it more. My job has taken me from the pews of Westminster Abbey to the knocking shops of Macau and to most places in between. I can't imagine what my life would have been like without it.

The world may hate journalists and journalism. And no doubt the world is sometimes right to do so. But as I leaf through the two decades of stories collected here, I leave you with this one true line – I know that I never will.

Tony Parsons
London 1997

Part One
Trouble with Girls

Introduction

The British media showed no interest in the murder of Gary Alderdice, but I became obsessed with his story from the moment I heard about it. Alderdice was a Hong Kong lawyer who fell in love with the highest paid prostitute in Macau, a twenty-year-old Russian called Natalia Samosalova. When she went back to her home town of Vladivostok, Gary Alderdice followed her carrying a suitcase full of money to buy her freedom. Samosalova's keepers took the money, but only after they had tortured and killed both Alderdice and the girl.

Gary Alderdice was a close friend of a close friend, but I would have been hooked by his story anyway. Not for all the obvious reasons – the sex, the romance, the exotic locations, the ex-KGB thugs who turned to pimping after the end of the Cold War; but because his life and death vividly demonstrate what a man will do for a woman he loves.

The story of Gary Alderdice was published in the Telegraph *magazine and it is included here with a selection of the columns that I wrote for* Arena, *the original magazine for men, during the ten years I spent working there. It feels like they belong together.*

The years 1987 to 1997 might well be the golden age of men's magazines. When Arena *started there was no orthodoxy, no traditions, no competition. We were in uncharted territory and there was no obligation to be any better or worse than you really were. As a writer you were free to pursue just one goal – truths about men that you could not read anywhere else.*

Like many of the men who read those articles in Arena *– and certainly the man who wrote them – Gary Alderdice was a man who dreamed of having his life transformed by love.*

7

Who Killed Gary Alderdice?

Telegraph Magazine, **12 November 1994**

Their love story could have been a remake of *Pretty Woman*.
Gary Alderdice was a good looking, successful middle-aged man
recovering from the break-up of his second marriage. Natalia
Samosalova was a beautiful young prostitute selling herself for
£500 a night. They met as client and hooker but very soon
became lovers who wanted to spend their lives together. The
only thing that stopped this true romance having a happy ending
was the character who was missing from the Richard Gere–Julia
Roberts film – namely, the girl's pimp. And it was this man – or
these men – who ensured that a love story that began in a Macau
nightclub ended with a double murder in a seedy flat in
Vladivostok.

Gary Alderdice, a 49-year-old Queen's Counsel, was one of
the most popular members of Hong Kong's legal community.
He was a warm, outgoing New Zealander whose passion for
tennis and golf kept him fit, despite the proximity of his fiftieth
birthday. In the often bitchy hothouse of Hong Kong's social
scene, Gary Alderdice was genuinely liked. The most negative
thing anybody in Hong Kong has to say about Alderdice is that,
according to another Hong Kong barrister, he had, 'sixty
seconds of charm for everyone he met. It would be – *hello,
mate, how you doing? Everything all right? Great!* And then
on to the next person. But that was just his way. I never knew
anyone with more friends than Gary.'

Alderdice was a gambler. Not a serious gambler, at least not
by Hong Kong's exacting standards, but he liked to bet and there
were as many racehorse owners, jockeys and trainers among his
friends as barristers and lawyers. But the only legal gambling in

Hong Kong is horseracing. In Macau, the Portuguese territory sixty kilometres west of Hong Kong, you can bet on almost anything. It was in the gambling resort that Alderdice met Natalia Samosalova, a blonde Russian escort who at twenty was five years younger than his oldest son.

Macau – which reverts to China in 1999, two years after Hong Kong – is only a couple of hours by jetfoil from Hong Kong but it feels like another world. This peninsula of the Chinese mainland is Hong Kong's weekend playground, where the stressed suits from Central, HK's business district, can come to unwind on the golf course and in the nightclubs after the pressures of their long working week.

In some of Macau's watering holes you will see hostesses, that peculiarly South-East Asian phenomenon of young women who will join your party for some conversation and a rather expensive drink, at the very least.

These hostesses operate in the gloaming between escort and whore. To take one of them off the premises, a man must pay her employers a 'bar fine' and then another fee to the girl for services rendered. As you would expect, most of the hostesses in Macau are Asian. But in a nightclub at the top of a plush hotel on Avenida da Amizade, some of them are Russians (and apparently all of the Russians are blonde, either by birth or bottle).

Natalia Samosalova had been working at the nightclub – a huge tacky cavern of a place, awash with chrome, mirrors and swirling lights – for six months when Gary Alderdice walked into her life last April. By May they were living together at Macau's most exclusive hotel. And at the end of June they died violently at the hands of Russian gangsters in a drab flat in Natalia's home town of Vladivostok, the lawless Russian port on the Sea of Japan.

The great irony of their love match is that Gary Alderdice was never one of those Hong Kong expatriates who dream of finding their very own Suzie Wong. The tart with a heart that fills the fantasies of many western men in Asia was never for him. Alderdice was never immersed in the hostess culture of the Far East, never one of the suits from Central who go looking for fun in Wanchai, the tenderloin area originally built to separate sailors from their money and now largely frequented by white-collar expats (at £30 for a girl's tequila, few sailors can afford 'the Wanch') who can pay a bar fine and take home a Filipina bar girl, like some sexual takeaway. Alderdice was never one of them.

'Gary was never into the bamboo,' says a Hong Kong barrister who knew him well. 'Gary liked blondes.'

He met his blonde of blondes April 1994. Among the hostesses of Macau, Natalia Samosalova stood out. She was very tall, very young and very beautiful. If she had been born in the West rather than in the town that is known as the capital of the Wild East, she would probably have been a model rather than a hooker. Men who saw her once have never forgotten her.

Her Russian passport showed that her trip to Macau was the first time Samosalova had ever been outside Russia. She arrived in August 1993, her application to be a dancer handled by an employment agency called the Society of Support to the Enterprises of Macau. She was issued with a Macau identity card and a six-month work visa. In March of this year the nightclub where she was working asked that she be given a six-month extension to her visa. She was at the start of her second six-month contract in Macau when she met Alderdice.

'A second contract is almost unheard of for one of these girls,' says one Hong Kong expatriate. 'But she had just started her second tour of duty when she met Gary. She was making a lot of money for them.'

She was not making her money by dancing. Reports suggest that by the time she met Alderdice, Samosalova was the highest paid whore in Macau. Gary Alderdice died – and Samosalova died with him – because he wanted to take her away from that life.

What makes their story remarkable is that Gary Alderdice was far from a naive man. He had spent a career around criminals – defending them and prosecuting them – and he had spent most of his adult life in the Far East.

Alderdice had been in Hong Kong for twenty years when he met Samosalova. After obtaining his degree in law from the University of Victoria, New Zealand, in 1968, he came to Hong Kong in 1973 and joined the Prosecutions Section of the Attorney General's Chambers. The legal journal, *Hong Kong Lawyer*, described him as 'a fair-minded, frank and reasonable prosecutor . . . always alive to the possibility of injecting humour into the tedium of court proceedings'.

Alderdice entered private practice in 1984 and his appointment to Silk in 1993 was, said the *Hong Kong Lawyer*, 'regarded by members of the Bar and solicitors alike as an appropriate recognition of his talent'.

But after a glittering career practising criminal law, by the start of this year Gary Alderdice was at a crisis point. He was coming up to fifty, he was tired of the relentless pressure of a legal career in Hong Kong and his second marriage was coming apart in dramatic fashion.

The *South China Morning Post* reported that in January 1994 Alderdice was treated for several wounds following an argument with his second wife, Pippa, at their home at 72 Chung Hom Kok, near Stanley on the south coast of Hong Kong (they married in 1986 after Alderdice divorced his first wife Christine, with whom he had four sons). Alderdice was admitted to Hong Kong's Adventist Hospital on 25 January, bleeding from a knife wound to his chest. He was released the next day but came back for more treatment on 31 January. The marriage, Alderdice's second, was over. Pippa Alderdice left for New Zealand.

When the *South China Morning Post*, Hong Kong's leading English language newspaper, made enquiries about the incident they received a call from Alderdice threatening a legal injunction to prevent publication.

'Two people know exactly what happened,' he said. 'One's in [another country] and the other one's me. I expect you realize that every time a story is told, it changes.'

After the break-up of his marriage, Alderdice was finding Hong Kong increasingly claustrophobic. The close-knit expatriate community can seem like a small town where everyone knows everybody else's business. He said he was tired of people asking him how he was and if they could help, and also disappointed that people he had felt close to had not stuck by him during the painful separation from his wife. He fled to Macau.

It is not difficult to understand what Gary Alderdice and Natalia Samosalova saw in each other. She offered the ageing, disillusioned QC a chance to reaffirm his virility. He offered the spectacular young call-girl respectability. They were both desperate to transform their life, both desperate for escape and perhaps both desperate for affection, even love. They had both had precious little of it in recent years. In many ways they were a perfect match.

Shortly after she met Alderdice, Samosalova stopped seeing other clients and began seeing Gary exclusively. It seems he kept paying her, although it is not known if she passed this money on to her employers. Certainly she very quickly stopped considering her relationship with Alderdice to be professional.

They moved into the most luxurious hotel in Macau – The Westin Resort on Coloane island, a secluded, exclusive resort built in classic Portuguese style. The adjacent Macau Golf & Country Club, with its endless palm-fringed greens rolling to the horizon under a cloudless blue sky, looks like a vision of the hills of heaven. You could see how a man could fall in love here. Or a woman.

Samosalova was never registered at the hotel but stayed with Alderdice in Room 705 for more than a month. And although some of Alderdice's closest friends in Hong Kong did not know of Natalia's existence, other associates knew about her because they saw the pair frolicking in the Westin's swimming pool. Alderdice did not tell his closest friends in Hong Kong about her, but he made no attempt to keep their relationship a secret in Macau. Indeed, Gary Alderdice seemed proud to introduce the young woman whose company he had bought.

And Natalia Samosalova was the kind of woman you noticed. The ornate lobby of the Westin is a vast area. It is quite a walk from the front doors to the lift. But one Hong Kong barrister remembers an attendant holding a lift for Samosalova as the statuesque blonde entered the Westin and crossed the lobby. She didn't hurry. She didn't have to. The same man was later introduced to Natalia at the hotel's swimming pool.

'I saw the girl – tall, blonde, absolutely stunning – before I saw Gary. At first I thought it was Rod Stewart. I really did. His hair was much longer than it was in Hong Kong and very fair from the sun. He was trying to look twenty years younger than he was and, I have to say, doing a pretty good job. He looked very happy. Like a man who was having the best sex of his life.'

Alderdice introduced the girl as 'Natasha'. This was his own name for Natalia. It was as if he had made her into someone else, someone different from the hostess he met in a nightclub, as if she was now a woman known only to him.

Alderdice was tanned and fit after a month of tennis, swimming and spending time in the pool with 'Natasha'. They drove around Macau in a rented jeep and, after the traumas of the messy separation from his wife, it must have seemed an idyllic existence. Gary told someone at the hotel that he was reluctant to go back to the pressures of his old life in Hong Kong.

'He didn't want to work any more, or at least not for a while. He said he was not looking forward to going back to Hong Kong because he didn't feel that he was cut out any longer to be a courtroom stiff in a pin-striped suit.'

And it wasn't only Gary Alderdice who was planning a change of career. 'There's no doubt in my mind he had told her she wouldn't have to be a whore any more,' says a lawyer who saw them together at the Westin.

Although he was not boasting about Natalia to his closest friends in Hong Kong – he told them only that he had met 'some nice girls' – in Macau Alderdice, with all the pride of a middle-aged man whose faith in his potency had been fully restored, was delighted to show her off in public.

Alderdice and Natalia regularly dined at Fernando's, a restaurant on Hac Sa Beach just across the bay from the Westin. There are those in Hong Kong who feel it was extremely unwise for Alderdice to parade his young love at Fernando's, which is one of the most fashionable restaurants on a small island, and where they were very likely to be seen by Natalia's former employers.

'He rubbed their noses in it,' says someone who knew and liked Alderdice in Hong Kong. 'You can't take one of their girls and say – darling, you don't have to do this any more. And if you *do*, you certainly don't parade her up and down. But that's exactly what Gary did.'

Natalia was just one of the many Russian women who come into Macau employed as 'public relations officers', 'dancers' or 'hostesses'. Their numbers are estimated at between fifty to two hundred – certainly you don't have to look far to see them, although they are not as prominent as they were when Gary met Natalia. Most of these young women are from Vladivostok (Moscow comes second by some distance). Their employment is arranged through a syndicate in Vladivostok and they are issued six-month employment visas by the Macau authorities. Most of the money they make – by knocking back overpriced drinks, by incurring bar fines and by sleeping with clients – goes to Chinese nightclub owners and Russian middle-men. But the girls still make a fortune compared to what they would earn if they stayed in Vladivostok. When they return to Vladivostok they employ bodyguards to accompany them, hired muscle to ride shotgun with them and their hard-earned money. But by May of this year, Natalia Samosalova had retired.

When it became clear that their star hostess considered herself to be Gary Alderdice's woman, the nightclub where she had worked terminated her contract and successfully applied to the Macau immigration authorities for her identity card and work permit to be revoked. Without a visa, Natalia had no choice but to leave Macau. With no chance of being allowed past the immigration authorities of Hong Kong (who are extremely unwelcoming to the Russian hostesses who flock to Macau – the women are forced to fly to Canton and make the journey to Macau overland through China), Natalia returned to Vladivostok.

But even if Natalia's visa had not been revoked, it is likely that her Arcadian life at the Westin with Gary Alderdice would have soon been over anyway. Alderdice – twice divorced, inveterate gambler and now a reluctant QC – had money troubles and was reportedly worried how he was going to pay his bill for a month's stay at the Westin. He returned to Hong Kong and a furious burst of work.

But the affair wasn't over. In late June Gary Alderdice followed Natalia to Russia, travelling to Vladivostok from Bangkok via Seoul. He paid in advance for accommodation in Vladivostok so that he could be issued with a visa but told the travel agent who booked the tickets that he would be staying with his girlfriend. His closest friends knew nothing of the trip.

What was he thinking of? There are those in Hong Kong who will tell you that the visit was prompted by pure lust but it seems likely that it was far more than that. When Alderdice arrived in Vladivostok he declared to customs officials that he was carrying US$150,000 in cash. And although Alderdice told at least one friend that he planned to leave the legal profession before Hong Kong's 1997 handover to China and invest in the fast-food

14

industry in Russia, it seems certain that he planned to use the money to buy Samosalova out of her employment. All the evidence indicates that by now Alderdice was very much in love with Samosalova. It seems that he was planning to build a life with his Natasha.

There is some dispute about the money Alderdice took to Vladivostok. 'I am not sure that Gary could have organized that amount in cash,' says one Hong Kong sceptic. Close friends of Alderdice have suggested that he was not in possession of such large sums of money. Gary Plowman, QC, Alderdice's best friend and another New Zealander, told a Hong Kong newspaper that he doubts that Alderdice would have carried that sum of money in cash.

'But it was not unusual for him to have large amounts of cash available in his accounts because he didn't invest in shares or property, he kept all his money in cash,' said Plowman. What is impossible to imagine is why Alderdice would declare US$150,000 if he didn't have it – especially as he was entering somewhere as potentially dangerous as Vladivostok.

The remote port was a closed city for fifty years. After the collapse of communism it opened up in 1992 and has since become a hotbed of organized – and unorganized – crime. A boom in trade and investment has been matched by a boom in murder, kidnappings and bombings.

Vladivostok is a major exporter of prostitutes. Since the city opened up, local girls have appeared in China, Turkey, Korea and Macau. It is a city awash with guns, and Dmitri Banov, a Vladivostok journalist, says several foreign businessmen have been killed in robberies. Gary Alderdice, who had spent a lifetime practising criminal law, did not realize how far he was from Hong Kong.

'Gary underestimated these Russian gangsters,' says one Hong Kong barrister. 'He had spent a lot of time around criminals and he thought he knew them. But he overestimated his own powers of negotiation. And – although he was a good barrister – he always did.'

Soon after arriving in Vladivostok, Alderdice checked out of his hotel and moved into Samosalova's dreary one-bedroom flat in the depressing First of May district. Sometime during the evening of 23 June, Samosalova let a man or men into her apartment. In the small hours of 24 June, neighbours complained of hearing strange noises coming from the flat, 'like people chopping wood'.

When police forced their way into the flat they found Alderdice's dead body in the hallway. He had been stripped naked and shot through the eye while sitting in an armchair. Samosalova was dead in the living room, her hands bound in front of her. She had been tied to a chair, tortured for several hours and then shot in the back of the head. A pillow had been used to muffle the gunshots, which had come from a Magnum .45 handgun. The money that Alderdice had declared at customs was gone.

News of Gary Alderdice's death sent shock waves through Hong Kong. With his friends and associates in every corner of Hong Kong society, from the legal profession to the horse-racing community, from Central to Victoria Peak to Happy Valley, it is not too much to suggest that Gary Alderdice was the most popular man in Hong Kong. And now he was dead, killed by gangsters because of an *amour fou* for a prostitute. Hong Kong – not a place that is easily shocked – was stunned beyond belief.

Alderdice's body was identified by Michael Lunn, head of his legal chambers in Hong Kong. 'Gary was the sort of man who could walk down Queens Road to court and he would be stopped by half a dozen people,' remembered Lunn. 'Maybe a jockey friend, a solicitor, a fellow tennis player or someone he had met playing golf.'

Sir Ti Liang-Yang, the Hong Kong Chief Justice, phoned Michael Lunn hours after Alderdice's death to express his sadness and to praise Gary's ability as a lawyer. But while Hong Kong grieved for Gary Alderdice, some said that his death was inevitable as soon as he bought a ticket to Vladivostok.

'The girl was boasting too much about her rich boyfriend,' says one Hong Kong lawyer. 'And loose lips sink ships. Especially out there.'

'Vladivostok is a very tough town,' says another. 'People get killed for far less money than Gary apparently had with him. But of course if it was merely a robbery, there was no need for that degree of violence.'

'I can just see him talking to them,' says a New Zealander who knew Alderdice well. ' *"She's beautiful, isn't she? She's beautiful!"* He would have believed he could reason with them.'

In the bars of Hong Kong, it is said that Natalia was sleeping with her Russian pimps in Vladivostok, even when Gary Alderdice was planning their future together. But a romantic, just off the flight from London, might speculate that trouble arose because she would no longer sleep with them.

'Let's not forget that she was a prostitute,' says one veteran of a thousand Wanchai nights. 'We have a saying out here – *you can take the girl out of the bar but you can't take the bar out of the girl.*'

'He didn't take the danger seriously enough,' says another Hong Kong associate. 'But that was one of the wonderful things about Gary. He didn't take anything too seriously.'

Why did Gary Alderdice have to die? Because Samosalova had a jealous lover? Because it was deemed necessary to send a message to the Russian girls still working in Macau – and possibly their clients? Because the pride of some sawdust psychopath was affronted by the breezy confidence of a man who was convinced he could live happily ever after with the Russian mob's most beautiful whore? Although to Gary Alderdice, Natalia Samosalova was no longer a whore. She was his Natasha.

At the start of July Gary Alderdice's body was flown to Wellington, New Zealand, where his ex-wives and three of his sons are living. But it is in his adopted home of Hong Kong where he is mourned most deeply.

On 30 August a memorial service was held at St John's Cathedral in Central, a symbol of colonial rule for nearly 150 years. Through doors made of wood from HMS *Tamar*, they came in their hundreds to remember Gary Alderdice.

'You can close your eyes and pray he'll come back, or you can open your eyes and see all he's left you,' said Gary Plowman in his address. 'Your heart can be empty because you can't see him, or you can be full of the love we've shared.'

The killers of Gary Alderdice and Natalia Samosalova remain free. And it is likely they will remain free. The two men suspected of the crime, both of them ex-KGB thugs with close links to prostitution in Macau, were questioned but released without charge. The Russian police have not asked the Macau authorities for any assistance with the case. Although bitterly missed in Hong Kong, Gary Alderdice is already just another statistic in Vladivostok.

The nightclub where Gary Alderdice first met Natalia Samosalova is quiet now. If you go there late on a Friday night you are likely to find it spectacularly empty. But it is still running and, if you ask politely, you can still get a Russian hostess to share a drink. The one I met at the end of the summer was a hard-eyed, busty young blonde whose previous employment was on an industrial estate at Inchon, Korea. There were two scars by the side of her mouth. She didn't look much like Gary Alderdice's Natasha. But then of course few women do.

Nobody really knows who killed Gary Alderdice. But what seems certain is that he died for love.

Platonic Love

Arena, **December/January 1995/6**

Nothing is quite as potent as a relationship that is never consummated. To love pure and chaste from afar – cynics will tell you that it just doesn't happen, that those feelings cannot be. But many men have a secret love, a passion they keep hidden from the world, a torch they carry with them down all the days. And platonic love never sets you free.

'*When I get what I want, I never want it again,*' sings Courtney Love. Naturally you know the feeling – what makes the Seattle widow one hell of a woman is that she thinks just like a man – but the flipside is that when you don't get what you want, then you want it for a lifetime.

But platonic love is more than just fancying someone that you never had the chance to knob. Platonic love is infinitely more than frustrated desire. It is the girl that got away. It is the baby that will never be born, the opportunity for salvation that will never be taken, the final chance for happiness that is missed – and missed forever.

Fantasists, dreamers, romantics of every hue – platonic love is made for them. Because platonic love can never be tarnished by habit, boredom or betrayal. A love that is never fulfilled is never tested in the real world. It does not wither and die with time. And so it grows stronger, deeper and ever more obsessional.

This kind of love can get out of control. For years you are locked into a courtship that never makes it to the altar – or even the bedroom. Platonic love is almost ludicrously romantic. A mid-afternoon cup of coffee in a sun-dappled café, an intense thirty minutes stolen between work and home, becomes an epiphany you will remember forever. Holding hands with your platonic love is more exciting than any blow-job. This is how you know that it is real. Platonic love grazes everything with magic.

Women are more pragmatic than us. Above the age of about thirteen, they will not spend too long mooning around after the unattainable. But there is a secret corner of every man's heart that keeps one woman separate from the rest. We are driven to find a love that we can never spoil.

Platonic love should not be derided too easily. The love that remains constant in a changing world is to be cherished – even if it is never given a road test. Platonic love is the real thing.

The hard of heart don't believe in it because they think that romance cannot exist in a vacuum. They think that real love cannot live without the exchange of bodily fluids, joint bank accounts, boring dinner parties and all the rest. But in a world where it is possible to sleep with someone without knowing their name, then it is surely possible to love someone without sleeping with them.

And, of course, you do sleep with them, if only in your dreams. Platonic love has a sexual charge that will never be diluted by the years. And if sexual technique is largely concerned with delaying the moment of release, then platonic love is when that moment is delayed for a lifetime.

It brings out the best in you. Platonic love puts you back in touch with yourself. It is true that your secret love never sees your dark side. You can't betray a platonic love, you can't leave the top off her toothpaste. But it would be wrong to say she doesn't know you simply because she only sees your good side. She knows what you were like before you were hardened by all the goodbyes, by all the messy endings. She knows you better than anyone.

Some argue that platonic love is the last refuge of the emotionally stunted, the ones who screwed too many of the wrong women and screwed over too many of the right women. Maybe. Except that there has to be something righteous in loving someone – truly loving someone – and asking for nothing in return.

Platonic love can be a great comfort in your darkest hours – to know that she is out there, that she lives and breathes, makes this world a better place. But it is also a relationship of sweet sorrow, of almost unbearable pathos. What if? *What if?* Could it

20

ever work? Would it be like all the rest? You will never know. But still you dream the impossible dream.

Because she always knows. You can't make your heart a hostage to someone who doesn't feel the same way. Fate, circumstance and quite probably her husband all conspire to keep you apart – but she knows how you feel and she feels the same way. Platonic love is requited love.

Don't feel bad about a love that lives only in your dreams. Don't feel ridiculous. You are not some lovesick teenager waiting for the telephone to ring. You know it is hopeless. You understand it can never be. But you continue to believe, you continue to want the best for her. You don't stop caring even when you know that there is nothing in it for you. And that's what makes platonic love feel like the greatest love of all.

How Many Women Have You Slept With?

***Arena*, May 1996**

'Come on then,' she smirked. 'How many women have you slept with?'

And he had to bite his tongue to prevent himself from coming on all Basil Fawlty. Oh, I don't know, what's normal? Because it's a very delicate subject. Perhaps the most delicate of all.

Women think size matters to us. They think this is the great issue. What very few of them realize – and what we never let on – is that numbers matter even more.

We are not talking about how your sex drive registers on the Richter scale. We are not talking about the quality of your private life. No, we are talking about the number of partners you have had. As simple – and crucial – as that.

When asked if he had any regrets in his long life, Sir John Betjeman replied, 'I wish I had had more sex.' More sex? Or more lovers? Far be it from me to put words into a dead poet's mouth, but every man in the world will know that what Betjeman really meant was: *I wish I had had more partners. As I stand on the edge of the abyss, gazing down into eternity – I wish I had put it about a bit more.*

How do we measure our relationships with women? By the number of times we have known true love? By the diversity of our experience – to have known both love and loss and all the tumult of emotions in between? No, it all comes down to *how many have you had?* Like perpetual adolescents, we care about quantity, not quality. For all our trappings of maturity, the company cars, credit cards and mortgage payments, we are still overgrown schoolboys obsessively counting the notches on our water pistols.

Tom Hanks has only slept with a handful of women – indeed, old Tom probably has more Oscars than former lovers. Peter Stringfellow, on the other hand, counts the number of women that have frolicked in his Jacuzzi in the thousands. Now there is little doubt that Stringfellow is the greatest living Englishman, but do we really believe he has had a happier and more fulfilled sex life than Tom Hanks? Do we really believe that? Yes, we do, because he's knobbed them by the thousand, the jammy old git.

But of course you don't dump a woman you love, a woman who keeps you fulfilled, a woman who feels like the other half of your soul. You stay with that woman, you hold on to her for dear life. It is only the cold, unsatisfactory sexual encounters that you are so quick to forget. So in that case, isn't it possible that Tom Hanks has had a fantastic sex life, full of deep, meaningful unions with a few choice women that he was mad about? While Peter Stringfellow has bounced from water bed to water bed simply because he has not known true happiness? Yes, it's possible. But whose memories would you rather have?

And it is not absurd to care about numbers. It's not morally wrong to desire a healthy number of partners. Numbers do matter, because how do you know how much you should appreciate what you've got unless you have lived, laughed and cried?

There is something a bit suspicious about the man who has only Biblically known a handful of women. What's wrong with him? Doesn't he like women? Chances are, of course, he likes them considerably more than the congenital knob merchant, because he has seen women at their best. To work your way through a sizeable number of females, you have to see women at their worst. The drunk and the stoned, the numb and the indifferent – all those girls who kiss on the first date. And nothing rubs the romance out of a man's heart like too much meaningless sex.

Most of us play a number of roles in the course of a lifetime. Most of us go through promiscuous stages and then go for – oh, *years* with only one woman. But while we all know the shiver of fear in John Betjeman's soul – my life will soon be over and I have lived so little – most of us would agree that periods of promiscuity very rarely coincide with periods of intense happiness. We know what we want – an endless variety of partners, the whole world a whorehouse. We also know that's not what makes us happy.

And yet we can't help but envy the great sack artists. Even if we know that numbers lose their meaning after a while, that there comes a point where you can't remember faces or bodies, let alone names. It is the knob merchants we envy, not the devoted husbands at home with their true loves. Is this the life impulse? A rage to keep the species alive? Or something more cynical, grubby and full of fear?

So, how many have *you* had? Ultimately it is a question that no man can truly answer. Because only boys know the answer to that one. Only the lads. A real man would have lost count years ago.

'How many?' she said, pressing him.

'Somewhere between thirty and forty,' he said.

'Practically a virgin,' she sneered.

And the awful thing was, he sort of agreed with her.

Sex with Madonna

Daily Telegraph, **17 October 1992**

She can't sing, she can't act, she can dance a little. But what has made Madonna the most famous woman in the world is her unerring talent for whipping up scandal. She is a Picasso of self-promotion, an Einstein of media hype. Madonna doesn't read her press clippings. She weighs them.

Currently she is all over the newspapers with her book, *Sex,* a work of celebrity pornography in which she acts out her sexual fantasies. *Sex* is published around the time that *Erotica,* her new CD, will appear in the record stores. Other celebrities promote their forthcoming records by writing their autobiography or making a video. Madonna gets her kit off and grapples with knife-wielding skinhead lesbians. For though *Sex* features Madonna baring her all in the soft porn pictures which have already appeared in parts of the national press, there is also sodomy, gang rape, gay sex, sado-masochism and group sex. All human perversion is here. Well, it would be wouldn't it?

Madonna's ruthless self-promotion would be harmless enough if she wasn't one of the world's biggest pop stars, if her constituency wasn't made up of young, inexperienced people who will perceive the ugly images in her book as some viable form of sexuality.

Sex is adult fare aimed at children. It is unlikely that someone would buy Madonna's celebrity porn if they did not buy her records. And the people who buy her records are kids. We are told that the book's £25 price tag will deter young buyers but why should it? That is no more than the price of a concert ticket.

Like many sleaze-mongers, Madonna is not quite as outrageous as she would like to be. The British serial rights were on offer for bids in excess of £100,000 but it was left to the *Observer* to pick them up for a mere £15,000. Still, there is no denying that *Sex* has served its purpose. Madonna is a very sacred cow. Even the staid ninnies at Radio One, those proscribers of such harmless pop songs as 'Relax' by Frankie Goes To Hollywood saw fit to declare Wednesday 'Madonna Day' and to bow down before the altar of her tacky fame.

She gets away with murder because those of us in our thirties and forties – men and women in positions of power – are the product of very liberated times. We came of age in an era when it was fashionable to believe that any form of censorship was wrong. We grew up believing artistic expression must not be restrained. But this unthinking acceptance of anything a cynical superstar dishes up is a tolerance that verges on madness.

Thirty years ago Mr Griffith-Jones QC asked – would you like your servants to read *Lady Chatterley's Lover*? The question was laughed out of court and an age of tolerance was ushered in. But now, after three decades of taboos being broken, we are afraid to even ask the question – would you want your children to see Madonna's *Sex*?

It seems self-evident to me that the answer is a resounding no – but the question is not voiced because any kind of censorship, even on the most personal level, is considered bad form. Madonna exploits this for all it's worth. She is a betrayer of the true libertarian values of the sixties and seventies. This woman gives tolerance a bad name.

Madonna's book finds her trotting out the line, 'Safe sex saves lives'. It is a depraved world where the condom has the power of life and death.

But I really don't want my twelve-year-old son to think that it is perfectly safe for him to engage in whatever sexual activity takes his fancy as long as he is wearing a prophylactic. I don't want him to believe that because it's not true. I would like him to be aware that condoms can break, slip, burst and generally let you down; that a one-night stand can kill you.

In the latest edition of US *Vogue*, Madonna says that women should not sleep with their boyfriends 'for the first five dates'. But she doesn't answer the questions posed by *Sex*. She neglects to tell us how many dates I should go on before allowing a lesbian skinhead to hold a knife under my crotch, or how well I should get to know someone before we do it in the middle of a busy highway.

The idea of Madonna being in a position to give anyone advice about sexual mores is ludicrous. It is like asking Dylan Thomas for advice about sensible drinking habits, or polling Keith Richards for his views on acceptable levels of drug abuse. But of course Madonna is in a postion to give such advice – because there are large numbers of young people who are willing to listen to her. And what message do they receive?

There is every kind of sexuality in *Sex* except the kind that most of us would regard as 'normal'. It is a sleazy – and violent – vision of adult sexuality. Love is nowhere to be seen. Any kind of affection or tenderness is surplus to requirements. Perhaps that is not surprising from a woman who, according to her biographer, Christopher Andersen, introduced herself to her boyfriend Tiny Ward by stubbing out a Marlboro Lite on his bare back. This is a role model from hell.

But Madonna is unconcerned about her effect on her audience. She has an undisguised contempt for her fans. 'Let's face it,' she said about some teenagers waiting for a glimpse of their heroine outside her home, 'they are not very bright.'

If they are not very bright, then that is probably because most of them are exceptionally young. If they are not very bright then that is probably because they do not yet have any real experience of the world. And if all they know are Madonna's words of wisdom, then God help them.

Sex contends that being tied up by a partner is an act of love – 'Like when you were a baby, your mother strapped you to your car seat.' There is another point of view, that bondage is a jaundiced sexuality's attempt to revive some very jaded taste buds. But you would never know it from *Sex*.

Madonna is the worst kind of hypocrite. She champions safe sex, Aids awareness and tolerance for minorities but the cause she cares most about is her beautiful career. She has made a little talent go a very long way because we are all so afraid of looking like old-fashioned, fuddy-duddy puritans.

In a world were nothing is taboo, the amoral slut is queen.

Camille Paglia

Literary Review, **March 1995**

Camille Paglia has reinvented feminist rhetoric by talking like a saloon-bar lech. 'As I say about girls wearing Madonna's harlot outfits,' she leers, 'if you advertise, you better be ready to sell!'

Know what you mean, know what you mean! But surely women have a right to all the freedoms accorded to men? Surely women should be able to act as they please without being treated like sex objects? Not according to Paglia.

'Going straight to a stranger's apartment on the first date', avers Paglia, 'should be correctly interpreted as a consent to sex.'

Say no more, Squire. Paglia has successfully portrayed herself as a new kind of woman by talking exactly like an old-fashioned kind of guy. 'Penis fits vagina,' she points out. 'No linguistic game playing can change that biologic fact.'

All this would be easy to dismiss as merely the soundbites of a controversialist who has made a lucrative career out of baiting the feminist orthodoxy. But while there is no denying that Paglia is the Stephen Hawking of self-advertising, her ravings usually carry the ring of truth. Because ultimately her message is that men and women are equal but different. In feminist terms, this is, of course, nothing short of heresy.

Sometimes she takes it too far. She is willing to defend every crotch-scratching, beer-monster builder who whistles at passing women. 'Men's guttural lunges are primal mating rituals, a crude homage,' she cries. But then Paglia's talent for excess is part of her considerable appeal. She puts her unique perspective down to her own sapphic tendencies: 'Because of my history of wavering gender and sexual orientation, I feel I have a special insight into these matters: I see with the eyes of a rapist.'

Women, Paglia maintains, do not need to subscribe to the victim culture of feminism because they already have more power over men than they could ever imagine. The way Paglia tells it, there is a missing piece in contemporary feminism's jigsaw and it is the vamp: 'the prostitute, seductress and high-glamour movie star wield woman's ancient vampiric power over men.'

Paglia's respect for the power of women means that she has a deep sympathy for the weakness of male flesh. And like the building-site workers she so closely identifies with, Paglia confesses that her sex life has not been all she would have liked. 'Cock teasing is a universal reality,' she sighs. 'What's a guy to do?'

Paglia is a true radical and the aspirations of feminism – jobs for the girls, a crèche in the office, hubby doing his share of the chores – do not figure in her dreams: 'Getting women out of the kitchen and into the office, we have simply put them into another bourgeois prison.'

Then what *does* she want? A return to basics – pagan basics, that is: 'We must reclaim the Whore of Babylon, the nature goddess of that complex city of arrogant male towers and hanging female gardens.'

Come again?

'I want to put the bomp back into bomp-de-bomp,' says Paglia, who never really recovered from that shining vision of freedom she glimpsed – along with the rest of the Woodstock nation – in the sixties.

Like *Sex, Art and American Culture*, the book that made Paglia the Boadicea of American academe, *Vamps and Tramps* is another spicy gumbo of post-feminist rants and reflections on lifestyles of the rich and famous. It is all hugely entertaining, but more than this, time and again you are reminded of Paglia's brash common sense, the reason why she was an agony aunt of genius for *Spy* magazine: 'What feminists call patriarchy is simply civilisation . . . the role of mother has been devalued . . . serial rape-murderers deserve to be executed . . . the date-rape and sexual harassment crisis claimed by white middle-class women is caused partly by their own mixed signals.'

Like *Sex, Art and American Culture*, a huge chunk of Paglia's new book is an advertisement for herself. There are fifty pages of quotes about Paglia, cartoons about Paglia, reprinted interviews and a recommended reading list. Sometimes it reads like a press release from hell.

Yet for all her little faults, Paglia is by far the most provocative, interesting and charismatic feminist fatale since Germaine Greer. She needs to restrain her appetite for self-promotion because at times it makes her unbearable. And she needs an editor who has the courage to tell her what should go into a collection of essays and what should be stuck in her scrapbook.

But most of all, as Camille Paglia seems to suggest on almost every page of *Vamps and Tramps*, what she really needs is a good shagging.

Howling Shame

Arena, **July/August 1995**

This summer marks the fifth anniversary of one of the bleakest events in the evolution of the modern male – the night in Italia '90 that Paul Gascoigne tackled a German player, got booked and promptly burst into tears. Gazza started a snivelling flood that has hardly stopped.

What was appalling about Gascoigne's blubbing is not that it made his great florid slab of a face look uglier than usual (as we know from every girl we ever went out with, crying does little for your looks). What was truly awful about the fat oik's tears is that they were purely tears of self-pity. Gazza didn't cry because England were on their way out of the World Cup – we weren't at that stage. He cried because if we made it to the final, his big Geordie rump would be parked on the substitutes' bench.

No matter. Gascoigne's tears made him the most famous footballer since George Best. Why? Because the nation mistook self-pity for passion. And also – after thirty years of feminist rhetoric about women *feeling* more deeply than us, the sensitive lambs – the world was ready for a lachrymose lad.

Now everyone is doing it. Chris Evans, the ginger jessy, bawls at the Bafta. Tom Hanks gets overwrought at the Oscars (every year). Paul Merson cries when he confesses to various appetites that would be more suited to a member of Guns 'N' Roses. And it always goes down very well. Crying is now considered appropriate for any occasion! Ten years ago a crying man would have been an object of scorn and derision. But now weeping reveals sensitivity, humanity and a man who is so in touch with his feelings that it hurts. Everyone likes it so much they pretend not to notice the snot on your chin.

But these big babies cry for *all the wrong reasons*. Do they shed a manly tear because there are crippled children in the world? Do they weep because of man's infinite cruelty to his fellow man? No – they cry because they did something naughty and now they have to pay for it (Merson, Gascoigne). Most sickening of all, they cry because they win some showbiz bauble (Hanks, Evans). Boys are taught not to cry when they lose. But nobody ever told us not to cry when we win. True, Bobby Charlton cried when England won the World Cup in 1966 but he was a special case because he had survived the Munich air disaster. Naturally he was an emotional guy. I don't think we would have liked it if Nobby Stiles had started blubbing because we had stuffed the Hun.

Today the taboo against men crying in public has gone. It no longer means you are a sissy. It means you are a wonderful guy. So Andre Agassi irrigates the Centre Court at Wimbledon. At the Barcelona Olympics that dinky little Pairs cox had a real old-fashioned blub – trembling chin and everything – when his team won their medal. And a real little twat he looked stood between two strapping rowers who somehow managed to refrain from such a self-indulgent outpouring of emotion.

It is not just girly tennis players and emotional coxes who do it. Even big, hairy-arsed politicians like Bob Hawke of Australia have boo-hooed in public. Where will it end? Soon men will be crying not because they have won a Bafta but because some other bastard has. Then we will know we have forgotten everything.

Should a man *ever* be allowed to cry? Of course. I cried when I learned that my father had lung cancer. And I cried when I heard that my friend Tom Baker had died. Loss, grief, that mind-numbing feeling that this world will keep turning despite your personal tragedy – cry, boy, cry. There was a picture of John Cleese in tears at the memorial service for Peter Cook. Fair enough. Cleese had lost a close friend (as opposed to gaining a bloody Bafta). My father-in-law cried when his dog died. I can understand that too. It is right and proper to mourn our most bitter losses. But the current vogue for weepy geezers cheapens all our tears.

And there comes a time when the crying has to stop and you have to start – a very old-fashioned notion – acting like a man.

Stoicism, dignity, a sense of emotional control – these virtues all have their place. And if not, then we have to accept that we are now no different from women.

The irony is that women have become much stronger in recent years. And it looks good on them. They take a power breakfast in the morning, buy you dinner in the evening and give birth during their lunch break. But while they have acted more like men, we have begun to act more like women. It looks bad on us.

We turn on the waterworks a little too easily. It has to stop. Don't cry when you win (or lose). Don't cry if you get hurt in love. Don't cry because you made your bed and now you have to lie in it. Save your tears for the real pain. Save your tears for something that deserves them. Time to pull yourself together, man. Or we will be shaving our legs next.

The Dating Game

Arena, **March 1996**

She was gone and she was gone for good. And even before he got beyond the bureaucracy of breaking up – dividing the collections of records and books, packing up, moving out, the thousand tiny cuts of two lives coming apart – there was something in his immediate future that he regarded with pure dread. He was going to have to start dating again.

Dating? That hardly describes the complex mating rituals of the modern, metropolitan world. But then all the words either sound too quaint or too callow. Dating and courtship are from an age we never knew, while pulling, picking up and getting off with some bird all sound like hobbies you abandoned in adolescence. Having dinner? Having dinner is just the start of it.

Yet if there is no appropriate word for it, the dating game certainly has its own language, a language learnt in adolescence and perfected in late teens and early twenties. But then you meet someone and they move in. And it is only much later, when they move out, that you discover that the language of dating has been lost to you. All you speak is pidgin that would embarrass a teenager.

But just when you are at your lowest ebb, just when your self-esteem has been given a good hiding, just when you are in all probability feeling the most negative about the opposite sex – this is the moment when you have to pretend to be God's gift to women and swan about with an urbane little smile. When confidence, hope and quite possibly your looks have all gone, this is when you have to re-enter the dating game.

'I know what I need is a good woman,' said my friend. 'But I don't think I should be around good women right now.'

'Why's that?'

'I keep bursting into tears.'

You could see how it would put a damper on the evening. But once you are out of a relationship, you can't stay out of the dating game for very long. Solitude is never really an option. A life built around memories, masturbation and meals for one palls after a while. But you are never match fit when you get back in the game. And invariably all the rules have changed.

Take my weepy friend. He had last been a boy-about-town in the early eighties when condoms had been the laughing stock of contraceptive options. But during those missing years, the rubber had made its amazing comeback. Suddenly carrying a packet of three was not an archaic, something-for-the-weekend-sir? joke. It was responsible sexual behaviour. And it disturbed him that he was a complete stranger to johnny etiquette.

What do you do? Do you get her engine warmed up before you put it on? Do you slip it under a pillow or do you jump out of bed and put it on there? Is it okay to turn on the light? And doesn't it spoil everything?

But long before you slip into your fashionable Featherlite, the dating game has untold humiliations in store. Abruptly released from a long-term relationship, the most sophisticated, well-travelled guy immediately becomes a bumbling lad. How do you attract a woman in your office without risking accusations of sexual harassment? Is it ever permissible to approach some perfect stranger? How do you know when they like you? How do you live happily ever after with someone when you can't even work up the nerve to talk to them?

Men that have been in solid relationships are simply not cut out for the hurly-burly of the dating game. It is possible that women who have been in solid relationships are not cut out for the dating game either, that they are as unnerved by the subtle semaphore of 'having dinner' as you are. But at least they have the luxury of being pursued. Even now – *even now* – the man is expected to make the running.

Far worse is when other people make the running for you. Nothing can drive you back into the arms of memories, mastur-bation and meals for one faster than the stilted dinner party that has been set up specifically to end your life as a spare prick. Because, naturally, if the woman you were being paired off with was worth having, then the sad cow wouldn't *be* on her own.

It is diffcult to find a balance when you are dating again. Some men chase everything with a pulse. Then there are those who fall heavily for the first woman who is kind to them. The former end up shagging everything that moves and dumping women who are worthy of love. The latter end up quickly making a match that is doomed to failure from the start. You either like women too much. Or you don't like them enough.

And if it all feels more difficult than it did when you were very young, that's because it is – and not just because you are out of practice. Now you have to deal with younger women. Older women. Women with kids. Women who have been divorced. Whatever kind of women they are, they are certainly not girls any more. When you get back in the game, you soon realize that it is not just you who is dragging around a matching set of emotional luggage.

Serial Adultery

Arena, November 1995

How do two people stay together for a lifetime? How *do* they do that? Paul Newman once explained the longevity of his marriage by extolling the virtues of monogamy, asking 'Why go out for a hamburger when you've got steak at home?' There's something in that, of course. But what nobody had the nerve to point out to him is that no man feels like eating steak every night of his life. Sometimes nothing goes down better than a hamburger.

Yet still we dream the monogamous dream. We pine for a love that will endure for a lifetime, a bond that will never be broken. The problem is that man is not biologically programmed for monogamy. All those vows, all those promises – they are promises to fight our true nature. We are not built to stay with one partner. We keep our wicks dry for other reasons – because we don't want to hurt our loved one, because we are afraid of disease, because we have formed an economic unit and, of course, because it is incredibly difficult to get shot of a woman once you have knobbed her.

We remain faithful not because man is the kind of animal that mates for a lifetime. Man is actually the kind of animal that mates when his wife is out of town. The kind of animal who mates when he has one too many. We stay faithful because of the mess the alternative leaves on the carpet. Men are socially conditioned to be faithful. But biologically programmed to fuck around.

There are good reasons to be faithful. Infidelity is corrosive. It shatters trust, encourages lying and the pleasure it brings is rarely worth the pain left in its wake. But these are all rational reasons. And as Sophocles pointed out, the sexual urge is like being chained to a maniac.

So why do we bother with marriages, relationships and special friends? Because we still dream of The One, the woman who will make us whole, the love of our life. And when we find her we always intend to be true. But it's hard.

Sometimes it is so hard that we lie to ourselves. I know men who believe that they have not been unfaithful unless vaginal penetration has occurred. They claim that a nosh – as Shaun Ryder so winningly refers to fellatio – doesn't count. But this is a very liberal interpretation of fidelity. Call me an old-fashioned romantic, but I maintain you are unfaithful the moment you get your cock out.

The a-nosh-doesn't-count merchants lie to themselves because they want to be faithful. None of us want to hurt the ones we love. None of us want to feel the disappointment and guilt that infidelity brings. But men are torn between the urge to build a love that will last forever, and the desire for the totally meaningless relationship. Hugh Grant's notorious nosh was more than a demonstration that men have a taste for forbidden fruit. It proved that sometimes men like bruised, over-ripe fruit that has been rolling around in the gutter. How can women ever understand that when we don't even understand it ourselves?

Monogamy is not what it was. Once it meant a lifetime commitment but now sticking together for six or seven years counts as monogamy. There is little genuine monogamy today, only serial monogamy. Or – to give it a more accurate description – serial adultery.

Serial monogamy has got a nice ring to it, a moral weight that makes it sound like an upgraded, modern version of what our parents had. But what it means in practice is half a decade of playing happy couples and then a few desperate months of secret meetings, tearful trysts and furtive phone calls from public telephones. What serial monogamy means in practice is merely deferred adultery.

But still men strive to be faithful. Because once you have strayed – where do you stop? Men try to stay faithful because once you have fucked around, in your heart you believe that a relationship is spoilt forever. And you are right. Once a man starts sleeping around, he has acknowledged the heartache in his dream home.

Will it ever end? Yes, because screwing around for a lifetime is as impossible as staying faithful for a lifetime. Sometime – probably just before your second by-pass operation – you will run out of jam. You will finally be able to be faithful when you are no longer worth having. Until that black day comes, you are condemned to a life of serial adultery.

The major consequence of serial adultery is that the important events in your life are all shared with different women. You are with one woman when your first child is born. You are with another woman when your first parent dies. And you are with another woman again when you finally start making proper money. And perhaps a string of relationships that last a few years is more fulfilling than one relationship that spans a lifetime. Perhaps not. But if you are a serial adulterer – and most of us are – you never really share a life with someone, only edited highlights.

As for serial monogamy, I can't see it ever catching on. If you are going to break up with someone, you might as well get laid.

Passion Killers

Arena, May/June 1995

Some offensive old git once remarked that a woman never farts until you marry her. A disgraceful remark. But beyond the gratuitous and, quite frankly, unforgivable sexism of the comment, there lurks a kernel of truth. A woman will often behave one way when she is after you and quite another when she has you.

Men, of course, are very different. A man will, metaphorically speaking, fart with equanimity before a wedding ceremony or after a wedding ceremony. A man will even fart during a wedding ceremony. Women are not that honest. They act one way during an affair and a very different way during a relationship.

Why do we see the wreckage of so many relationships all around us? Because the typical man and the typical woman want very different things from their union. A woman wants a partner. A man wants a lover. They yearn for a meaningful bond. We pine for meaningless sex. Women want security. Men crave excitement. They dream of watercress. We dream of waterbeds. Women want relationships. Men desire affairs. So they give us the latter so that they can get the former. They think it is a fair trade. We see it as trickery.

The affair is man-bait, designed purely to tempt you into a relationship. During the affair a woman will be all the things a man dreams of. She will have sex in the strangest places – a car, a field, even the butt.

But she will only do these things during the first flush of an affair, when the embers of romance can fan into flames or just as easily fade and die, she will only do these things *when there is still the possibility of losing the man*. Once you have been

40

lured into her silky web she puts away the lace underwear and starts picking out curtains. And no man's cock ever stood up and saluted for curtains (although they do have a lovely selection in Habitat on London's Tottenham Court Road right now).

Every man has seen this happen. Every man has seen his wild cat become a pussycat. Every man has seen the heartbreaker become a *hausfrau* virtually overnight. Every man has seen – and seen it many, many times – that horrible moment when the affair ends and the relationship begins. To them it no doubt feels like a wonderful thing. To us it is an intimation of the grave.

An affair means passion, lust and rapture. A relationship means all these things turning into mere affection. During an affair, the two of you are happiest alone. During a relationship, when you no longer have anything to say to each other, you hang out with other couples. Or – even more extreme – you go to dinner parties where you are immediately separated from your true love and placed next to a stranger. An affair, by its very nature, can only last a short time. But relationships last for eternity. At least it *feels* like an eternity.

To a woman, the start of a relationship is when love truly begins. But to men it is the moment when love starts to wither and die. Men and women think of different things when they think about love. And that is why we will always be calling to each other from different sides of the sky.

Men can see the appeal of a relationship. Yes, it is a good feeling to be with someone you trust and like and know. There are none of the pressures of an affair – the constant need to make dazzling conversation, the requirement of giving constant, undivided attention, the commitment to make every sexual act feel like an event in the Winter Olympics.

A relationship can seem peaceful and soothing compared with all the blood-boiling madness of an affair. After the fever of intense letter-writing, blissful dinners, bouquets of white lilies, and semen on the ceiling, a relationship is like slipping into a nice warm bath. And that can be pleasant for a while (usually thirty minutes maximum). But it gets old. It gets stale. And you start to feel that you are existing on a diet of yesterday's croissants.

For centuries men have been accused of dividing the female population into two kinds of women – the Whore and the

Madonna. The theory goes that, moral hypocrites that we are, we think that one is for sex and the other is for love. One is for blow-jobs and the other is for bringing up baby. One is for motels and the other for marriage.

But this is pure myth. We know from bitter experience that women always divide themselves into the two categories.

The intelligent thing would be for women to combine both sides of their nature – to be your dream fuck and also your best friend. But, sadly, a man knows that you – almost – always have to choose between the two.

Is there no hope for us? Is there no way for a man's need for an everlasting affair to combine with a woman's need for a never-ending relationship?

Are we doomed forever to see every new love die?

Probably – until more women wake up and realize that what it takes to win us, it takes to keep us. A tip, girls – if you want that relationship to last, make sure that the affair never ends.

Younger Women

Arena, **July/August 1994**

The younger woman never really crops up until a man is in his middle thirties. It is around that difficult age that he often finds himself dating a woman who was born around the same time that he was losing his virginity. You look at her one night and say to yourself, 'My God. She has never heard of the Daleks.'

You lose shared cultural references if you go out with someone not your own age. You haven't watched the same television programmes, read the same books, thrilled to the same events. If you are in your thirties and going out with a woman fifteen years your junior, the chances are she will have no idea why 1977 was important for British music or 1966 was crucial for English football. She will never have heard of *Zen And the Art Of Motorcycle Maintenance* or the Glitter Band. But so what? If you want to talk about The Clash, Bobby Moore or the Daleks go down the Rat and Trumpet with your mates. Heterosexuality is a celebration of differences. And few things emphasize those differences more than a generation gap.

Grown men dream of a woman who will make them feel like a teenager again. But of course teenage boys dream of a woman who will make them feel like a man. Bobby Goldsboro put it best: 'I knew nothing about love – she knew everything.' Promising a masterclass in carnal knowledge, the older woman is a major love object for a growing boy. Then the fantasy changes.

We need to define our terms here. A younger woman is around fifteen years younger than you are. An older woman is around fifteen months older than you are. They mature so much faster than we do.

43

Why do men love a younger woman? Women will tell you that it's sexual fascism, a physical thing. That comes into it, of course – but far more than for her bright eyes and bushy tail, men like a younger woman because she turns up on your doorstep with far less emotional baggage than her older sister.

Adultery, divorce, broken homes – all the major life-rending traumas that are unavoidable in the modern world lie somewhere in the future for a younger woman. Yes, her eyes are bright and her flesh is firm. But far more than this, the younger woman is appealing because she faces the future with an open, optimistic heart. No kids! No tears! No ruined years! Isn't that preferable to some embittered crone moaning about her ex-partner?

Naturally there are plenty of younger women with squawking brats and memories of being mistreated at the hands of rotten men. And there are older women who never married, never divorced and have passed through life relatively unscathed. These women always seem to get on fine with their ex-boyfriends. But as a general rule the older woman has far more reasons to be bitter than the younger woman. And that is why the older woman is such hard work.

But let's not feel sorry for the older woman. In the past she may have got a lot of stick – from Joe Orton's *Entertaining Mr Sloane* to Joan Collins' jokes to the ooh-you-are-awful hags of a hundred situation comedies. But these days the older woman can date younger men without anyone batting an eyelid, she can keep time at bay down at the gym and then round it all off by having a baby when she is fifty. There is no longer any shame in being an older woman. These days the younger woman gets all the rotten publicity.

The younger woman is caricatured in Woody Allen's *Husbands and Wives* as an empty-headed bimbo susceptible to screaming scenes and every passing fad. She parades on high heels through the tabloids, breezily wrecking the happy homes of Tory politicians. And finally she is demonized for the man on the Clapham omnibus as that firm-breasted appendage – the Trophy Wife.

This is very unfair on the younger woman. A trophy is something to be won, cherished and prized – so in a very real sense, surely every wife is a Trophy Wife? And if your wife is no trophy then you almost certainly married the wrong girl.

What you get from an older woman that a younger woman can't offer is something that feels like wisdom. Even when adolescence is a dim and distant memory and you are not looking for a crash course on sexual technique, an older woman can still teach you a thing or two.

'There are a lot of nice people in the world,' I was once told, just after making some improbable declaration. And she was right. But a younger woman would never tell you something as priceless as that.

But not all older women are fonts of wisdom. They can be desperate, grasping creatures – their body clock ticking like a faulty pacemaker – who see you as their last chance for hearth, home and suburban bliss. There are few greater turn-offs in this world than being seen as someone's last chance in the global dating bureau. There is one thing a younger woman has that an older woman does not – and that is time. Ultimately the younger woman is irresistible because she still has the room to get things wrong. Just don't mention the Daleks.

Before She Knew Me

***Arena*, November 1994**

We have a strange relationship with the ex-partners of our partners. In many ways they are our dark side – the black sheep of the family, the bad seed, runaway brothers who did the dirty deeds and disappeared, and who must be spoken of only in whispers. Darth Vader to our Luke Skywalker, Cain to our Abel, a fraternity of restless ghosts – and the most recent one is always the most restless of all. The man she knew before she knew you.

We know about old boyfriends because women always tell us – even if we don't want to know. Even if you put in earplugs, turn up the volume to full blast and tell yourself again and again that your love began in year zero, sooner or later you get the old boyfriends speech. And what a sorry tale it is! For these old loves are always dangled before you as a bad example.

Even when a woman is cursing the day you were born, she will never say, 'If only you could be more like Tim, Mick or Larry – now there was one hell of a guy.' She will never compare you unfavourably to an ex-boyfriend because women never get dewy-eyed about old flames. Men do – in our secret hearts, a sentimental candle is forever burning for all our old girlfriends. Unless, of course, she got hideously fat.

But not women. Old boyfriends are forgotten but not forgiven. A woman in love will forgive almost anything. She will forgive boorish behaviour, infidelity, drunkenness, throwing up in the cab, going to bed with your socks on and premature ejaculation – *even all on the same date*.

But the one thing a woman will never forgive in a man is cold feet. The one thing no woman – not even a woman in love – will ever forgive is a lack of commitment. This is why their ex-boyfriends always get such a rotten press.

When women tell men about their previous affairs there is always one man who gets a particularly savage review. He *hates* women, you are told. He *fears* women. And what did this monster from the deep do? Fuck her sister? Beat her up? No. It usually transpires that his only crime was that he wasn't ready to commit himself – at least not to her. And that is the great unforgivable.

Once women dreamed of love. These days they dream of commitment. They all seem to have an unhealthy, pathological yearning for unqualified commitment. They want commitment more than babies, more than BMWs, more than *anything*. Real Commitment has replaced True Romance as the ultimate goal of the modern woman.

The irony is that men – a loyal, devoted, dog-like breed – are actually quite capable of making a commitment, which is really nothing more than a promise to love and honour for an unspecified length of time (usually about five or six years).

But women are commitment junkies. They are never satisfied. Commit yourself to thirty minutes and a woman expects you to stay all night. Commit to a night and a woman wants a relationship. Commit yourself to a relationship and pretty soon she expects you to leave your wife and kids.

And of course if you commit yourself to a marriage she wants to stop you being who you are – the poor, pussy-whipped sap she allegedly fell in love with – and change you into someone else, someone who will not complain about going to Sainsbury's on a Saturday afternoon. Too often women confuse commitment and domestication.

Commitment – that holy grail of female aspiration – is a vow that love, lust and affection will be translated into something more concrete. Not much to ask for! Men want exactly the same thing. What is unreasonable is that men who make their excuses and leave when it's make-your-mind-up time get vilified by the women who are left behind. Don't they understand that you can't commit to all of them?

When women speak of the men they have loved and lost, their tone varies wildly from amused disdain to righteous loathing. But these men – the feckless playboy, the adulterous husband, the mummy's boy and the rest – all have something in common. They were all found wanting, usually in commitment.

And, yes, sometimes a man's lack of commitment looks a lot like a lack of human decency. A reluctance to commit is often an excuse to fuck around, to lie and cheat, to have your cake and your neighbour's cake too. A fear of commitment is sometimes just a fear of growing up.

But it is equally true that nothing is more repellent to a man than a woman who is desperate for commitment, a woman who is *gagging* for it. There's something so impersonal about these commitment junkies – you feel that she doesn't really want commitment from you but from *any* man who can eat lunch without getting food on his chin.

Men should always take the old boyfriends speech with a pinch of talk. If you actually met the flesh and blood behind this fraternity of ghosts – shared a beer with them, talked some football, flicked a few wet towels in the locker room of life – you would probably find that they are a lot like you.

When she speaks of old flames, don't believe a word. Nobody is that unlucky in love.

Thy Neighbour's Wife

Arena, October 1996

The Bible had specifically warned him off his neighbour's wife. She was clearly mentioned in the Tenth and final Commandment, right there with the admonitions to also keep thy greasy paws off thy neighbour's manservant, maidservant, ox, donkey or 'anything that is thy neighbour's'. But he fell for her anyway.

Him and Mrs Jones – they had a thing going on. It grew quietly, they circled around each other politely at first. He watched her from a distance. Walking her young daughter to her red car. Going to the park for a run. She was the nice lady who lived just down the road. And she made his head swim.

Love with the neighbour's wife started with proximity, opportunity and a discreet desire. Just like an office romance, they became strangely close without arousing suspicion. And without even really noticing themselves. Then it began.

She decided when it began. Perhaps women always do, and we ludicrously overrate our seduction techniques. But certainly the neighbour's wife decided when it began – after one of those eighties dinner parties where everybody ate too much, drank too much and imagined that their little patch of real estate would go on rising in value forever. And as they said good night on her doorstep, instead of placing a kiss on his cheek, she placed a kiss on his lips. Then she laughed. But she wasn't joking. Suddenly he saw he had a chance with this beautiful creature.

He had always liked her, liked her from the start when he had knocked on her door to offer neighbourly sympathy after a bungled burglary. She was suspicious at first. Who wouldn't be? The family silver was still piled up in the hall. And he could have

49

been after her video. But later that day she came up his garden path with a big grin. And he liked her. He liked her a lot. She was a dazzler – beautiful, young and foreign. Tall, funny, talented – every time he walked past her Victorian bay window, she was amusing herself with a different musical instrument. But he had thought that when her front door closed, she was happy. He had thought that her marriage was rock solid. And he was wrong.

They crossed a line with that kiss and after that it all moved very fast. There was a trip to the cinema, innocently arranged at yet another dinner party, arranged in front of their partners (perfect cover). They kissed again – after the film, on the edge of Piccadilly Circus. Not so chaste this time. The next morning they went to bed for the first time as eagerly as only adults can, two grown-ups worried how many more chances for true happiness they would be allowed. 'The important thing,' she told him, 'is that when this is over, we are still friends.' But the possibility of friendship was already gone. They existed on a diet of forbidden fruit. And it was exciting to have to meet in secret, arrange trysts in quiet pubs and occasionally to have the impossible luxury of spending an entire night together.

They were at the vanguard of a new kind of relationship. Inevitably it will become more and more common to get involved with the woman next door as more of us work from home. The golden era of the office romance is over. This is the future – the fax, the modem, the neighbour's wife. From now on you will make your living and find your love on the street where you live. But I don't think that he will ever do it again.

There comes a point in the affairs of men when, if you could, you would surely keep life like this forever. If you could press a button to keep life as sweet as this for always, you would. It usually happens when you have two women and both of them are happy. The first one doesn't know about the second and the second one believes that one day she will replace the first. But the moment passes. And what you're left with is two unhappy women.

It wasn't all wild, ecstatic sex and vows of undying love. She was, after all, the neighbour's wife. And both of them had already pledged their troth elsewhere. There were excuses to be made, lies to be told, betrayals that when discovered would leave wounds to endure for a lifetime. Guilt always ferments into resentment and a hardening of the heart. You end up blaming the innocent party for your own crimes. Soon there were screaming rows in both their houses. Angry lights burned deep into the night.

After drifting through the years, their worlds were suddenly awash with bitterness, tears and a happiness that made him giddy. Life without each other was unimaginable. He couldn't give her up. Could he? Of course he could. Our tragedy is that we can learn to live without anyone.

It was wonderful while it lasted. Then she confessed everything to her husband, which at least meant he wouldn't have to go to quite so many eighties dinner parties. But her confession wasn't the problem. The problem was that it started to trouble him that they were neighbours. It troubled him because he felt that his part could have been played by almost anyone. That she loved him because he was there. Not so much Mr Right as Mr Escape Route.

Were they in love with each other? They said they were, although of course that means less than nothing. Yet even now there are times when he feels that for a few months he was closer to her than he has ever been to any woman. But perhaps that is only because it ended sooner than it should have. Perhaps that is only because she was the girl that got away.

It all came to a screaming, messy end with the neighbour's wife. He started to fuck around, the emotional coward's way of avoiding commitment. Sleeping with her *au pair* was the final straw. She was a woman of pride as well as beauty and she wouldn't put up with his bullshit. She moved out of the marital home and out of his life. She didn't leave a forwarding address. By then they were no longer lovers. Or neighbours. Or friends.

It was only later that he realized how wrong he had been. Getting involved with the neighbour's wife hadn't been the mistake. Letting her get away had been his big mistake. At least he had learned something. He had learned that you are asking for your heart to be given a beating when you get involved with your neighbour's wife – because nothing can ever be the same again. Not for you. Not for her. Or for the silent partners you betray. An affair with the neighbour's wife is an *hors d'oeuvre* of bliss, an *entrée* of misery and a punch in the cakehole for dessert.

And, as the Bible warns, you are also asking for serious trouble if you ever get involved with your neighbour's donkey. But that's quite another story.

Waitresses

Arena, July/August 1996

A man who is tired of waitresses is tired of women. How could anyone ever grow weary of these metropolitan sweethearts? Waitresses come in every shape and size and from every race and class.

There are nubile students moonlighting in the holidays, enigmatic Eastern Europeans paying for their language classes and slim Asian babes whose tiny hands can shred a Szechwan duck in seconds. And from Chinatown to coffee house to bar and grill, what they all have in common is that they are the one section of the female population who are obliged to talk to us.

At least they have to take your order. They all have to ask, 'Can I get you anything else?' Of course they are also free to drop the soup of the day in your lap if you get lippy. And quite rightly, too. There are few things lower in this world than a man who is rude to a waitress.

The opening scene in *Reservoir Dogs* is dominated by two women. One is Madonna and the debate about the meaning of 'Like A Virgin'. But the other woman – who is discussed with even greater passion – is the unknown waitress whom one of Tarantino's wise guys refuses to tip. It is left to Harvey Keitel's Mr White to put her case.

'Waitressing is the number-one occupation for female non-college graduates in this country,' he says. 'It's the one job basically any woman can get and make a living on. The reason is because of tips.'

What Harvey is saying is that the waitress is worthy of love.

Men are meant to fantasise about schoolgirls, French maids, nuns, nurses, traffic wardens – this is the clichéd lexicon of lust.

But what really gets your trousers crowded is a top-of-the-range waitress. But nobody ever hails the allure of these short-order sirens. Nobody ever sings the praises of waitresses.

Or almost nobody. Camille Paglia – a woman who knows a thing or two about women – has called the waitress the Eternal Mother. The waitress taps into our most basic instincts and ancient memories. The Eternal Mother feeds us, sustains us, gives us fuel to face the world. Every waitress reminds us of the first woman we ever knew, our first female ally, the first woman who ever looked at us and said, 'Is he hungry? Is he? Is he?'

But the waitress is more than a mother substitute. There is something profoundly romantic about the waitress. They have dreams, these girls. You are always aware that she might not be there next week. Every waitress soon moves on.

Like flowers – like female beauty itself – waitresses are soon gone. They don't last long. But a good one can make you return to a swanky restaurant or a humble caff again and again. 'I've got a Ferrari,' says Martin Clunes at his most gooey, lost in rapture for the blonde goddess who brings his pizza in the commercial. We know how he feels.

This country is not like France or Italy, where there is a career in serving, where the same wizened old git who brings you your *café au lait* today will still be there when you return next year. For the Mediterranean male, waitering is a vocation. But in the English-speaking world, waitressing is always what a young woman does between different lives. It makes the waitress an object of obsession.

What *Lolita* did for jailbait, Glenn Savan's novel *White Palace* did for the waitress. Savan's hero is Max, an advertising man whose life is turned inside out by desire for Nora. She is earthy, lusty and dirty. Above all, she is a waitress. Her job frames their whole love affair, with Max usually portrayed as a passive observer, waiting for extra helpings from Nora the action woman.

'The grey double doors on the kitchen flew open and Nora burst through, holding a folded tray-stand in one hand, and balancing a big oval platter loaded with food on the high-held palm of the other. She hesitated, her eyes going flat, and her platter gave a dangerous wobble.'

Savan captured the way the waitress turns every man into a

voyeur. You watch them coming and then you watch them walk away. You love them when you can.

Actually date a waitress and you suffer the torments of purgatory – left at home all evening with a burning jealousy, tormented by visions of all those half-cut guys evaluating the way she fills out that apron, having to wait until after midnight when the staff are settling down for their meal before you can pick her up. Loving a waitress takes real commitment.

Savan's novel recognizes the waitress as urban heroine, bringing glamour and romance to the city just as surely as she brings the menu to your table. And it is a hard job. Long hours, small pay and assholes all come with the territory. You have to admire their bravery, the grace and good humour with which they play their role. But all the best women have done it at least once in their life.

So God bless and protect this noble breed. And let every man learn to respect, honour and cherish the ever-changing army of young women who approach our tables with the magical words, 'Would you like any pudding?'

Part Two
Real Men

Introduction

Whenever I write about my son I always feel a little like Judy Garland dragging Liza Minnelli on stage for a song and dance routine. I feel proud, guilty – but most of all I feel like I just can't help myself.

This section is predominantly a collection of homages to and interviews with men, but the final piece is about the two men who have meant the most in my life – my father and my son; my dad and my boy.

Part of me would prefer not to explore this kind of thing in public. I don't want to invade their privacy and I would much rather tell you about Will Self's unexpected warmth and generosity, or the way Elton John's hair doesn't move, or Nick Hornby's relationship to the novelist Anne Tyler, or what it is like to share a pint with the footballer who makes Vinnie Jones look like a Teletubby. But I know that the best writing comes from closest to the heart. So I keep coming back to my incredible father and my beautiful boy.

The question that drives every journalist up the wall after they have done an interview and then written it up is – yeah, but what's he really like? Surely if your article doesn't tell the reader what the subject is really like then you have failed? And yet in a way it's a fair question.

One or two thousand words very rarely capture someone's true nature. You don't have the time to shine your policeman's torch into their inner psyche and they don't have the inclination to let you. All you can get are a few hints, clues and pointers.

What's he really like? It's probably not a question you can answer about someone who is trying to promote their record, book or film. The only person you can legitimately ask that question about is yourself, and then spend a lifetime looking for the answer.

It seems to me that our best chance of finding the answer comes when we reflect on our relationships with our parents and our children. If you asked Liza Minnelli, I'm sure she would tell you exactly the same thing.

The Lost Boys

Arena, June 1996

Years ago, in a suburb far away, I could see my friend John whenever I wanted to. If I wanted to see John – and I always did, because we had such a laugh – I just knocked on his door and his mum would let me in. But when boys become men, the nature of friendship changes.

The friendships of adult life are no less profound than the friendships of childhood. In many ways the bonds we form as men are more serious than the alliances we have as boys, because now they are tested by all the trials and tribulations of maturity. You drift through the years and friendship seems to amount to meeting your mate in some crowded restaurant or bar every month or so. But stick around and sooner or later you will see your friend through love gone wrong, problems with children, career trauma and all the other horrors of adult life – and he will do exactly the same for you. That's when, if he is a real friend, you will realize that you care about him just as much as the friends you had as a boy. But still – you can't knock on his front door without a very good reason.

And sometimes I miss the years when I didn't have to look into my diary to work out when I could see my friends. Now and again I miss the intensity of the friendships we had as boys. And I miss my mate John.

I remember sitting up a tree with John, having a farting competition. This is going back a bit. But I clearly remember that we sat up that tree, laughing ourselves to the point of nausea and back again. Just two vulgar young lads sitting up a tree in the backwoods of Essex – but I will remember it for the rest of my life.

In those days John could knock on my door day or night and be guaranteed a warm welcome. Or I could go to John's door and know that I would be fed, entertained and given a place to rest my cropped head. It was like having two homes. It is not like that any more.

And of course it's not like that any more! John and I didn't have diaries. And the reason we didn't have diaries was because our lives were simple and carefree. Beyond the school gates all we had to worry about was entertaining ourselves. Work, the great dictator of a man's life, had yet to begin its fifty-year reign of terror. Apart from John's paper round.

And naturally these days I can't barge into the home of my friends and interrupt what they are doing – quality time with their children, a small dinner party, tea with the in-laws – with loud demands for a farting competition. I realize that it can never again be like it was for John and me. But I don't think it is wrong to mourn those days when friendship came first.

When you're a boy, friends are a permanent presence in your life. They are ally, companion and support network. Perhaps it is only when we are boys, unencumbered by all the baggage of adult lives – careers, family and exhaustion – that we truly understand the nature of friendship.

Now friends – even friends I love like brothers – are more distant figures. These friends, even the ones that will be there forever, are on the margins of my life, just as I am on the margins of their lives. Our meetings have to be meticulously scheduled because time is so scarce. And while I do understand the need for that formality, sometimes it seems like a negation of friendship.

Total, all-consuming friendship is the province of boys, not men. Yet the years of total friendship last for a surprisingly long time. Even when you have grown to young manhood, friends are still central to your existence: there is still that unspoken assumption that whatever you are going to do, you will do it together.

It lasts until you get serious with a girl. It lasts until you decide to narrow down your world to one sweet face. And we let our friends slip away too easily. There are always millions of fantastic women in the world. But there are only ever a few special mates. You don't need any more.

What happened to John and me? Grew apart, I guess. I don't even have his telephone number. And if we met, I don't honestly know if we would have that much to say to each other. Sometimes you take off in different directions and end up calling to each other over a vast, empty space.

Friends are no different from women or colleagues – we go in and out of each other's lives like bus boys in a restaurant. Yet, just as separating from a woman does not mean that you never loved her, so growing apart from a mate doesn't mean your friendship wasn't real.

So, John, if you're reading this – I would love to get together for old time's sake. Yes, life has changed out of all recognition. But I am up for a farting competition, if you are.

Your club or mine?

The Strangeness of Comfort:
Ian McEwan

Arena, **November/December 1987**

Under a wispy Beatle cut that is now etched with silver, a frown passes across Ian McEwan's watchful mandarin face. He is considering all those people who think he is a sick man. 'I have this troubled streak in me,' he says finally. 'It happens less now but I would become possessed by, say, the deadpan voice narrating *Butterflies*.'

Butterflies was his short story about a very young girl who gets violated and killed down by the canal. 'It took a long time', recounts the charmer who narrates the story, 'pumping it all out into my hand.'

'I would become possessed by that voice and take immense *pleasure* in getting it right,' McEwan says in his soft, classless, rootless voice. 'It is what Graham Greene called the chip of ice. You *don't care*. In that sense all writers are sickos.'

But no other writer has charted the blackest, most diseased legions of the human psyche as brilliantly and with such relish as Ian McEwan. He has been sending despatches from the dark side for more than ten years now. His two collections of short stories (*First Love, Last Rites* and *In Between the Sheets*) and his first two short novels (*The Cement Garden* and *The Comfort of Strangers*), all of them with taut, horrific plotlines hewn in McEwan's sparse, gleaming prose, have made him one of the very few British writers trusted by both public and critics ('Genius' – *The Times*, is one of McEwan's more restrained reviews).

In the past his work has dealt with themes that run the gamut of debauchery and degradation. He has built his career on tales of suspense, mystery and imagination splattered with blood, vomit and semen. But paradoxically these stories have been told in the most concise, pristine, gem-hard prose imaginable. At his best McEwan has matched even the work of Martin Amis, the smirking champ of British fiction.

Children in particular have had a tough time in his work. They have been fucked, murdered and been made to throw up at the most inappropriate moments. More than one of the poor little mites has cross-dressed. Women too have been forced to sniff the short end of Ian McEwan's spiteful stick.

There is a Nabokovian voice he does very well, full of laconic decadence and cultured, fastidious malice, and McEwan seems to enjoy making the rich and sophisticated do unspeakably low deeds. There is the man who owns the famous forgery of a Rodin sculpture who shares his bed with a storeroom dummy (*Dead As They Come*). And the diplomat's son who plays master-slave games so enthusiastically that his wife ends up a cripple (*The Comfort of Strangers*).

Every one of his readers has his favourite McEwan moment, when Ian has sunk lower than you would have dreamed possible. For my money the purest Black Mac moment is in *Psychopolis* where the man and the girl are eating dinner in a restaurant in Los Angeles. The man is telling the girl that she is the best thing that ever happened to him, that he loves her so and that he would do anything for her, anything at all. So the girl tells him what she would like him to do.

'I want you to urinate in your pants, now. Go on now! Quick! Do it now before you have time to think about it.'

And he does. And he sits there in a puddle of piss staring at his dream girl. And then she tells him that the middle-aged couple who just walked into the restaurant are her parents and she calls them over to meet him . . .

McEwan's first collection of short stories won the Somerset Maugham Award in 1976 and his second novel was shortlisted for the Booker Prize in 1981. He has enjoyed even more early success than Martin Amis, but as McEwan enters his fortieth year it seems his future could be considerably less golden than his past.

Many of the promising young British novelists of the last ten years are in the middle of a crucial change of life. McEwan, Amis, Julian Barnes, Peter Ackroyd, Timothy Mo – all of them are coming up to or just passing their fortieth birthdays. You cannot go on being 'promising' and 'young' forever – not even in publishing. It is time to deliver.

Amis considerably upped the ante with his triumphant study of a porn gourmet, *Money*, while Mo, Ackroyd and Barnes have enjoyed more modest success with, respectively, *An Insular Possession*, *Chatterton* and *Staring at the Sun*. But Ian McEwan, most lavishly praised word-brat of this insular set, with whom not even Kingsley's boy could live in the seventies, *that* Ian McEwan has published a novel, *The Child in Time*, which even his staunchest supporters are finding difficult to admire.

It was time for McEwan to prove that, for all the austere beauty of his prose, he was not merely a talent which has horror and cheap thrills at its foundation. He has done himself little good with *The Child in Time*. Even before its official publication date dissenting voices were wondering if the book proved that McEwan was a major talent who had lost his way or a minor talent that has for a long time been vastly overrated.

'Tries to be sensitive and clever,' *Vogue* said of the book. 'Just ends up being vague and wet.'

'*The Child in Time* operates on various levels of achievement,' said the *Literary Review*. 'Which is a fancy way of saying that it is uneven and not very well constructed.'

The Child in Time attempts to prove to the world that Ian McEwan is more than the thinking man's Stephen King, more than the Roald Dahl of the heavyweight lit set.

In the background of *Butterflies*, as the young girl is being slaughtered by the canal, a gang of young boys are roasting a live cat over a fire, just to rub your nose in it, you understand, to show there is absolutely no hope for mankind. But with *The Child in Time*, Black Mac discovers that this can be a wonderful world. Incredibly, at times he is positively *cloying*.

Set in a post-Thatcher, authoritarian England of the near future, *The Child in Time* is the story of Stephen Lewis, an author of children's books who is conscripted onto a government commission to help create a definitive childcare handbook, which will be the blueprint for bringing up the next

generation. It is a liberal nightmare – Victorian values choreo-
graphed by Orwell.

Stephen daydreams his way through endless committee meetings, forever haunted by the kidnapping of his three-year-old
daughter Kate, who was silently snatched from her father's side
during a trip to the supermarket. The loss of the child has
wrecked his marriage because neither Stephen nor his wife can
come to terms with the tragedy. McEwan glumly charts the disin-
tegration of their union. Meanwhile Stephen's best friend
Charles betrays him by secretly drawing up an alternative
government childcare handbook, the one the rotters planned to
use all along. Charles then betrays himself by quitting politics,
London and adult life and moving out to the country where his
wife becomes his mother and he reverts to a macabre conkers-
and-bogies childhood, dressing up in short trousers, carrying a
catapult, building a treehouse and talking like Just William.

Stephen is eventually reconciled to his estranged wife, the
bovine, hammock-breasted Julie, and though the kidnapped
Kate is never brought back, the book ends with the woman
giving birth. It is a madly ecstatic rather than a happy ending,
and while it would be wrong to knock McEwan for being overwhelmed by the sight of a child being born, I have to confess that
I found his mawkish eulogies to milk-gorged tits a little hard to
stomach.

Parts of the book – especially the moment Kate disappears
and the description of Stephen paralysed by grief, struck so
numb by a despairing inertia that all he can do is watch game
shows – are McEwan at the height of his powers. But such
moments are few and far between. You have to search out the
good things in *The Child in Time* whereas in McEwan's past
work there was no fat, no gristle, nor a steely phrase wasted.
Though only a shade over two hundred pages, *The Child in
Time* is almost twice the size of McEwan's other novels and he
seems lost in all that space. Despite the rare times when he
shows himself still capable of tightening the muscles around your
throat, the overall impression is clumsy and hifalutin. The work
is shot through with reflections, thoughts and little lectures on
the nature of childhood and time.

The longtime McEwan fan will no doubt second Paul Taylor's
final judgement in the *Literary Review* – 'He should stick to

being Ian McEwan' – but the chances are that *The Child in Time* is a fairly accurate reflection of what middle period McEwan is going to look like, just as *Einstein's Monsters* revealed where Martin Amis is going to be for the foreseeable future.

Both writers are changed men, and it is having children that has changed them. Fatherhood has made these former *enfants terribles* concerned for the world – though it is a concern that can sometimes sound like special pleading – and it has humanized their voices. Neither McEwan nor Amis are the haggard masturbators they were in their twenties, lapping up the black side of life like maggots inside a body bag, though so far Amis has certainly incorporated this new-found humanism into his work more ably than McEwan. Has all this personal joy (McEwan and his wife have two small sons) dulled the cutting edge of his work? Has Ian McEwan gone soft?

'Well, this would be the very romantic view of literature that through *suffering* . . .'

I don't mean you have to be tortured and starving in a *garret*.

'If you say having children is a positive thing in your life then you mean it in its totality,' McEwan says. 'It brings out things in you that for a man come out reluctantly; degrees of tenderness, the experience of serving someone else – something you don't do if you are living alone and running around town. A lot of things about having children are quite difficult and you have to cheer yourself up, tell yourself you are being extended and that you would not be without this love affair with this child. You become sensitized – towards tenderness and anxiety. You become a kind of hostage to life.'

I meet up with Ian McEwan in the ritzy Bloomsbury offices of Jonathan Cape. We are in a very small room that is stacked high with cardboard boxes full of copies of *The Child in Time*, spiderishly autographed. McEwan is soon on the phone with the director of *Sour Sweet*, the Timothy Mo novel that is soon to be a minor motion picture, its screenplay written by McEwan. It seems there is a problem with the film's budget and McEwan is being consulted on how to keep down costs while maintaining the movie's artistic integrity.

'I suggest we cut the stunt and the scene with the Buddha,' he murmurs into the telephone.

All these guys do *something else*. Amis interviews writers who are older than he is, Julian Barnes had his post-Clive James TV column in the *Observer* for years, Mr Mo works for a boxing magazine and, most lucrative of all, McEwan writes for the screen both large and small. His teleplays like *The Imitation Game* and *Solid Geometry* (notoriously banned by the BBC in 1979 for featuring a large penis preserved in a jar of milky liquid) and the screenplay for *The Ploughman's Lunch* have done as much to enhance his reputation as his books.

There is a copy of the *Literary Review* on the desk in front of him. I feel a little sorry for him. He has the bruised authority and hurt pride of a monarch who has survived a messy coup attempt.

'At least it is well written,' he says, tapping the *Review*.

I really *enjoyed* all that sensationalist stuff you used to write. Have you come to look down on your past work?

'No, I enjoy that stuff too,' he says in his neutral sixties voice, an accent untouched by the taint of class or emotion. 'But my sense of what is extraordinary has extended to something I saw. It is an extraordinary thing to see one human being coming out of another, it is as bizarre a thing as I ever clapped eyes on . . .'

I guess I know what he means but I still think it's a raw deal (for him as well as the rest of us) that McEwan lets his joy and wonder at the process of procreation turn his steel to mush, his icy sagacity to clumsy pretension. I wonder aloud if he has been a little *too* lavishly praised over the years and if the adoration of the critics hasn't made him overreach himself. McEwan thinks not.

'It is too drawn out a process, writing a novel is such a long haul and, in the end, the critics cancel each other out. The reality is a quiet room and what you can do.'

If McEwan has doubts about his latest novel then he is keeping them well hidden. For more than ten years people have been telling him how impossibly hot he is and now that they are saying he has fallen flat on his fleshy, expressionless face, he just doesn't believe them.

'In a way *The Child in Time* feels like my first novel because it is the first time I have ever used the freedom allowed by the form of a novel to expand, use different strands and have a more complicated structure.'

But it is not only different in structural terms.

'The world it describes is bleak and menacing but it hangs onto a flimsy kind of optimism. I see it as a continuation, there are many things in the book that I was writing about even when I was writing short stories – children and the degree of control exercised over them by adults. The child that is within you. The idea of regression and – again – the sense of *threat* that I feel and expressed in various ways.'

But it is so strange to see you this reverential about children. In the past, the world you have had them inhabit has been a global concentration camp . . .

'Well, the child in the book gets stolen, which is in many ways the worst thing I can think of. But I am more concerned with the child within us and the deal it gets. I'm concerned with our relationships with the total accumulation of our lives and what we deny when we get older and more pompous.'

The things you have put kids through in your work have made people wonder about your moral health.

His shrewd, blind eyes glisten with mild bewilderment.

'Someone once wrote "The idea of being Ian McEwan's child is absolutely chilling." I thought, I could get offended by that. But life's too short. If you write first person narratives you run into this problem. Actors don't get it. Nobody goes up to Jonathan Pryce and says, you fucking murderer, I saw you in *Macbeth* last night, you should be locked up – you and your wife . . .'

In *Solid Geometry* the man says to his wife, 'You don't even have the blessing of an unhappy childhood.' Do you think that maybe an unhappy childhood is good preparation for life because it is *not* all trips to the seaside and R. White's lemonade out there, but dog eat dog and cat eat mouse?

'No, I think a happy childhood is a much better preparation for the world – we can argue about definitions but I mean being secure and loved which means you are able to love, and I would count an unhappy childhood one where you were neglected, abused, unloved, fucked around – and you become the kind of person who does those things as an adult and contributes to the world's unhappiness rather than partaking in its happiness. But I actually think that a happy childhood is quite a rare thing. A lot of us are walking around with bruises.'

There seems to have been a lot of dislocated love in

McEwan's own childhood. It is probably no coincidence that he is at his heart-thumping best when writing about loss and grief. He was born in the barracks town of Aldershot where his soldier father was stationed. His father was posted overseas to Africa and the Far East – this was in the fifties, when the sun was setting on the British Empire, but very slowly – and young Ian sometimes travelled to these far away, exotic bases but often did not.

His mother, a Scot like his dad, had two children from a previous marriage but they were much older than Ian so he grew up as a kind of hemmed-in only child. Once he hid behind the sofa when his father came home on leave, not recognizing him. Another time he came down the stairs piping, 'Please, I want to be a girl,' just like the youngest boy in *The Cement Garden*, who wants to be a girl because girls don't fight and get hurt.

The Armed Forces made McEwan a painfully class conscious child (lower-middle, he says, explaining that his dad only joined up to escape the dole), and he did not enjoy those army occupied beaches where the children of the ranks, like him, were segregated from the gilded offspring of the officers.

Mediocre at boarding school, his brain only woke up after he had read literature at Sussex University and gone on to take a post-graduate course at the University of East Anglia. He started writing here when he was part of Professor Malcolm *The History Man* Bradbury's writing programme. Someone on the same course remembers McEwan as manipulative and calculating, setting out even then to be a rich and famous Great Writer. The suggestion clearly upsets McEwan much more than criticisms of his latest book.

'When I was at UEA I certainly didn't have any clear idea that I was going to be a writer,' he says, this most mild-mannered of men turning suddenly heated. He quickly comes off the boil. 'If I had wanted to get rich and famous then writing short stories and sending them to *Transatlantic Review* would not have been a very clever way to start. I was really just enjoying myself at UEA. There was a lot of experimenting with drugs – which is an absurd thing to say, they were just consumed – and it excited me to be writing into the night, no matter how badly. I had no clear sense of wanting to be a writer. That only happened when *I came back* and was yearning for some stability.'

Where Ian McEwan came back from was the hippy trail to Katmandu. He had bought a magic bus in Amsterdam and headed for the North-West Frontier. It was 1972. 'Psychotropic drugs', he has written, 'were consumed in large quantities.'

Three years later when *First Love, Last Rites* was published to ecstatic reviews, McEwan was already living modestly on what his short stories earned. In the early eighties the writer moved from the ascetic squalor of his South London pad to the lusher pastures of Oxford. Today he lives in a spacious house with his wife Penny Allen, an alternative healer, Penny's two teenage daughters from a previous marriage and the couple's two young sons, William and Gregory. McEwan was present at both births and eighteen months ago he delivered his youngest son himself. McEwan seems to be happier now than he has ever been.

But what is Ian McEwan *for*?

'I would like – it sounds pompous – I would like to make people feel more alive. I am a closet moralist with a puritan streak that I am finding harder to control as I get older. Not that I am pointing the way to better behaviour but I would like to make people . . . more alert to whatever is within them.'

And just how good is Ian McEwan? Did he peak ten years ago or is the best yet to come? My view is that it is too early to put his name down for a place in history but writing his obituary is also a little premature. As the Bard said – it's not over till it's over . . .

'Posterity? I only think about it when I am in my cups.'

Your friend Martin Amis told me that it is the only thing that matters. Being read afrer you are dead. And he was serious.

'Martin did an interview where he talked about how much posterity means to him and the article had a very witty cartoon with Martin hanging off London Bridge, staring into the Thames, and the reflection he was getting back was Shakespeare.' McEwan laughs out loud. 'But I am not sure that the final judgement belongs to the future . . .'

And so we take our leave of Ian McEwan. Tonight he is staying with Amis in Westbourne Park and tomorrow he will go home to Oxford where there is a light that never goes out. I hope that he comes back.

'Horrific things are a lot more interesting than nice things,' he says. 'You paint the world black to find out what is good. It is like

Portia's line – I'm paraphrasing – about the candle in the darkness and how far that little candle throws its beam, so shines a good deed in a wicked world. It is immensely satisfying for a writer like me to light that one candle.'

But you have taken so long to get your matches out, Ian.

'But they were always in my back pocket,' he says, and seals it with an adjective. 'Rattling.'

Will Self

Daily Telegraph, **October 1993**

'The English are like a nation waiting at a literary bus stop,' says Will Self, sucking on a Camel. 'And *every* time a bus pulls up it's the *wrong number* or they *don't like the driver* or it's *full*. They are all standing there in their plastic macs and their head-scarves, refusing to get on.'

What's your idea of hell? For a large number of literary critics it seems to be the emergence of a writer who was named as one of the Twenty Best Young British Novelists *before* he had published his first full-length novel and who then had the nerve to promote that debut with what they perceived as the double-whammy of horror (the book's first chapter features a sex scene with a decapitated tramp) and hype (the author's name is such a gift to headline writers that for a while it was assumed he had made it up).

No novelist has ever made the transformation from great white hope to *bête noire* as quickly as Will Self. Not so long ago his collection of short stories, *The Quantity Theory of Insanity* and his hermaphroditic novellas *Cock & Bull* (wherein a man grows a vagina and a woman sprouts a penis) had the likes of Martin Amis, Doris Lessing, Ruth Rendell, Salman Rushdie and Beryl Bainbridge forming a queue to anoint him with lavish praise that was unprecedented for a writer whose career had just begun.

But earlier this month came the publication of Self's first novel, *My Idea of Fun* (Bloomsbury, £15.99), a Faustian narrative surrounded by the furniture of life in the nineties, and it has inspired a torrent of abuse that is equally unprecedented. The quality press have given *My Idea of Fun* a ferocious

74

kicking, often comparing the author unfavourably to his literary antecedents. 'Comparing Self to William Burroughs is like comparing Roald Dahl to Kafka,' said one. 'He writes like Martin Amis going cold turkey with a thesaurus,' spat another. '*Alice In Wonderland* brutally synthesized with *The Naked Lunch*,' sneered a third.

'There are a load of nerdy literary journalists,' retorts Will Self (his real name). 'A bunch of nerds who all have hairless ankles and have come straight out of Oxford and sat down in a library for ten years.'

In the pale, personable flesh, Self is supremely self-confident, a naturally combative man. And yet he is reluctant to plead not guilty to all the charges against him.

'It *is* a very nasty book,' he concedes. 'It was a very disturbing book to write because it is about the conflation between neurosis and evil. And the thesis of the book is that ugly thoughts can be ugly actions.'

In *My Idea of Fun* a lower-middle-class boy called Ian Wharton with an upwardly mobile mother and an absent father is taken in hand by a retired businessman who turns out to be The Fat Controller, who may or may not be Satan's chief personnel officer.

By the time Ian is a thirtysomething marketing man – promoting a chain of restaurants called 'Just Lettuce' pitching the idea of a CD full of fridge noises – he is tearing the head off a tramp, killing an office worker for his suit and having oral sex with a dead pit bull.

'The problem is that literature is competing with the three-minute attention span and cultural fixes that can be obtained so much more easily elsewhere,' says Self. 'I am not going to come the Jeanette Winterson, but ordinary people that read it don't have any problem with it. Literature has to compete with film. That's why I am not afraid to tackle extreme violence, sex, whatever. You have got to provide entertainment value.'

The gory cameos are actually a tiny part of *My Idea of Fun*. What seems to truly offend Self's critics is how successful he has been at marketing his book.

'And I have been thinking lately that if I was a punter I would be turned off, which depresses me,' he admits. 'Because it is ALL about getting the book read. To me the book is about the decline of patriarchy, the crisis of fatherhood in our society – very much in response to becoming one myself. [Self is married with two small children]. What are fathers *for*?'

Self's alleged insatiable appetite for publicity overlooks one important factor – he is great copy. Although only thirty-one, he is a man with a past. 'A dosser stands out a mile but a junkie is a member of the plain clothes division of debauchery,' he writes in *My Idea of Fun* which – apart from being a black comedy, moral fable and reflection on the nature of evil – also contains the story of his life.

'The most hurtful thing is not people saying that it's rubbish but when someone said there's no real anguish behind that text. Because that is a really anguished book. People talk about callow, self-regarding prose but that is what my life was *like*, that's what it was *like* being brought up in Hampstead Garden Suburb with crashingly literate parents and finding myself up at Oxford and a heroin addict at eighteen. Of course it is self-regarding! What else could it be like?'

There are some amazing flights of fantasy in *My Idea of Fun*, – at one point Ian visits The Land Of Children's Jokes, which is populated by the likes of Doug (as in, 'What do you call a man with a spade in his head?'). But when Self writes about the wretched inhabitants of the backstreets of King's Cross, it seems horribly real.

'The observations on the junkie hinterland are straight auto-biography. I know what I'm writing about. There were a lot of us middle-class junkie kids in the late seventies when the Iranians hit London with all that good brown gear. Everybody was taking it, it was almost socially acceptable. And it was the antithesis of a spiritual life. It was the most material and deadened existence I can think of – here I am, every opportunity in the world, crippled by a ridiculous drug addiction.'

We are in Bloom's on Whitechapel High Street in the East End, tucking into chicken casserole and dumplings as Self – who has recently been accused of anti-semitism, along with everything else – discusses his Jewish heritage.

'Only my mother was Jewish and she was a very deracinated Jew. She was completely *schiz* about it – on the one hand she would say, nobody knows I'm Jewish, nobody knows I'm Jewish! And would be quite paranoid about it – and being an American living here, she had good cover. But on the other hand she would say – everybody knows Jews are more intelligent than everyone else! In English society, at the end of the day if you are a Jew you are a Jew. Even if, like me, you have half non-Jewish blood, you're still not quite pukka.'

If you read Self's reviews he sounds remarkably like Bret Easton Ellis, the *American Psycho* man, a purveyor of amoral mayhem. If you actually read his work you see he is more like a delinquent William Burroughs or a darker shade of Ian McEwan. But his closest literary relation is widely regarded as Martin Amis.

'We are both middle-class boys that got sent to quite tough schools when we were at a young and brutal age,' Self says of Amis. 'And we were put in these environments where the values around us were not the values in our homes. That's the similarity we have in sensibilities – a determination to embrace life outside the bourgeoisie. They won't let me be myself, of course. I have to be the new Martin Amis.'

Ultimately Self has a unique vision. Yes, when the cameras are rolling he can be a ham. But he has not been promoted harder than anyone else. Just better.

'I do believe it is important to write proper, grown-up, high art novels. But that doesn't mean that high art shouldn't acknowledge the culture it's in. Or that you shouldn't try to win an audience. But that's what gets up people's noses – and I don't blame them. But you have to have some sort of aspiration if you are alone in a room writing a book for two years.'

Self is currently working on a book of drug essays which will be followed by a large-canvas novel exploring the gloaming of London's ethnic communities. Our talk in Bloom's, he insists, is his valedictory interview. Not only is all this promotion exhausting his muse, but his publisher reports stacks of letters from females seeking information on this interesting-looking man. Will Self is in danger of becoming the thinking woman's crumpet.

'That's no help, the sex stuff,' he says, embarrassed for the first time. 'I think *that* winds people up. It is staggering to me that I could be a sex symbol of any description. I think I've got a face like a bag full of genitals.'

Paul Smith

***Guardian*, 21 November 1992

Paul Smith is sitting comfortably. 'The name's made up, of course,' he says. 'I'm actually one of the Von Heidelbergs.' Of course. I always thought it was too pat that Britain's most successful designer should have such a spectacularly British name. Paul Smith Ltd has an annual turnover of £54 million with shops in twenty-five countries all selling a little bit of England. That unassuming label – a neat black autograph on a white background – always seemed just too perfect.

But, of course, the name is not made up. Paul Smith is just kidding, breaking the ice in his office above his shops in Covent Garden's Floral Street. The room is a mad jumble of clothes, magazines and antiques but I soon feel at home. Paul Smith makes sure of it.

This tall, youthful man – still gawky at forty-six – somehow combines a bluff Northern warmth with a smooth, cosmopolitan charm. There is something eminently approachable about Paul Smith. It is the secret of his success.

Paul Smith makes people feel comfortable. His clothes attract arty types of every hue – Hockney, Jagger, Bowie, Jack Nicholson, Alan Parker, Norman Foster, George Michael, Richard Rogers and Mick Hucknall have all flashed their plastic in Floral Street – but he also gets brokers and builders.

On a Saturday afternoon, his shops ring to the sound of every kind of accent. Paul Smith has taken the embarrassment out of men's fashion.

'A lot of clothes shops around the world make you feel like you need a stiff drink and a new hairdo before you walk in the door,' he says. 'And I hate that. I want people to get a tingle of excitement when they walk into my shops.'

His clothes are high quality, hard wearing and reasonably priced – but their appeal goes way beyond these purely practical terms. Like Giorgio Armani, Paul Smith has an aura. His clothes convey a silent blessing. You are a man of taste and wealth (they are not *that* cheap).

Paul Smith's clothes make you feel that you are quite a guy. Like Armani, Paul Smith whispers – you're doing fine. And he is bloody good. Let's not lose sight of that. Unlike Versace and Gaultier, Paul Smith's clothes do not make you feel like a screaming nelly. They let you be yourself – or a slightly improved version of the real you. Paul Smith's clothes allow you to be an individual – but not so individual that people throw rocks at you in the streets.

'It's not Jimi Hendrix,' he says. 'But I allow you to quietly show your colours. It's like the Mods being into regimental ties. I love that.'

Paul Smith actually allows the modern male to be as wacky as he wants to be. The two most colourful items in my wardrobe are a Paul Smith shirt (a riot of primary-coloured circles) and a Paul Smith waistcoat (an explosion of autumnal leaves).

But his suits could be worn to any office in the land. He sells a kind of seditious elegance, a Mod Nouveau sensibility that is much loved by both the creatives and the ordinary salarymen who buy his clothes.

'I allow the wearer to put their personality into my clothes,' he says. 'The clothes allow people to express their character rather than overwhelming it. That's why I have a lot of creative people as customers because they appreciate that. It's the difference between being a dandy and a fop. A dandy is into the way he looks and a fop is an attention seeker. Paul Smith is for the dandy element.'

'He manages to combine two strands of the British character,' says Peter Howarth, style editor at *GQ*, 'which is an innate conservatism with flashes of eccentricity. He's tapped into that and it is a very solid philosophy. And he has lasted. You go to the big menswear shows in Paris and Milan and the only British designer up there is Paul Smith.'

And how has he done it? He ascribes his success to being 'an okay designer and an okay businessman', but surely so are lots of other people. 'It's actually almost impossible to find both those qualities in a designer,' says Sarah Mower, fashion features director at *Harper's Bazaar*. 'Most designers just want their clothes to sell to twenty-five people at one nightclub in London. Paul Smith is more grown up than that. In many ways he is a very MOR designer. But he is a brilliant retailer who knows what regular guys want.'

Paul Smith shops are famous for selling stuff as well as clothes. Right now it is plastic spaghetti sculptures. In the past it was pink and lilac vacuum cleaners. Back in the eighties he discovered some of the emblems of the decade – such as boxer shorts ('His gift to Marks & Spencer,' says Sarah Mower) and the Filofax. A lot of people get stuck in a decade. How did Paul Smith manage to transcend the eighties?

'I was never a man of the eighties,' he says. 'Yes, I was the guy who found the Filofax, but all I did was introduce it to the world – somebody else made it foul. I am definitely not an eighties kind of guy – I hated the greed, the corporate expansion, people *going for it*. All I did in the eighties was let it roll.'

Although Paul Smith once seemed as much a part of the eighties as Mrs Thatcher, red braces and getting pissed on dessert wines at three o'clock in the afternoon in Alastair Little's, the people who know him best agree that he was never a part of the greed-is-good era.

'That image of him being the darling of the yuppy bankers was always a media invention,' says Peter Howarth, who once worked for Smith. 'In a world that is built on myth and marketing, he is a remarkably genuine and honest man.'

'The main thing about Paul is that he is really, really generous,' says Nick Logan, the publisher of *Arena* and *The Face*, and a good friend of Smith's. 'He is totally selfless. He has helped so many students, people starting out and businesses who got into trouble.'

When Jason Donovan successfully sued *The Face*, Paul Smith was one of Nick Logan's greatest allies in helping raise the magazine's legal fees and the damages award to Donovan. Smith designed and sold two excellent T-shirts in aid of *The Face*. His support was emotional as well as financial. On the Friday that the jury delivered its verdict, Paul Smith turned up in *The Face*'s local pub with a gift – one of his shirts – for Nick Logan.

Paul Smith was born in Nottingham in the summer of 1946. He hated school and left at fifteen to carry garments around a clothing warehouse. As a boy he was obsessed with racing bikes and dreamed of winning the Tour de France.

'I was only interested in being a cyclist,' he says. 'I was in bed at nine, eating certain foods, very serious. And then I was hit by a car and ended up in hospital for six months. I realized that there's more to life than riding a bike. I never really had any kind of social life before the pub I started drinking in was, by chance, the one where all the kids from the art school hung out. Then suddenly I became aware of things I'd never heard of – Bauhaus, pop art, Warhol – and I was completely fascinated. It was another world where everyone was into graphics, music and clothes.'

He began to learn about art and design. He began to think that he was pretty cool. Then on his twenty-sixth birthday he met a woman who made him realize that he wasn't cool at all.

Pauline Denyer was a London college lecturer with two young sons, Jason and Marcus (now thirty-two and twenty-nine) who had come to Nottingham to teach. She wore dark glasses. Even at night. Paul Smith was thunderstruck.

'She had studied at the Royal College of Art with Hockney and Allen Jones. She actually knew people that I had only ever heard about. She worked for a design company where Patti Boyd was the house model. Meeting Pauline made me realize that I was just a provincial guy. She had all this knowledge plus – she liked me! And she encouraged me to start my own business.' Paul Smith moved out of his parents' house and moved in with Pauline, her sons, and a menagerie of cats and dogs. They have been together now for twenty-five years.

'She taught me everything I know,' he says. 'She was – and still is – an inspiration. I was working as an assistant in this other clothes shop and Pauline said – you've got so much energy, so many ideas, you should have your own place and do it your way.'

The empire that Paul Smith built was started in 1970 with £600 savings. That first shop in Nottingham was more of a box – a twelve-foot square space down a back alley. Smith stuck a sign at the end of the alley saying Vestes Pour Homme and opened two days a week. The rest of the time he made a living

81

and served an apprenticeship that would give most designers the vapours.

'From Monday to Thursday I did things to support my new found family. I used to commute a lot. Hippy shops in London would want velvet trousers made and I would find a factory up near Nottingham that could make them. I even did alterations on my mum's sewing machine. And I went to night school to learn pattern cutting. Between 1970 and 1976 I was learning my trade and keeping my shop going. In October 1976 I had the confidence to have something made with the Paul Smith label.'

And 1976 was the year that – urged on by Pauline – they relocated to London. Three years later Paul Smith opened his first shop at 44 Floral Street.

'I came to London to be anonymous. You can be too famous in a provincial city. Pauline made me understand that. I rejected the bad things about provincial life – the small mindedness, the little cliques – but I've kept my roots. It's very down to earth and I value that. Did you know that Nottingham is literally the centre of the country? But I had to get out. So then it was London. And then the world!'

Paul Smith is big in Japan. Very, very big. Out of that £54 million turnover, a staggering £33 million is earned in Japan, where he has seventy shops. In Japan, Paul Smith is bigger than Armani, bigger than Chanel. Every year he sells 70,000 suits to the Japanese; 5,000 people pass through his flagship shop in Tokyo's Shibuya every month.

They are buying high quality clothes of course – Paul Smith's stuff lasts for years – but also a taste of western promise. Apart from clothes, his Tokyo shop sells vinyl from the sixties, first edition photography books and old copies of *The Face* and *Arena*. But none of that explains how Paul Smith has conquered Japan while so many other European and American companies have failed.

'So many people have the wrong idea about Japan,' he says. 'When I give any kind of talk, the first thing businessmen want to know is: how do you get into Japan? And the answer is you go there to learn, to enjoy it, to get a feel of the place. The attitude of a lot of the foreigners in Japan is absolutely disgusting. You don't go there with contempt for the people and the culture. You don't go there just to make money. I have been to Japan thirty-one times. I am a success in Japan because I go there with love in my heart. I respect the people, I have tried to learn their ways. I love the place. A lot of important designers are not successful in Japan and they don't deserve to be.'

Think global, act local, he tells his staff. Learn about the local culture. Never assume. But hasn't Paul Smith felt the cold winds of recession?

'Not at all. Sales in Japan are 14 per cent up. Here we are taking spring orders now, which are the same as the winter orders – 30 per cent up on last year. The shops are all doing well.'

Paul Smith is a very wealthy man. He and Pauline have a house in Holland Park and another in Tuscany. You might think that these millions would turn the head of a boy from Nottingham. But he says all the changes that money brings happened long before he moved down to the capital.

'I had five Porsches before I ever moved to London,' he says. 'I lived fast. Hung out in Studio 54. Some men have a mid-life crisis because they never did it when they were young. They get to their forties and suddenly need the fast car or the young girl. I did all that in my twenties. I drive a 1956 Bristol that I bought for two grand. I don't need any more Porsches.'

He travels for six months out of every year, supervising his shops in two dozen countries and opening new ones (a big one in Paris in early 1993). No doubt this peripatetic lifestyle has helped him maintain a relationship for twenty-five years. I remind him of an old Japanese saying – a husband should be healthy and absent.

'Pauline's been enormously patient with me,' he says. She was involved in the fashion business until the mid-eighties then she went to school to learn the history of art, fine art and painting. She's a painter now. And she's so disciplined. She's had to be because of me travelling so much. But what's so wonderful is that she has allowed me to do that. Our relationship has continued to blossom. It has never been better.'

Though he has railed against the parochialism and inefficiency of the British fashion industry – he dropped out of the British Designer of the Year award earlier this year because he considers it 'irrelevant' and 'self-congratulatory' – he doesn't seem remotely jaded. Paul Smith still has the passion of a very young man and this rubs off on both his staff and his clientele. Unlike every other leading menswear designer in the world, when you walk into a Paul Smith shop there is always the possibility that the man whose name is on the label might be the man who serves you.

'One of the most stupid things about designers is that they fail to meet the people who pay their wages. I deliberately have this office above the shop so that every day I walk through and can see if it is clean, looking good and if the staff have the right attitude.'

He says that when he opened that first shop in Nottingham he was facing the problem that most men liked to spend their money on cars, beer and women. Possibly his major triumph is that he has helped clothes to elbow their way into that manly company. Paul Smith has taught a million men that Narcissus was an okay kind of guy.

'That first shop in Nottingham was just like a club,' he says, a little misty-eyed. 'People came from Sheffield, Leicester, Manchester. I got all the kids from the all-nighters at the Northern soul clubs. And I remember one time there was this solicitor trying on a grey flannel suit right next to a young guy trying on a Hawaiian shirt. Suddenly that kid did two perfect back flips and said, "Okay, I'll take it." And that is what Paul Smith is all about.'

In Bed with Mick Jagger

Marie Claire, **December 1992**

They say that the only woman in the Rolling Stones camp that Bianca could stand to be around was Shirley, the wife of Charlie Watts. Bianca is said to have liked Shirley because she believed that the drummer's wife was the only Stones woman who Mick hadn't fucked. True or false, it illustrates one central point about Mick Jagger's turbulent love life: he has been spoilt for choice. 'Jagger is about as sexy as a pissing toad,' said Truman Capote. Armies of women have disagreed and have fallen prostrate before Mick's grotesque beauty.

Jagger squired Marianne Faithfull in the sixties, Bianca in the seventies and Jerry Hall in the eighties (she may yet be his choice for the nineties). All three would, in their day, have been a candidate for any 'Most Beautiful Woman in the World' award. But there have been others. 'Mick sleeps with many women but he rarely has affairs with them,' Bianca said.

'They are all trying to use him. They are all nobodies trying to be somebody. I'm up against this every day,' said Jerry Hall. 'I'm not talking about just groupies. One girl, a famous singer, said to Mick when she first met him, "Should I put my diaphragm in? Or should we talk first?" Mick said it put him off so much. It's so unromantic.'

But romance has never really suited him, at least not in his public persona. Though he has written some tender love songs, on record Jagger has always seemed most at home when tormenting his women. 'Under my thumb is the squirming dog who just had her day,' he gloated as a young man, and this theme of crotch-scratching belligerence has dominated his work. And he *is* Mick Jagger, the lead singer of the ultimate rock and roll band. Next year he will be fifty. It can't be easy.

In 1992 Jagger became a grandfather for the first time and a father for the fifth time. When he fled Jerry Hall after the birth of their third child for the arms of a young nubile or two, it was tempting to see his errant behaviour as a symptom of Mick's menopause. But while the effect of being called 'Grandad' and reaching his half-century should not be discounted, the tabloids who condemned his infidelity as the pathetic antics of an ageing swinger ignored one crucial fact – Mick Jagger has always fucked around.

'Which songs are about me?' Jerry once asked him.

'They all are, darling,' he replied.

Sure.

'You can't stop having affairs if they come along,' he has said. 'But there's a difference between that and trying to be with every girl you meet.'

So what kind of women does Mick Jagger like? As we see from the years he spent with Marianne, Bianca and Jerry, he likes women in their prime. Or even a bit younger – many of his brief flings have been with girls who you could imagine getting over the affair by throwing themselves into their A levels.

Those who have chronicled life on the road with the Stones – Robert Greenfield in his book *A Journey Through America With The Rolling Stones*, Stanley Booth's *The True Adventures Of The Rolling Stones* – suggest that when he is touring, Mick will sleep with almost anyone. Playboy Bunnies. Backing singers. Lowly groupies. The wives of the rich and famous. Anyone. In this he is no different from any other rock and roller. But being Mick Jagger, he has a bigger choice than anyone else.

Off the road, his tastes are much more refined. He likes to win girls who are desired by other powerful men. 'Far and away the most beautiful lady you have ever seen on a catwalk,' said Donald Trump of Carla Bruni, the model Jagger was linked to after the rift with Jerry, while Jerry herself sat between Mick and Warren Beatty on their first big date. 'They were both being pretty keen,' remembered Jerry. But Jagger can fight off the stiffest competition.

He likes posh girls. The upper class has given him some of his most spectacular erections. Carla Bruni was born into the aristocracy, as was Marianne Faithfull, the daughter of a baroness, and Bianca Rose Perez Moreno de Macias, the daughter of Nicaraguan toffs.

Faithfull and Bianca were both his social superiors and Jagger, a terrific snob, has often used his relations with the opposite sex as a chance for social mobility. He is a sucker for true class. In many ways, Jerry Hall – who comes from a huge brood of dirt-poor Texans – was an aberration. But what Jerry has going for her – apart from the fact that she is a cosmic amalgam of legs, hair and teeth – is that she is an easy woman to be around. She wants to please her man. 'My mama told me that a woman should be a maid in the living room, a cook in the kitchen and a whore in the bedroom,' Jerry once informed me. Jagger likes a strong woman who doesn't attempt to be his equal.

His first love was Chrissie Shrimpton, the kid sister of Jean Shrimpton. She was a seventeen-year-old student when they began courting in the early sixties. Jagger allegedly proposed marriage but quickly changed his mind when fame deposited a legion of women on his doorstep. They spent four years together. 'He kept her under his thumb,' said Marianne Faithfull, adding that when the affair with Shrimpton was over, 'he never saw her any more.' If Jagger stays friends with an ex-lover then it is probably for the sake of the children. He is infinitely more dutiful as a father than he is as a husband and has a deep bond with the son and four daughters that he sired with three different women (three with Jerry, one with Bianca and one with Marsha Hunt). But though he loves his kids, it seems that too much domestic bliss makes him claustrophobic. He will never be comfortable smiling from the pages of *Hello!*, God bless him. Probably a contributing factor in the split with Jerry was that it was all getting a little too cosy.

He never played happy families with Marianne Faithfull. True, she had a small child that Jagger doted on, but domesticity was staved off by jealousy, mental confusion and drugs. There are those who see Faithfull as the love of Jagger's life. 'I think of all the girlfriends he's had, he loved her the most,' said Jerry Hall.

The daughter of Baroness Erisso, Faithfull was educated at St Joseph's Convent in Reading. She was seventeen when she met

Andrew Loog Oldham, the iconoclastic young manager of the Rolling Stones (he dreamed up the headline, 'Would You Let Your Daughter Marry A Rolling Stone?'). Oldham admired her pretty face, her sweet, melancholic grace and no doubt her mother's title. One night she spent thirty minutes recording a Jagger/Richard song called 'As Tears Go By'. It made her a pop star.

Faithfull was the epitome of liberated sixties womanhood, the First Lady of Swinging London. 'I lived in a Renoir painting,' she said. 'Long blonde hair, sunny days, straw hat with ribbons.' The reality was not quite so wistful. 'My first move was to get a Rolling Stone as a boyfriend,' she told *NME* in 1975, ten years after 'As Tears Go By'. 'I slept with three and then decided the lead singer was the best bet.'

She had married a Cambridge undergraduate called John Dunbar but by 1965 it was over and Faithfull – and her young son – were living with Jagger. While most of the Beatles were setting up home with their provincial childhood sweethearts, Jagger and Faithfull were the couple of the age. The fallen convent angel and the neanderthal rocker. He gave her notoriety. She gave him class. He also gave her a paltry £25 a week to keep house in Cheyne Walk. She was the first woman to complain of his stinginess, though not the last.

Perhaps Jagger was not so different from a Beatle husband lording it over his little hairdressing *hausfrau*. Faithfull says that Jagger resented her ambitions. 'You can't have two stars in the house,' she said, although she admits that she in turn was jealous of his achievements, especially his ability to turn her drug problems into great songs. 'I was jealous seeing him going out and doing better and better work,' she said. 'All my traumas and all my unhappiness he changed into brilliant songs and it made me sick to see him, like a really good writer or any really good artist, turning the traumas in his own home into work. All artists are totally selfish.'

Their *amour fou* floundered as the sweet dreams of the sixties were turning very sour. In Sydney, where Jagger was to make a film about Ned Kelly, Faithfull – depressed by her fading relationship with Mick and the death of Brian Jones – took 150 Tuinal sleeping pills. Jagger woke up and summoned help quickly enough to save her life. He is good in a crisis (Jerry Hall says that he was incredibly supportive when she was wrongly arrested in Barbados for possessing 20lb of marijuana).

As the sixties drew to a bitter end, one cold Chelsea night Faithfull grabbed her son and some clothes and left Jagger. For months he tried to win her back. But she was sinking deeper into heroin and one day Jagger walked in to find that she had done something unforgivable. She had become fat. And then he no longer wanted her.

Years later someone asked Jagger if he felt responsible for destroying Marianne Faithfull. 'Marianne nearly killed me, man!' he replied. 'I wasn't going to get out of there alive.' Guilt does not come easily to him. On the rocky road to the seventies, Jagger had a brief relationship with Marsha Hunt, a black American who danced naked in the hippy musical *Hair*. Jagger has always had a soft spot for black girls and their union would have been unremarkable if it had not produced a child, Mick's first. At the time, Hunt refused to name the father of her daughter – although his identity was widely known. 'He's no longer involved with us,' Hunt said. 'At first I thought I cared for him a lot, but I found out afterwards I didn't really know him at all.'

In her autobiography, Marsha Hunt says that Jagger told her he didn't love her and never had, only a couple of weeks after their daughter Karis was born. Happily, Hunt, Jagger and their daughter Karis have since established a much warmer relationship. Jagger can be very adult about these situations.

As the new decade dawned, Narcissus discovered his reflection and was immediately smitten. Apart from looking like a female version of Jagger, the woman who would become his wife (his first and, I believe, his only wife) embodies many of the qualities that Mick seeks in a lover. Bianca had class. She was exotic. And she was hard to get. They met at a Stones show in Paris in 1970 as Faithfull unravelled back in London, and Bianca was 'an Inca princess dressed like a Dior mannequin', according to Philip Norman, 'watching the proceedings with the slightly contemptuous detachment of an Egyptian royal cat.'

And Jagger was on the rebound. The wounds inflicted by breaking with Faithfull were too serious to be soothed by blowjobs from an endless succession of groupies. Mick married his glossy Latin beauty in St Tropez on 12 May 1971.

They had a fight on their wedding day – always a bad omen

– because Bianca initially refused to sign a wedding contract stipulating whether their property was to be held jointly or separately (the contract was required by French law rather than Jagger's parsimony). Bianca thought that such clinical legalities had no place in romance and wanted the wedding called off. Jagger got angry. 'Are you trying to make a fool of me in front of all these people?' An intensely proud man, he does not like to lose face, and Bianca relented.

After a chaotic civil marriage and a quiet religious ceremony where the organist played the theme from *Love Story* (Bianca's choice), the happy couple retired to their wedding party accompanied by assorted Beatles and Stones. The groom, always the exhibitionist, took to the stage to strut his funky stuff and Bianca stormed off, sulking for reasons unknown. Perhaps she did not want to share Mick Jagger with the crowd. She later said her marriage ended on the day of her wedding. Marianne Faithfull heard about the wedding on her way to Paddington to catch a train to see her parents. She went into an Indian restaurant and eventually became so tired and emotional that she passed out with her lovely face in a plate of curry. She spent the night in Paddington Green police station. Five months later in Paris, Bianca gave birth to a daughter called Jade.

'The music's not as good,' sniffed Marianne Faithfull of Jagger's new muse. But for a while the couple were in Biba heaven, defining the new age as surely as Mick and Marianne had in the sixties.

The St Tropez wedding of these two pouting beauties marked the start of the transition of rock stars from grubby bad boys to jet-setting Nigel Dempster fodder, hanging out with Andy Warhol and Halston in the VIP room at Studio 54.

But Mr and Mrs Jagger were soon arguing on two continents. What did they argue about? Everything. Careers, their daughter, their friends (none of them mutual). Perhaps the only thing they didn't argue about were Mick's casual fucks. Bianca was always too sophisticated to play the part of the jealous wife, and in these pre-HIV years, the exchange of bodily fluids really did not seem to count for very much. But like some seminal Princess of Wales, what Bianca objected to was the privileged, oppressive world inhabited by her husband. And though widely perceived as a gold-digger who wanted only to further her career as an actress and model, she seems to have genuinely hated the sordid scenes that surrounded the band. She despised the sycophantic courtiers, the sexual and chemical gluttony, the endless travelling, all the things that look quite appealing from a distance and are no fun being married to.

Though their marriage would drag on for a few more years (their divorce was finalized in 1980), Jagger and Bianca were leading separate lives by the time he found something stirring in his trousers for a young Texan model called Jerry Hall. She was going out with someone else at the time. But Jagger never lets that stop him.

Jagger invited the prairie rose and her boyfriend Bryan Ferry to a Stones show in 1976 (backstage at a Stones concert is always Mick's favourite singles bar). After the show they went back to Ferry's house in Holland Park. Jagger is never shy in declaring his feelings. 'I'd go in the kitchen to fix some more tea and Mick would follow me and Bryan would follow him,' wrote Jerry in her wonderful autobiography, *Tall Tales*. 'He was real jealous that Mick was flirting with me. Finally Bryan got really upset and said, "I'm going to bed." He stomped off and everyone started to leave. And Mick tried to kiss me but I didn't let him.'

She did eventually. After her dinner date sitting between Jagger and Warren Beatty at that New York restaurant, Jerry ended up in bed with Jagger (he enjoys stealing women from under the nose of another sex god). Jerry was guilt-ridden for betraying Ferry and told the rubber-lipped Lothario that it could not happen again. But it did.

After the dirty deed was done, Jagger sent flowers, he called – he can be the perfect gentleman when he wants to be – and though she tried to fight him off, once again Jerry's long, golden body ended up in Mick's bed. And as Jerry fretted about whether she could stick with Ferry or submit to Jagger's lascivious charms, Mick would sit on the floor, get out his guitar and sing her an old blues song by Robert Johnson. 'Stop breaking down/Mama, please stop breaking down/The stuff I've got will bust your brains out baby/Girl, you're going to make me lose my mind.' He is quite capable of turning the romance up to full volume. Then Jerry's father died. She was devastated. Ferry was touring. Jagger was there for her and genuinely sympathetic.

That clinched it – she would leave Ferry for Jagger. But if this lasts a year it's a miracle, thought Jerry.

Seven years later their first child, Elizabeth Scarlett, was born. Her brother James arrived a year later and baby Georgia was born at the start of this year. They are all cherubs wreathed in golden ringlets with bee-stung lips, little Micks made angels. Typically, Jagger has lavished love and attention on his children but has not let their presence interfere too much with his sex life. During his relationship with Jerry, Jagger has had a number of outside interests. The press has linked him with Catherine Guinness in 1979 and Lord Longford's daugther Natasha Fraser in 1980. 'Purely platonic,' said Jagger. 'He's my new boyfriend,' Natasha is said to have told friends. 'Stay away from my man,' said Jerry.

Then there was teenage New Yorker Gwen Rivers in 1982. The same year Mick was seen dancing at a nightclub with a US deb Cornelia Guest, eighteen, the *Sun* tells us. 'They later had breakfast together.'

1982 – the year before he turned forty – was the year of living unfaithfully for Jagger; the year when he went astray in a spectacular fashion. 'He decided to take advantage of the way girls are,' said Jerry. She immediately retaliated with an affair with horse-loving tycoon Robert Sangster. Stung, Jagger pursued her. And he gives very good phone.

He won her back but, ten years on, Jerry Hall is faced with exactly the same problems with this year's models. At the time of going to press, there are rumours of a reconciliation. Anyway, talk of Jagger and Jerry divorcing is almost certainly academic. Last year they went through a Hindu wedding ceremony in Bali but were unable to supply the Indonesian government with all the documentation needed to make the ceremony legally binding – passports, birth certificates, doctor's letters, divorce papers and – most important of all – a letter from a Hindu priest stating that the couple have converted to the Hindu faith. Neither Mick nor Jerry are practising Hindus. Was it just coincidence that Jagger went through a wedding ceremony that did not actually marry them? Or did slippery old Mick know exactly what he was doing?

And what happens to Mick Jagger's women? Jerry Hall once told me that when Jagger went through his phone book from the sixties, half the people in it were dead. His women have fared slightly better. Chrissie Shrimpton is forty-nine now, the mother of four children and living in south London with her husband Mike Von Joel. In 1976 Jagger won a High Court injunction forbidding her from publishing his love-letters in one of our sleazier tabloids. 'I shudder to think of being married to Mick,' shuddered Chrissie. 'He takes a lot of pleasing.'

Marianne Faithfull, the girl from a Renoir, exchanged Mick Jagger for heroin. She spent a lot of time in the early seventies roaming Soho trying to feed her habit. Later she kicked her addiction, worked in the theatre, made some critically acclaimed albums and is currently working on her autobiography. She is philosophical about her love affair with Jagger. 'We loved each other,' she said. 'We wanted to keep it and we couldn't in the end. You need time to be together. He was so busy that I really tried to hold myself back. And it nearly destroyed me. The effort of restraining myself and not working was terrible. And I ended up on drugs.'

She does not blame Jagger for her descent into hard drugs. 'People always assume I was already a junkie when I was with Mick – but I wasn't. At that stage it was still an experiment.' Faithfull married a punk rocker called Ben E. Ficial (not his real name), but is now single. She does not regret the night she walked out of Cheyne Walk and Mick Jagger's life. 'It would have killed me staying with Mick,' she said. 'He has always been quite brutal towards his women. I still love him in a way but everything happened for the best. If I was Mick's chick I'd be just that.'

Marsha Hunt is now a successful novelist and the daughter she had with Jagger is a university graduate (Mick attended her graduation ceremony). Bianca Rose Perez Moreno de Macias flirted with acting but that didn't work out. Now she does good works on behalf of her country, raising funds and visiting trouble zones in Nicaragua and other Central American countries. 'I have survived,' she said. 'I was the Nicaraguan who married a rock star and now I am someone else. I have no regrets and we are still friends.'

Bianca was bad-mouthed as an upmarket bimbo but she has turned out to be a woman of real courage, real integrity, real substance. And she looks great. She lives in New York, but I saw her at a private club in London last year and – on the verge of becoming a grandmother – she looked like dynamite.

Jerry Hall's future is assured. She has hired out her lovely face to promote goods as varied as Bovril and Bentley, and has launched her own range of luxurious swimwear. She has such huge supplies of Texan charm that she will always be loved in this country. What she has to decide is if she wants to give Jagger another try or if she has been hurt enough.

The talk of the getting-back-together grows louder every day. By late summer Mick and Jerry were eating dinner together at the Mansion On Turtle Creek restaurant in Dallas. They were said to be spending their son's birthday together at La Fourchette, their château in the Loire valley. Sweetest of all, the happy couple were spotted cuddling backstage at a Dwight Yoakam concert in London.

My guess is that they will attempt to drag their relationship around the block one more time but that eventually there will be more betrayal, more tabloid headlines, more young lovelies kneeling before the altar of Mick Jagger's celebrity. And so it will go on until Jerry runs out of patience or Jagger runs out of juice.

But how about some sympathy for the old devil? Warren Beatty may get all misty-eyed every time he smells a soiled nappy but Warren has just become a father for the first time. Jagger has been a father for over twenty years. And Warren is an actor. Mick is no actor – as anyone who has seen any of his films will testify. Mick is rock and roll, where the love of a good woman can never truly compete with the love of a good time. Something that has been inside him all his life refuses to let him settle down. It's a blessing when you are a young man. By the time you are forty-nine, it is a kind of curse.

Jerry might believe that Jagger loved Marianne Faithfull more than any of his other girlfriends. Personally I think his great love is Jerry Hall. Jagger has, I believe, loved her as much as he can love a woman. If she can't hold him, no woman can. Which of course is a distinct possibility. He is, after all, Mick Jagger, the lead singer of the Rolling Stones, growing old disgracefully. What else did we expect?

Elton John

Daily Telegraph Magazine, **8 April 1995**

'Anyone can have an opinion about me,' says Elton John, the man who once received a £1 million settlement from an errant tabloid. 'Just as long as there's some truth in it. You can call me fat, bald, untalented pig – but if you tell a lie about me . . .'

Up close, the most famous hair transplant in the world looks just like the real thing. Dirty blond bangs flop down over the face of a slightly debauched choirboy. The rug operation is said to have cost £15,000, and yet it is easy to forgive Elton John's little vanities because he has never seemed like one of Mother Nature's rock stars. Elton always had to work at it.

Unlike Bowie or Jagger, he has wrestled with his weight, fretted about his hairline and wept when his football team lost in the Cup Final. Even back in the seventies, when he overcompensated for natural shyness by turning himself into a rock 'n' roll Liberace, he always seemed closer to his audience than his peers. What other member of the rock aristocracy would take to the stage dressed as Donald Duck? But this man-of-the-people image is deceptive. In terms of records sold, scandals endured and appetites indulged, Elton John is the biggest star of them all.

He makes more money – and gives more of it away –than any other British musician. His earnings for last year alone were more than £17 million. Two years ago he established the Elton John Aids Foundation, which receives the proceeds from all the singles he releases everywhere in the world. It has already given away $7 million to AIDS charities.

In the twenty-five years since 'Your Song' made him famous, Elton John has made more than forty albums and sold more than 200 million records. He was the first British superstar to emerge in the wake of the Beatles and America has always been mad about the boy – he has had at least one single on the *Billboard* chart every year since 1970 and he has now won an Oscar for Best Original Song. Commercially, he is the most successful solo artist since Elvis Presley. But beyond the cheery, gap-toothed grin, he has also been the most tormented. Cocaine, alcohol and Sainsbury's cockles – you name it, Elton John, the original sinner from Pinner, was once addicted to it.

'I was not a happy budgie,' he says in his suite at the Relais Carré d'Or, an exclusive residence (Stevie Wonder is in the suite next door) on Avenue George V in Paris. 'Not a happy budgie' turns out to be one of his favourite phrases. He is possibly the only major rock star who constantly compares his well-being to that of a domestic budgerigar. But until he changed his lifestyle, he was a very self-destructive budgie indeed.

'I took cocaine and I drank a lot because I felt that might help to loosen me up. I wanted to join the in-crowd. As a kid I was always on the fringe of everything. I wasn't part of the gang. Going out to the cinema with mates, I was always the last one to be asked. I thought that by doing coke I would finally be in with everybody else. And then I got the taste for it.' He was also bulimic, existing on the Elvis Presley diet plan – four pots of Sainsbury's cockles, three bacon sandwiches and a pint of Häagen-Dazs vanilla ice cream was standard fare. 'Then I would go and throw up and then do the whole lot again.'

Five years ago, Elton John checked into the Parkside Lutheran Hospital in Chicago to reclaim his life. His boyfriend of the time was with him and they both had to write down all the things that were wrong with each other. Elton's partner wrote, 'He is addicted to cocaine. He is an alcholic. He is bulimic. He has terrible fits of rage.' Elton wrote, 'He doesn't tidy up his CDs.'

'It was either clean up or die,' he says. 'Even though the dark side of me was thinking, well, you might as well die, I was saved by being all mouth and no trousers. I wanted to live. I wanted to give myself a chance. I wanted to be proud of myself and my life again. I finally saw what my life had become and how intolerable I had become. And I didn't want that any more.'

'I had forty years of pain and nothing to cling to,' he sings on his remarkable new album, *Made In England*. There are songs here, such as 'House' and 'Believe', that suggest Elton John has finally reached a state of grace. He no longer drinks or takes drugs. The only reminder of his wild years is his abiding passion for Sainsbury's cockles.

'We have some in the fridge at home. I still eat them. But not to the same extent that I did before.'

He says that he always worked best when not immersed in the fog of booze and cocaine. Now that he has emerged from the long, painful process of recovery, he has rediscovered his muse. After years of pleasant power ballads and politely up-tempo party numbers, *Made In England* has the resonance of autobiography. It is his strongest album for twenty years.

He describes the title track as 'a precis of my life'. It is all here – the strangely isolated childhood, the struggle for sexual identity, the historic action against the *Sun* (who forked out one of the largest settlements in British legal history after falsely accusing him of a multitude of sins, including dalliances with rent boys and removing the voice boxes of his guard dogs) and, above all, the successful battle against his multiple addictions.

'I feel closer to this collection of songs than to anything I've done for twenty years', he says. 'Bernie [Taupin, his longtime lyricist] has watched what has happened to me and tried to give me a set of lyrics I can relate to. I felt more involved with this album than I have for twenty years. With the advent of technology, I began to tune out. I wouldn't be there for half of it. I would go shopping or play tennis. I didn't want to do that any more. I think I coasted for a while, if I'm honest. An artist doesn't let someone else finish off his paintings for him, does he?'

He is using Paris as a convenient base for a week of promotion, commuting daily to perform chores on Spanish and German television. Home is in Holland Park, in London, which he shares with a young American called David Furnish.

He came out as bisexual almost twenty years ago, although after his brief marriage in the eighties to a German recording engineer called Renate Blauel, he now calls himself gay. Elton John wasn't quite the first rock star to admit to being something other than heterosexual – David Bowie did it a few years earlier, but at the time Bowie was a cult act trying to break into the big time. When Elton did it, he was already America's red-blooded sweetheart.

'I have never had any qualms about coming out and it's never held me back. It did in America for a while with the Bible Belt. But English people have always camped it up. English comedians, straight or gay, have always jumped into drag. That's one of the things I adore about England.'

He even looks back fondly at the regular ragging he took from away team supporters when he was the openly gay chairman of Watford Football Club. 'I took abuse – but it was good-natured, it was that English thing with a sense of humour.'

It says volumes about the courage and humour of the man that he can smile about 10,000 football supporters singing, 'Don't Sit Down When Elton Is Around' to the tune of 'My Old Man Said Follow the Van'. 'But I never felt afraid at football, and I never felt threatened,' he says. 'The abuse I got at football is completely different to the kind I got from the tabloids.'

His demeanour is matey, with only sporadic outbreaks of camp, such as when he refers to himself as 'her' and 'she'. ('In my office they were going, "She's finally lost it, she's round the twist",' is how he describes the reaction to one of his famous temper tantrums.)

He is wearing a grey two-piece check suit that would probably seem loud on anyone else, but looks rather sedate on the Little Richard of the Home Counties. The only sign of his old flamboyance is the triple gold band he wears around his right wrist. A dark, good-looking cameraman is filming our conversation for an Elton John documentary. This affable young cameraman turns out to be Elton's partner, David.

'We have been together for quite a while now – two years – and David gives me a lot of love, which I find very difficult,' says Elton. 'And yet it is what I've always wanted. One of my nicknames was Sharon Picket-Fence because I always wanted the relationship to go on forever. I always thought that my relationships failed because I was impossible. And I was impossible. But you can't have drugs in a relationship; it won't last. Every relationship I've ever had has always become a threesome instead of a twosome – me, my partner and cocaine. Now there are no more distractions. I have someone who is prepared to support me. I've got everything in my life back in order. I hope this one with David will last to the end.'

Elton Hercules John (his real name – he changed it by deed

poll) was born Reginald Kenneth Dwight in Pinner, Middlesex, in 1947. His father Stanley, an RAF squadron leader, was a distant figure and he was raised by his mother, Sheila, and his grand-mother, his beloved Nan. 'I had a love-me mother and a quit-me father,' he sings plaintively on the new album (Stanley Dwight died in 1991).

'I think being raised by women shaped my personality because I spent a lot of time on my own, in my room, playing records. It made me a loner. It made me shy with other kids. I created my own world. I was immersed in music and records even at that young age. But I don't really think being brought up by women had anything at all to do with my being gay. Because I think that's a genetic thing.'

There's a famous photograph of him as a small child sitting at his piano, immaculate and eager to please: he looks like a good little boy – almost impossibly good. He came very late to rebellion. When he went off the rails in the mid-seventies he discovered that he was blessed – or cursed – with the kind of constitution that would turn Keith Richards green with envy.

'I have the constitution of an ox. I would stay up all night for five or six days in a row and then go and do a rehearsal for a tour. After a while it takes its toll.' Throughout Elton's lost years he continued to work, touring and recording, often releasing two albums in the same year. His dissipation revealed itself in bizarre displays of temperament. One morning he looked out of his suite at the Inn on the Park and demanded that someone do something about the wind in Hyde Park.

'It's funny to look back on,' he says ruefully. 'But I was coming down off cocaine. I woke up in the morning and the wind was blowing – I blamed the hotel. On drugs I was divine, lovely and fabulous. Coming down off drugs, I was a nightmare. I used to fly over anger and land in rage. My personality couldn't handle the cocaine come-down. But I still get those rages. When you finally stop taking drugs you are still stuck with the person-ality you were when you started out.' Did he almost kill himself by trying too hard to be Elton John? Or by trying too hard to bury Reg Dwight of Pinner?

'I don't like being called Reg,' he insists. 'Reg is the unhappy part of my life. Eric [Clapton] still calls me Reg and it makes me cringe. I'm Elton. I'm not Reg.' The higher he climbed, the more bitter the self-loathing became. There was a theatrical suicide attempt in 1975 when it was 'Elton John Week' in Los Angeles. His hands had just been immortalized in Hollywood Boulevard cement, he was playing a string of sold-out concerts and staying at a mansion in the Hollywood Hills. As his proud family basked in his triumph, Elton took sixty Valium and jumped into the swimming pool with a cry of 'I'm going to die!' As they fished him out, he heard his grandmother say wistfully, 'I suppose we all have to go home now.'

'She was seventy-five at the time and didn't stand for any nonsense. She raised me more or less, with my mother. I grew up in her house. My family are very plain-speaking. And that made me very uncomfortable at times when my mother would say, "Listen, I don't want to be around you, I'm going".'

His mother, who had remarried in 1972, found his behaviour so painful that she left the country to live in Menorca, though she has since returned to England. He always remained close to the two women who brought him up.

He dedicated his Oscar to his grandmother who died the week before the Academy Awards. 'She was the woman who would sit me down at the age of three at a piano and make me play,' he said.

Elton John was forty-two years old when he entered rehabilitation, the same age Elvis Presley was when he died. Elton had met Elvis – and got his autograph – just before his death. But it was meeting a teenage haemophiliac who had been infected with the AIDS virus by a contaminated blood transfusion that made him determined to fight for his life.

After contracting AIDS, Ryan White had been persecuted at school and shunned by his neighbours to such a degree that his family were forced to abandon their Indianapolis home. White continued to campaign for greater awareness of the AIDS virus to the very end of his life. Profoundly moved by the dying boy's bravery, Elton John flew to his side and remained there to the end, comforting White's family, helping to organize his funeral and finally carrying his coffin. Ryan White was eighteen. Elton John would never be the same again.

'It made me realize what an insane, fantasy lifestyle I was living. Seeing Ryan and his mother forgive all the people who had been so vile to them, who then came to say they were sorry.

Seeing how brave that kid was – I just knew then that my life was completely out of whack. I had never really confronted the fact that I was a drug addict and that was why my life was a pile of rubbish. And it wasn't long after that I went in and got myself sorted out. I know that my mother had to leave the country because she couldn't stand to be around me – that's a pretty savage indictment of someone who thought that he was having a successful life. And in fact my life wasn't a success. My career was a success. But my life was pretty miserable.'

When he first entered treatment, Elton had to write a good-bye letter to cocaine. 'I wrote it as if I was saying goodbye to a boyfriend. I said, "I don't want you and I to share the same grave. I'm fed up with you. I don't want to die like that. You have been my whore. I've flown you in on planes. I've sent cars for you. I've even sent trains for you. I've spent lovely nights with you. I have always come back to you when I've left you. And this time it's got to be goodbye." '

How to explain the appeal of Elton John? He has a classic pop sensibility, of course, but that scarcely explains sales of 200 million records. Perhaps it is simply because people like Elton. If he seems like the most accessible rock star, he is also surely the most vulnerable. He has fought all of his battles in public. And although he has plumbed the depths of rock star indulgence, he has always felt like a force for good. After his victory over the *Sun*, the tabloids were never quite so cavalier with the truth again.

'There are a few things I've done in my life that I'm proud of – and I'm proud of the way I fought the *Sun*. It was a year and a half of sheer misery, but I was prepared to spend every penny I had. There were some days when I would get up and look at the front page of the *Sun* and just cry my eyes out. It was a constant battle. At the time that was going on I wasn't a particularly well budgie so you can imagine the trauma it caused me.'

But now he has just released his strongest record since *Goodbye Yellow Brick Road* and is living with a man he considers the love of his life. Elton John – happy at last? Not quite.

'There's an inner peace now,' he says. 'But there are times when that inner peace is rattled and I become the dark, broody, unhappy person I was before. Recovery is a never-ending process. I don't go to AA meetings any more, because there are certain parts of my nature that can't be solved by going to an AA meeting. Those demons that will always be inside me sometimes rear their ugly head. But they usually don't win any more.'

Albert Goldman

***Vox*, November 1992

Albert Goldman is a dirt-sucking, sleaze-licking, turd-sniffing sack of prurience. And I can't wait for his next book. Book? Albert Goldman doesn't write books. He issues *fatwahs*.

Goldman is the writer who has made a million dollars – and a million enemies – by combining a tabloid hack's love of sleaze with a serious biographer's depth of research.

His 1981 book *Elvis* was the result of six hundred interviews and four years' word-processing. In 591 pages of well-researched spite, Goldman revealed that Presley was a pervert, a junkie and a gun fetishist. Well, nobody's perfect.

The Lives Of John Lennon in 1988 was the result of 1,200 interviews and six years' work. Goldman alleged that Beatle John was a bully, a sadist and a junkie. Bad to his wife, bad to his son, bad in bed. These two books have earned Goldman a reputation as the Rasputin of rock writing and a sizeable collection of death threats.

The next subject – make that victim – of Goldman's attention will be Jim Morrison. This will be the Lizard King with his leather trousers down; a book to make Oliver Stone's film look like a French kiss. It will not be a pretty sight.

For years Hollywood stars like Monroe and old showbiz types like Sinatra have suffered at the hands of biographers eager to sniff their dirty laundry. But Albert Goldman was the first man to bring this lust for soiled sheets to the fun-filled world of pop.

The King of Rock and Roll? An obese racist, says Goldman, stuffing in every kind of drug at one end while pooping his XXL baby diapers at the other. And John Lennon? Lethargic, impotent, talentless. Every rock star is a rat and Albert Goldman is Rentokil.

His publishers call him a 'master of the world of pop culture' but he is not that. A bald old jazz fan, Goldman *loathes* pop culture. He comes not to praise rock 'n' roll but to bury it. Every page of his books hums with the electricity of pure spite. This makes his books highly entertaining – hate is rarely dull – but also somewhat curious. I mean, they may have made a few groupies cry but so what? In this sad world full of murder and misery, they are just pop stars. They have killed nobody except themselves. It's only rock 'n' roll.

The motives for most rock books are love and money. Usually just the latter but sometimes both. The bad rock books – and most of them are complete crap – are written quickly, often by people who have never looked their subject in the eye. The best ones – Anthony Scudatto's book on Dylan, Jerry Hopkins and Danny Sugerman's Jim Morrison memorial *No One Here Gets Out Alive*, the Marvin Gaye biography by David Ritz – are labours of love written by people who respect the man and love the music.

Goldman is not like that. Neither love nor money interest him very much. Of course the money is nice, but ultimately he is in it for the pure sadistic joy of sticking the blade in the soft, white guts of some cultural deity.

Goldman loathes rock's heroes, loathes the pale children who consume it, and loathes the fact that it has dominated popular culture in a way that Goldman's beloved jazz never did and never will.

Goldman's books are fun. But like a public hanging, they leave a nasty taste in the mouth. Praise of the subjects is thin on the ground and, if he doesn't think that Presley or Lennon made wonderful music, how in the hell can we trust his other judgements? Still, there's no denying that his reports of life inside Graceland or the Dakota building have the awful ring of truth about them. And life inside Morrison's leather trousers? It is going to be very messy. Goldman is not a great writer but, hot damn, he is effective. He is effective in the way Nobby Stiles was effective. Albert Goldman goes in with his studs showing. Albert Goldman always goes over the top.

What's wrong with his books is that, despite the long years

researching every great subject, this is not his world. He is an outsider. He subjects never touched his heart or moved his feet.

For twenty-three years Goldman was a Professor of English and Comparative Literature at Columbia University, New York. He wrote a book about comedian Lenny Bruce, but Goldman only discovered his destiny when he turned to Presley.

Goldman's great subject is Elvis. He has written two books on the subject, the monumental *Elvis* and the slim follow-up, *Elvis: The Last 24 Hours*. He is obsessed with the King. He has hounded him beyond the grave. The ultimate rock star, Presley is the biggest target any enemy of pop culture could have.

I suspect that originally he stumbled on Elvis Presley's horror. That he researched the ultimate hero and found that he had stinking feet of clay. This fitted all his prejudices and then it became his gimmick, his routine. The two books are as biased as propaganda. Presley, Lennon, Morrison – all of them produced work of bright, shining glory. Unfortunately Albert, this literary Darth Vader, inhabits only the dark side. To find some joy and light, you have to return to the music.

But Goldman is a grafter. This is both a strength and a weakness in his books. Sometimes you stumble across great undigested clumps of research that one of his team has brought back from Liverpool or Memphis, but other times he turns up a gem, such as some hired hand telling him about Yoko sprinkling cat shit on the carpet for our John to tread in.

But though Goldman does his worst to destroy his subjects, ultimately they are out of his reach. Goldman can dance on Presley's grave until his legs fall off, but 'King Creole' still sounds good to me. Jim Morrison says more in one song than Albert Goldman will say in a lifetime. And there is more love, joy, torment and pain in one of John Lennon's farts than Goldman and his team of researchers could muster from here to eternity.

Goldman is a seething sack of negative energy and that is why he will never achieve the greatness of his subjects.

You suspect Albert knows this and – curses! foiled again – it gives him the mad passion to carry on tearing down the false idols of rock music. It makes reading his books more fun than pulling out the wings of butterflies.

Michael Jackson

***Daily Telegraph*, 14 June 1995**

Michael Jackson may be weird but he is not stupid. In a machiavellian marketing move, Jackson's first album since the child molestation allegations of two years ago, *HIStory* (Jacko's capitals), yokes the glories of his past to the traumas of more recent times. *HIStory – Past, Present and Future – Book I* (to give the double CD its full, laborious title) asks just one question of Michael Jackson's audience: Don't you love me any more?

HIStory (geddit?) is half greatest hits package, half personal testimony. The first CD, *HIStory Begins*, features fifteen of Jackson's remastered hits, while the second CD, *HIStory Continues*, comprises fifteen new songs with titles such as *Tabloid Junkie*, *Money* and *Scream*. You get seventy-five minutes of euphoric moonwalking exuberance followed by seventy-five minutes of paranoid, mind-curdling autobiography.

HIStory Continues is an angry record. Jackson has played the angry man before but the rage was usually directed at imaginary wicked women (*Dirty Diana* et al) and has always seemed synthetic. Clearly, this is the real thing.

HIStory Begins is an exhilarating reminder of why Jackson united the pop audience the way nobody had done since the Beatles. Hearing again *Billie Jean*, *Thriller* and *Beat It*, you understand why the album *Thriller* sold 47 million copies, making it the biggest-selling album of all time (and likely to remain so). Like his late father-in-law, Michael Jackson desegregated music. These songs exist beyond categories such as soul or rock. Everything on *HIStory Begins* sounds like a celebration. It seems a lifetime ago.

There is not much joy on *HIStory Continues*. There are

weepy power ballads about an expiring orphan (*Little Susie*) and what we are doing to the planet (*Earth Song*) plus a lovely boy-loses-girl torch song (*You Are Not Alone*). But this is a world where the saccharine is always waiting to rub up against the grotesque.

The press release for the record comes with seventy-four 'Michael Jackson Facts' and lurking among the guff about 'the success of the Michael Jackson doll' and 'the Michael Jackson Good Scout Humanitarian Award' is fact number 23 – 'In August 1993, reports surface in the media that Michael is under criminal investigation for child abuse by the Los Angeles Police Department . . . An out-of-court settlement, which both sides have been working towards, is agreed for an undisclosed sum.' Fact number 23 haunts every groove of *HIStory Continues*.

This is the most personal record that any major artist has released since Bob Dylan's *Blood on the Tracks*. But where Dylan mourned a broken marriage, Jackson rails against a shattered life – his own – and a world that he obviously believes is out to destroy him.

Paranoia abounds in the lyrics. 'Somebody's out to get me – they really wanna fix me' he sings on *This Time Around*. 'Just because you read it in a magazine or see it on the TV screen don't make it factual, actual,' he snaps on *Tabloid Junkie,* adding the cute coda, 'They say he's homosexual.' It goes on and on – *Scream*, *Money* and *2 Bad* all lash out at backstabbers, hypocrites and the wicked media. This is the King of Pop seemingly on the verge of a nervous breakdown.

HIStory Continues is protest music, but perhaps Jackson protests too much. His lawyers settled what was potentially the biggest case in show business history this side of O.J. Simpson, so it is difficult to sympathize with demands for justice. An out-of-court settlement – 'which both sides have been working towards' – surely suggests that a kind of justice has quietly and privately been done.

HIStory Continues is big on defiance, fury and self-pity. But nowhere is there any indication that Michael Jackson's problems might – rather like his nose – be at least partly of his own making. What made *Blood on the Tracks* one of the greatest records of all time was that Dylan accepted his share of guilt for his smashed relationship. Michael Jackson embraces his status as victim. Everybody else is to blame for his misery. Being the King of Pop means never having to say you're sorry.

Instead what you get amid all the bile are the usual homilies to the little ones. Inside the CD there are photographs of children waving placards stating 'GOD BLESS MICHAEL' and 'MICHAEL IS THE BEST', while Jackson writes, 'I lovingly dedicate this album of my music to all the children of the world: let us dream of tomorrow where our children are nurtured and protected and nourished.'

I know he hasn't been found guilty of anything, but isn't the out-of-court settlement a little close for this Pied Piper routine?

Incredibly, Jackson still sees himself as a heroic figure – *HIStory*'s cover features Jacko as one of those monumental Russian statues that went out with Marxist-Leninism (it should be a joke, but I fear it's not) and there's a spirited cover of the Beatles' *Come Together*, John Lennon's late hippy plea for brotherly love.

But I am afraid it is far too late in the day for the world to come together over Michael Jackson. I doubt if there is anyone more likely to divide public opinion. 'It's been my fate to compensate for the childhood I've never known,' he explains on *Childhood*, the closest he gets to an alibi for his troubles.

In a curiously touching finale, *HIStory* concludes with Jackson's version of the old standard, *Smile* – yes, as in, 'Smile though your heart is aching, smile even though it's breaking'. The song is done without irony and is strangely moving, perhaps because trapped inside that pale, remodelled flesh and those stupid military uniforms there is an old-fashioned song-and-dance man struggling to get out.

The show must go on despite everything, and there's the real tragedy of Michael Jackson. *HIStory* is the sound of a man who has brought joy to millions and salvaged so pathetically little for himself.

Dean Martin

***Daily Telegraph*, 5 April 1994**

I grew up with the music of Dean Martin. My father loved Dino's lazy, Latin charm, and my childhood echoed to the sound of *That's Amore* and *Relax-Ay-Voo*. But I could never understand his appeal. All those cod Italian ballads with lyrics like 'When the moon hits your eye like a big pizza pie – that's amore' and all that falling around pretending to be drunk made Dino seem irredeemably corny. Dean Martin, I thought, was just showbiz ham.

But in his brilliant new biography of Dean Martin, Nick Tosches argues that Martin was the missing link between Bing Crosby and Elvis (who carried the ghost of Dino in his voice – I can see it now). Tosches insists that Dean Martin was the coolest man who ever wore a tuxedo. Most of all, says Tosches, he embodied 'America's holy trinity of flash, trash and cash'. Tosches says it was Dean Martin not Frank Sinatra, who epitomized old-guard cool. Nothing impressed Dino – not the Kennedys nor the Mafia. 'I have so much respect for you,' one Mafia hit man said, trying to place a kiss on Dean Martin's cheek. 'Save some for yourself, pally,' Dino said, brushing him off.

Now that's cool. Tosches's book, *Dino – Living High in the Dirty Business of Dreams* (Secker, £16), is one of the greatest books ever written about showbusiness. It traces Martin's life from the steel town of Steubenville, Ohio, through the nightclubs of New York and Chicago to the end of the rainbow in Hollywood and Las Vegas. It is the story of fifty years spent in the fleshpots of Tinseltown. No wonder he needed a stiff drink.

Dean Martin breezes through the book with inebriated

insouciance. The stage persona was not exaggerated. Drinking only heightened what was already a laid-back nature.

This is a strange book because Tosches clearly isn't in love with Martin's music. But then, neither was Dino. What interests Tosches – and what he sees as the key to Dino's success – is that gap between Martin and his work. He always maintained *lontano* (distance) from the world. Nothing ever really reached Dean Martin. 'If you want to talk,' he told chorus girls, 'go see a priest.'

Born Dino Crocetti seventy-five years ago, Martin grew up dealing craps in the local mob joint. Running moonshine, gambling and the numbers racket were part of the scenery. It was a world he understood.

'Love was Dean's racket,' says Tosches. Martin was not interested in art. 'All he ever wanted was broads, booze and money – with plenty of linguini on the side.'

And that appealed to people. Dino didn't go in for *ersatz* showbusiness sincerity. He sang of eternal love while openly ogling the chorus girls. The critics called him King Leer. Clearly, this man was in it for whatever he could grab. And people loved it. Fifty million Americans regularly watched *The Dean Martin Show* in the late sixties. In 1968, he sold more albums than Jimi Hendrix.

A lot of Dino's films, music and TV shows were second-rate – 'straight from the heartland of mediocrity', says Tosches – but that was almost the point. The book reveals a man whose boundless charm was matched only by his infinite cynicism.

He believed that showbusiness is full of phonies, that love songs are just the sweet lies of seduction, that Hollywood is just another racket. Millions of his fans felt exactly the same way.

Twenty-five years on, I think I finally understand why, when my father arrived home from work, the records that he played were by Dean Martin.

Burt Bacharach

Daily Telegraph, **16 September 1995**

The first indication that Burt Bacharach was about to become the coolest man on the planet came last year when Oasis, the great pale hopes of British rock music, featured his face on the cover of their debut album. Bacharach – composer of such three-minute rhapsodies as *Walk On By*, *I Say a Little Prayer*, *Make It Easy On Yourself*, *The Look of Love*, *Close to You*, *Anyone Who Had a Heart* and dozens more – has never gone out of style with the generation who fell in love to his songs back in the sixties. But now he has been discovered by the generation that was conceived to that music.

'Is it the melodic content they've been missing?' Bacharach speculates when we meet in Saint-Paul-de-Vence on the Côte D'Azur. 'Perhaps they are learning that melody is nothing to be ashamed of. There's nothing wrong in writing something that people can whistle.' Suddenly music you can whistle is everywhere. EMI recently released a compilation called *The Sound Gallery*, featuring brassy instrumentals from the sixties including Alan Hawkshaw's *Nightrider*, better known as the theme from 'the lady loves Milk Tray' advertisement. This autumn A&M will release *Indigo Moods – an Easy Listening Compilation*, featuring Herb Alpert, Chris Montez and Sergio Mendes, which will coincide with the relaunch of the Indigo Club in Soho, where trendy young things chill out to the soothing sounds of Andy Williams. A&M is also re-releasing Bacharach's 1968 solo album, *Reach Out*, and the Sandpipers' *Guantanemera*. And all this aimed at the under-thirties.

Why is easy listening suddenly becoming a growth industry? One theory is that the generation that boogied till dawn in the late eighties is all raved out. Another is that the easy-listening fad is just an ironic, kitsch-is-cool offshoot of the nostalgia industry. But what it really represents is a growing interest in the other side of the sixties. Not the decade of peace, love and mind-altering substances of popular legend, but the sixties as an age of romance, sophistication and affluence which, in these trou-bled times, seems even more exotic and distant (the evocative titles on *The Sound Gallery* album include 'The Penthouse Suite', 'Girl in a Sportscar' and 'Life of Leisure'). And if the Beatles embody the psychedelic sixties, then nobody expresses the cool, urbane side of that era like Bacharach.

Yet, while Bacharach's aching melodies and lush orchestra-tion place him comfortably in the new easy listening, he is not really a part of it. Bacharach and his lyricist, Hal David, were the Lennon and McCartney of middle America. There is a yearning at the heart of their music, a sweet-and-sour romanticism that infuses every note of songs such as 'I Just Don't Know What to Do With Myself', 'A House is not a Home' or 'Trains and Boats and Planes'. Emotionally obsessive, melodically unforgettable, this was major trauma transformed into heavenly music. Calling Bacharach and David easy listening is like calling Beethoven a deaf guy who knew a good tune when he saw one.

Bacharach is in the south of France to perform two shows in Monaco. The craggy good looks of his youth are still visible. This is the man Sammy Cahn called, 'The only composer who doesn't look like a dentist'. He is here with his fourth wife, Jane, and their two-year-old son, Oliver (his previous wives were the singer Paula Stewart, the actress Angie Dickinson and the songwriter Carole Bayer Sager). Jane is about thirty years his junior. Like his songs, Bacharach's women don't seem to get any older. 'I kept her up all last night,' he says. 'I wish I could say in a good way, but I have a thing about air-conditioning. I don't like it.'

I have brought with me some tokens of Bacharach's new street credibility – the Oasis CD and a copy of *The Face* calling him, 'a genius long due for irony-free re-evaluation'. Bacharach is polite, but he is clearly unimpressed. 'Oh yeah, I heard about this,' he says, gingerly holding the Oasis record. Perhaps he feels that, at sixty-six, he does not need the stamp of approval from a bunch of twentysomethings.

Although Bacharach is identified with the sixties, he is some fifteen years older than the likes of Paul McCartney and Mick Jagger. He was Marlene Dietrich's musical director when the Stones and the Beatles were still schoolboys. Formed by a sensibility that pre-dates the sixties, his attitude to music is very un-rock and roll. 'It's good to know something about what you're doing. It's good to be able to write music down. It's good if you know how to read music. I think it's very important. You have to learn the rules before you can break them.'

Born in Kansas City but raised in New York, Bacharach studied music composition and theory at McGill University and Mannes School of Music during the day and went to hear jazz bands at night. He was too realistic to try to make it as a jazz musician – 'I wasn't good enough' – and too ambitious to pursue a career as what he calls a serious composer – 'You end up teaching in some university' – but he knew that music was his way into the world.

Playing in a band at Forest Hills High School had saved him from his multiple complex about being short, shy and Jewish. 'I pretended not to be Jewish, which is a terrible thing to do, but I liked the Catholic kids I grew up with and they always spoke disparagingly about Jews. When we played football against a Jewish team we would be in a huddle and my team would say, 'Let's go and kick the shit out of these Jews'. So I never let them know. I was also very short – there was not a girl in a school of three thousand kids smaller than me – so I had enough to get on with without admitting to being Jewish.'

Bacharach dreamed of being a sports hero like his father, Bert (with an e), who played football and basketball before becoming a syndicated journalist. 'But he was big and I was small. So being in a danceband was my way to meet other kids. I even got to meet a couple of girls. And they looked at me a bit differently because now I was sort of important.'

At the start of the fifties, Bacharach served two years in the US Army in Germany, playing boogie-woogie piano to casualties of the Korean war. After he was discharged, he worked as a pianist, arranger and conductor for a number of artists, including Vic Damone, before getting his big break as musical director for Marlene Dietrich's nightclub act.

The young composer and the ageing film star worked together for three years at the turn of the sixties. In the words of

American journalist Hubert Saal, under Bacharach's direction Dietrich's career 'blossomed into a beautiful Indian summer'. 'I learned a lot from her,' says Bacharach. 'A belief in perfection. And hard work. And how to deal with musicians. I remember Quincy [Jones] coming backstage one night and saying, "What are you doing here, man?" As though I should be on the road with Aretha Franklin. But music is music.'

By now Bacharach was writing his own material. But his first effort, 'Night Flight to Heaven' – one of those aspirational titles – was not recorded and his first hit was an inauspicious debut, a song written for a low-budget horror movie called *The Blob*, recorded by the Five Blobs. Then Bacharach met Hal David, brother of his co-writer, Mack. Hal also wrote lyrics and was looking for a partner.

Bacharach and Hal David had a few hits, including 'Magic Moments' for Perry Como and 'Tower of Strength' for Frankie Vaughan, but it was not until 1962 that they decided to work exclusively together. They were an odd couple. Bacharach was handsome and athletic, David avuncular and a chainsmoker. But one of the most successful partnerships in the history of popular music had begun. (One industry insider estimates that combined record royalties, sheet music, and having his greatest hits played in the airports and elevators of the world must have made Bacharach between $30 million and $40 million.) They churned out hit songs seemingly at will, instant standards built upon words and music that together captured what Albert Goldman called, 'The pathos at the heart of the American hullabaloo.' 'I always tried to make songs that were like mini-movies,' says Bacharach. 'A song like "24 Hours From Tulsa" – it told a story, there's a balance between its highs and lows. And there's a lot of drama.'

The music of Bacharach and David was where the spirit of the sixties collided with old-fashioned showbusiness. They wrote songs for films – *Alfie*, *The Look of Love* and *What's New Pussycat?* – that became huge hits. They banged out a hit Broadway show, *Promises, Promises*. And only Lennon and McCartney wrote more number ones for more artists. Even their bits of fluff could do no wrong – 'Raindrops Keep Falling on My Head', written for *Butch Cassidy and the Sundance Kid*, won an Oscar for Best Song and Bacharach picked up another Oscar for the film's score. By now he was married to the beautiful young Angie Dickinson. And he wasn't short any more.

At the start of the seventies, Bacharach and David were still breaking artists – a young duo called the Carpenters were given a massive shove to stardom by 'Close To You', a ten-year-old Bacharach/David song – but the winning streak was about to come to an end. 'What did us in was a picture called *Lost Horizon*. I worked on the score, which was interminable, and it was tough. I was still working and Hal was playing tennis in Acapulco. And it didn't feel good. It would have been okay if the picture had been good. But it was rotten.' Bacharch ended the partnership because he felt the workload was unequal.

Bacharach also broke up with Dickinson. 'I almost respect Burt more than I love him,' Dickinson had said a few years earlier. 'His music has revolutionized the world. It's so much more important to the world than anything I can ever do.' But by 1976 Dickinson had become a star, thanks to a cop show called *Policewoman*, while Bacharach's career was on the wane. He had been making records since the sixties, mostly instrumental versions of his hits with the occasional crooning in his battered baritone, but now he reinvented himself as a performer. 'At first I couldn't understand why people would pay me a lot of money to see me conduct an orchestra and do my material. But I learned to appreciate it. And the reality is that it's easier to go out and perform material that is already written than it is to sit down and write something new.'

The seventies were a lucrative wilderness for Bacharach. But in the eighties he found a new song-writing partner when he teamed up with Carole Bayer Sager (lyricist to 'Groovy Kind of Love', 'When I Need You' and the James Bond theme 'Nobody Does It Better'). He says it was a very different partnership to the one he had with Hal David: 'I didn't go home and sleep with Hal.' Bacharach and Bayer Sager married and together they wrote 'Making Love' for Roberta Flack, 'On My Own' for Patti Labelle and Michael McDonald, 'That's What Friends Are For' for Dionne Warwick and 'Arthur's Theme (Best That You Can Do)', which won an Oscar, Bacharach's third. But in 1991 the marriage ended.

Music had been his way into the world. He admits he has also used it to keep the world at bay. 'I like to be isolated and that's a great way to split up, to be able to go into your narcissistic world. I had my music, so I could always isolate myself at the times I wanted to. When I was single in New York I would get rid of a girl by telling her I had to write an orchestration. Just to get her out of the house. But maybe she wasn't a great girl to spend the whole night with anyway.'

Did women expect the man who wrote 'The Look of Love' to be more romantic than he really was? 'At one time, I was very good at being what they wanted me to be. I was faking a personality without even knowing it. It wasn't conscious. It was something to do with the desire to please.'

Bacharach had more success with Carole Bayer Sager than most songwriters have in a lifetime. Yet it was hard to fight a sense of anti-climax. The sixties were never really his decade – he was already in his thirties when they began – but as much as Jagger or McCartney, Bacharach has to live with the incredible weight of past glories and the thought that the best could well be over.

'Listen, I don't know if I'll have another hit song. I don't know if you get a ration of success, you get a ride, and that's it. I don't want to say that the new material is not as good as the old material – but that's possible. I take music very seriously. But I don't take it as seriously as I did. Why is that? I've got a kid who is two. I've got a nine-year-old boy I'm crazy about. So some of the attention goes there. And then there are the horses.'

Bacharach has owned horses for almost thirty years but now he also breeds them at a little farm in West Virginia. His horses have run in the Kentucky Derby for the past two years. 'I've always been very good at obsessing and you can get very obsessive about horses. They can break your heart.'

The last thing I see of Bacharach is him playing with his two-year-old son and a plastic golf club. No, there probably will not be many more songs to rival 'Walk On By' or 'I Say a Little Prayer' from this man. But it will never really be over for him because, in a supposedly disposable art form, Bacharach wrote songs with David that will last for ever. The Cranberries recently covered 'Close To You', the song that broke the Carpenters a quarter of a century ago, while Oasis's decision to put Bacharach on their album cover was no mere affectation. The new easy listening will come and go, but Bacharach will always be in fashion with anyone who knows how it feels to nurse a badly bruised heart.

The words of his mentor still sum him up best. 'I wish I could say that he is my composer.' said Marlene Dietrich. 'But it's not true. He is everybody's composer.'

Robert Lenkiewicz

Arena, **September/October 1989**

The furry face of the artist puckers up with imperious disdain. 'People only ever want to ask me three things,' sighs Robert Lenkiewicz. 'How many children do you have? Who are you sleeping with? And what have you done with the dead body you stole?' The answers to these pressing questions – fifteen, almost anyone, and it's a secret – are but the vaguest of introductions to the wonderful world of Robert Lenkiewicz.

Both his life and work – massive murals covering whole sides of buildings and huge, quasi-cinemascope canvases – are teeming with humanity. Children, wives, patrons, models and lovers cram his Rabelaisian private life, while his work is replete with the life of Plymouth, his adopted city and for centuries the murderous heart of British naval power. Lenkiewicz is not nostalgic for the days when Francis Drake set out to sink the Armada from these grey docks.

'This city limps like a psychic cripple between the dockyards and the military and Methodism,' sniffs Lenkiewicz, with his usual elegant contempt. 'The fact that I am here is entirely circumstantial. I could be anywhere.'

But it is Plymouth where Lenkiewicz landed at the end of the sixties and Plymouth that he has spent twenty years recording. There have been seventeen exhibitions on various aspects of the city's life, from alcoholics and prostitutes to mental handicap and (a subject close to his heart) orgasm. For his latest exhibition, on education, Lenkiewicz used as his models everyone from school governors to school children who are involved in the Fascist Column 88 movement. As usual, the show was ignored by the London art establishment. And, as usual, none of the work was for sale.

'I do not want to get involved in the sordid business world,' says Lenkiewicz. 'I have about twenty patrons. Some are rich, some are not rich. They pay my bills, buy my materials and give me things. Every once in a while they choose a painting.'

The wealthiest of his patrons is the Earl of St Germans, one of the largest landowners in the West Country, while the more modest patrons are the owners of small restaurants and cafés on the waterfront where Lenkiewicz has his studio, and who ensure that the painter and his associates (including visiting journalists and photographers) never have to pay for a meal.

The work these art-loving philanthropists receive for their support is full of an ancient sense of wonder focused on dirty, violent modern England. There is a classical grandeur, a heroic scale, that pays unreserved homage to his heroes, Rembrandt and Giotto, and it is possible to see echoes of the big city German expressionists such as Max Beckmann and George Grosz in his elevation of the everyday, the mundane and the prosaic to mythic, sometimes terrible, proportions.

'Except that someone like Grosz was socially and politically committed,' says Lenkiewicz. 'And I regard politics as the asshole of culture, the very lowest level of human perception. Nothing haunts more deeply than the plain fact of a thing. What amazes is the fact that something exists, and not the way it exists. I am thought of as a portrait painter or a figure painter. I see myself simply as a painter.'

He sees his work as an amoral, all-seeing eye, the recording of his dislocated, apolitical documentary of modern times. His paintings can veer from an everyday, fleshy stillness that breathes the silent air of Lucian Freud's work to a roaring fascination with the wilder shores of British society that, coupled with his love of religious trappings (saints and stained glass and the cruel T-shape of the crucifix), can summon forth the ethically barren but emotionally powerful work of Gilbert and George.

Lenkiewicz's work often produces strong reactions. An elderly man recently collapsed with a heart attack while contemplating his large canvas *The Fight* at the most recent exhibition. His show of prostitution was closed down by the authorities and all the work was seized. His 50m mural, *The Last Judgement*, depicting a mountain of writhing, naked flesh (all based on local council leaders and various Plymouth big shots), was inspected by the police to see if it was obscene (it wasn't). And yet it is not for his considerable body of work ('Over ten thousand canvases stored in warehouses all over the city,' he says. 'It is a form of art pollution.') that Robert Lenkiewicz, the Bluebeard of British art, is best known. Never a stranger to controversy, the hysteria around him reached fever pitch when he stole the corpse of Diogenes from the hospital where he died, and then refused to give the body back.

Diogenes was a former tramp called Edward McKenzie who Lenkiewicz had befriended, renaming him after the legendary Greek figure who lived in a large earthenware jar because McKenzie had once resided in a barrel. When his friend died and was destined for a mean pauper's grave, Lenkiewicz stole the body, had it preserved in embalming fluid and refused to give it back.

Diogenes remains safe in the artist's care ('rather like a large paperweight'), his whereabouts unknown, though there is a large, ornate gold coffin at the foot of the painter's four-poster bed. Incredibly, the authorities of Plymouth – often exasperated but almost always tolerant of the wild man in their midst – have let him keep the pickled corpse of Diogenes.

Lenkiewicz tries to play down the controversy – 'The body of Diogenes will not be exhibited,' says a haughty sign in the window of his studio – and yet there is a dominant element of his nature which revels in and rejoices at the reactions to his outrageous behaviour.

He has a lively, learned mind, his conversation peppered with quotes from Kant, Descartes and Nietzsche, yet he has an almost childish desire to shock that is wed to a genuinely anarchic attitude to life. Apart from the snatched body and the fifteen children from almost as many women (the youngest child is a year old, the oldest at university), there are fourteen small studios around Plymouth – 'Every one a relationship,' he says, his small fleshy mouth twisting in a lewd smirk – and a passion for the shameless and shocking statement. 'AIDS shows the witty indifference of nature to the human race,' he says. Or, 'There is not a woman between the age of three and eighty that I am not attracted to.' Or, 'It can be quite sweet to have sex with the mother of your girl-friend – which is something I have done quite a lot.'

And all this over one cup of tea (served free by a patron in the Barnacle Bill café).

He stands under *The Barbican Mural,* a Bohemian Santa Claus in a paint-splattered smock, scarlet scarf and work boots. His giant haystack of hair is the colour of dead wheat, his blue eyes twinkle with mad mischief. Lenkiewicz stands discussing the erection of scaffolding with two workmen. Soon *The Barbican Mural* – subtitled 'A survey of Elizabethan culture 1580–1820: Alchemy, Jewish Mysticism, Philosophy, Cult of Chivalry and General Metaphysical Thought', a not untypical lapse into pretentiousness – will be sealed and a new mural, *The Dance Of Death* painted over the same 3,000 square metres. When the work is in progress, Lenkiewicz will sleep on the highest level of scaffolding. He says he sleeps in a different venue every night of the week, though the closest he has to a home is the building next to the mural.

In this neighbourhood – The Barbican is the oldest part of Plymouth, a working-class neighbourhood on the waterfront – stands the painter's shop (where nothing is ever sold), his library (where he writes and draws in huge, monastic-style ledgers that form the intellectual spine of his exhibitions) and, up a steep, narrow flight of wooden stairs, the two floors that serve as both gallery and studio. When, as now, the gallery is exhibiting, Lenkiewicz only uses the area as a studio at night. A secret door-way leads to the master bedroom, containing the four-poster bed where his youngest child was born on his lap, plus the gold coffin, religious icons and many sexually explicit paintings, often featuring the artist himself as the randy leading man. Other paintings show him with a baby in his arms, another with a dead rat in his mouth. Though he can be defensive about his intellectual abilities, he is dismissive of his skill as an artist.

'Four great painters come along every hundred years,' he says. 'I am not one of them.'

Lenkiewicz is the son of middle-class refugees. His mother was a German Jew, the daughter of the court painter to mad King Ludwig of Bavaria ('A mediocre painter,' yawns his grandson); his father a Russian Jew, a trainee rabbi and horsebreaker (there was a huge cleft in his face printed there forever by a ferocious hoof). His parents' families perished in Auschwitz and Buchenwald, but they themselves escaped, married, started a hotel in London and baby Robert was born in 1942. He was painting at nine and attended St Martin's School of Art and the Royal Academy, from which he was expelled. After careers as a teacher, an arm wrestler (he is as powerful as a bull), a tourist portrait painter and a thief (he was sent to jail for two years for stealing antiquarian books from a Plymouth museum), Lenkiewicz began his long quest to record the life of a city. Though he is no longer the patron saint of alcoholic tramps, he still gives a Christmas dinner for them every year, filling Plymouth bus station with a beggars' banquet over which he presides like a ragged-trousered Pied Piper. He has a love for the theatrical gesture and often it seems that his painting is merely foreplay for his life.

'I love those melodramatic Hollywood films about great artists,' he says. 'Charles Laughton as Rembrandt! Kirk Douglas as Van Gogh! *Charlton Heston as Michelangelo!* Awful schmaltz. I love it. Rather marvellous.'

Tonight Lenkiewicz has three sittings in his studio for his next exhibition, shyly entitled 'The Painter With Women'. Lenkiewicz is passionately, hysterically heterosexual. 'I would rather sleep with a camel than another man,' he says. 'An *attractive* camel.'

He has been married three times, and the latest union has not been affected by the birth of his newest baby daughter to another woman. The first sitting in the studio, the night-time deserted gallery, is with a young dancer, the second with a teenage son (who is allowed to keep on his white socks), and the third with a Rubenesque young deaf girl. All are painted quickly, with calm, quiet direction, but the deaf girl is painted while sitting on the artist's velveteen, Pollock-stained lap.

'What people call love is a pathological disorder,' says Lenkiewicz. 'A little bit of pain brings people together – they share their sandwiches. But intense pain tears people apart – you don't share your sandwiches in Auschwitz. Likewise a little bit of pleasure brings people together but intense pleasure tears them apart. So I am over all that.'

The deaf girl skips off to the master bedroom to wait for Lenkiewicz. Painting, his foreplay to life, is apparently over for the night.

Justin Fashanu

Evening Standard, **28 January 1991**

'I had a blood test before I joined Torquay Football Club,' says Justin Fashanu. 'That's okay. They have been very supportive to me down there. But they know I'm gay. And I know people worry about AIDS. It doesn't bother me because my lifestyle is such that I know I don't have to worry about HIV and AIDS. They can give me as many blood tests as they like. I'm not worried. But I'll tell you who *should* worry and that's all the promiscuous heterosexual footballers because they are all sleeping with exactly the same girls. Up and down the country, it's the same pool of girls. And once one of those guys catches the HIV virus then they are *all* going to get it. When one goes – they all go.'

When Justin Fashanu, Britain's first million-pound black footballer, announced that he was the country's first openly gay footballer it seemed his playing days were over.

Football is not theatre. It is not fashion. Football is a tabloid-reading, working class world and attitudes are as enlightened as those of the public bar and the factory floor. 'Fashanu?' said one manager when asked if he would consider signing the 29-year-old striker. 'You mean that poof?'

But one year after coming out, Fashanu is captain of Torquay, leading their struggle from the wastelands of the Third Division.

'Football is a cut-throat business,' he says. 'I have learned that everyone is alone. *Everyone*. Of course I get stick from crowds. But my fellow professionals are supportive to my face. Behind my back – who knows? It's a hard game. Everybody is in it for themselves.'

This is not the first time that Fashanu has survived something that might have been expected to crush him. That million-pound transfer went very sour when he fell out with his new manager – Brian Clough, who during one memorable bust-up called the police to have Fashanu removed from the ground. A few years later a crippling knee injury led one specialist to wrongly diagnose he had polio.

But the knee was nursed to health after Fashanu sank £200,000 of his own money into operations, and his homosexuality has not killed his career. There is a thread of steel in him that dates from his childhood. When he was four years old Justin and his younger brother John were taken into the care of Doctor Barnardo's.

'It's hard to say how Doctor Barnardo's affected me. I have always been very determined and it's very likely a lot of that comes from there. They were hard times. But I was brought up in a loving environment – my foster parents were white, upper middle class. I actually come from a more privileged background than most professional footballers. Unlike some black people, I'm not intimidated by good restaurants, expensive hotels, big cars. But I never denied my blackness. My mother once told me that when I was young I said I wanted to be white. But I don't remember that. I never want to be anyone's Uncle Tom.'

When Fashanu talks about his mother and father he is talking about his foster parents and not the young nurse and the Nigerian law student who were his real parents. His family have been supportive of his decision to come out of the closet – apart from his brother John, the Wimbledon striker.

'I wouldn't like to play in the same team as him or even get changed in the vicinity of him,' John said of Justin. They are no longer speaking.

'I love my brother,' says Justin. 'I am closer to John than anyone in the world. We have been through so much together. He's straight and he hates these FASHANU IS GAY headlines because he doesn't want people to think it's him. But I have to be true to myself. I hope that he will come to understand that. None of this has been done to hurt him.'

Sipping Earl Grey in the lounge of a Piccadilly hotel, Fashanu is nobody's idea of the average professional footballer. He is definitely *not* opening a boutique, Brian.

124

'The average footballer's life revolves around birds, booze and bookies,' he chuckles.

But for all his media skills, Justin Fashanu is a different proposition on the football field. He once left a Bristol City defender 'with his nose all over his face'. So will these macho performances change preconceptions about homosexuals?

'What's macho?' he says. 'Is it macho to be a drunk and a wife-beater? Is that what we call being a real man? I think we have to revise some of our attitutes about what constitutes a real man. Some chest-beating drunk – that's a real man? I'm a nice guy. But push me beyond a certain point and then I am not a nice guy. I can deal with that kind of confrontation. If you want to keep pushing me then I am not afraid to get physical with you. It's not a problem for me.'

Fashanu says he did not realize he was gay until he was in his twenties.

'As a teenager I was very determined and focused on my career. There are always women throwing themselves at young footballers. Lots of them. And at that age, to be crude about it, as long as you are relieving yourself somewhere then it doesn't matter much who it is with! Then I became a Born Again Christian – and they disapproved of sex outside marriage. So I stopped having sex with my girlfriend, who I was living with, and that's when I started to have homosexual feelings. When they were more than feelings – when they were actions – then I had a double burden of guilt. But when I meet my Maker I have to account for myself. Did I lead an honest life? Was I truthful about myself?'

He says he is not our only gay footballer, merely the only one to admit it.

'I would say more than 25 per cent of football is gay. It's got to be higher than average. It is a very physical, closed world, a man's world, and you form deep bonds with people that you hardly know. There are a lot of gay people in football.'

Fashanu's ex-lovers include footballers and a married Conservative MP. He acknowledges that his old *amours* must be nervous about his decision to admit he is gay but says he came to believe he had no other choice.

'I decided to come out when I met a young kid in Canada whose parents strongly disapproved of him being gay. He had become a prostitute and I later learned that he had killed himself. Thrown himself off a roof. I don't see myself as a role model but I had a gradual realization that I had to be true to myself. The world is more homophobic than it has been for years. But it would never have been a good time to admit it. Martina Navratilova said Magic Johnson would not have received all that public and media sympathy if he had been gay. She's right but I wouldn't expect it to be otherwise.'

Fashanu points out that he is no stranger to bigotry.

'I've spent my life fighting prejudices, being something other than what people expect me to be,' he says. 'When I started in football some managers had their theories about what a black footballer was like – we couldn't play as part of a team, we only played well when the sun was shining. They were wrong. Now I intend to be something other than what they expect a gay person to be. Limp wristed? Effeminate? Forget it. That's not me.'

Intelligent, articulate, hard as nails. That's Justin Fashanu. His brother should be proud of him.

Red Card Roy McDonough

Daily Telegraph, 6 January 1996

Roy McDonough is a football legend. You will not find him trading badinage with Des Lynam on *Match of the Day*. He is not sponsored by Nike. But in the tough, semi-professional world of non-league football, where the rewards are slight, the crowds are small and the tackles are as hard as you will encounter anywhere, they all know his name.

Down where the wild things are, McDonough's reputation as football's Vlad the Impaler precedes him. It is said that opposing centre-halves call in sick when they know they are playing against him. Crowds buzz with anticipation. Referees watch his every move. For McDonough – aka 'Red Card Roy' – has been sent off more times than any player in football. 'But I am not a maniac,' he insists. 'I am one of the most easy-going blokes in the world. My girlfriend says I'm a soft touch.'

It is true that in the flesh McDonough is a warm, outgoing man, a 6ft 1in Brummie who looks younger than his thirty-seven years. But on the field he is something else. 'Roy is the most ill-disciplined and occasionally terrifying player I have ever known,' said Dave Cusack, who was McDonough's manager during his one-year spell at Dagenham. 'He could eat Vinnie Jones for breakfast.'

Sipping on a soft drink, the man who could digest the Wimbledon Rottweiler like he was so much muesli tries to work out how often what he calls 'the sending-off situations' have occurred. He thinks it has been nineteen or twenty times. Losing count is perhaps understandable under the circumstances. 'There were thirteen in the Football League, three or four in the Vauxhall Conference, I can think of two in the FA Cup. I have certainly been the most sent-off in the Football League. But then I have been around a bit longer than your Vinnie Jones or Julian Dicks.' (Jones, at twenty-nine, has been sent off eleven times, Dicks, at twenty-seven, nine times).

McDonough has been called the dirtiest player in football, but this is untrue. He never gets his 'retaliation' in first. His dismissals invariably occur when he feels that opponents are not playing the game fairly. Taking liberties. That's the one thing he can't stand. People taking diabolical liberties. It is a manly creed that has surprisingly left few scars on Roy McDonough. 'I've still got my nose. I've still got all my own teeth. I've only had about a dozen stitches in my face. I've looked after myself.'

The line between glory and obscurity is painfully thin in football. Although McDonough was always a jobbing striker (he has been at seven professional clubs), he very nearly made the big time as an eighteen-year-old at Birmingham City in the old First Division. But, frustrated in his role as understudy to England striker Trevor Francis, McDonough accepted a transfer to Walsall. The week after he left, Francis was injured. It could have been McDonough's big chance, but he had already gone. 'It was the biggest mistake of my football career. I needed a bit of guidance and didn't get it. I was next in line for that position and I think if I had stayed I would have been a First Division footballer for a long, long time. But I went to Walsall. I had a couple of good years, but then they wanted to cut my money. Then I went to Chelsea. Couldn't cope with London. And it went on from there.'

You could be forgiven for thinking that football in the nineties is a middle-class leisure activity. After Nick Hornby's *Fever Pitch*, literary football books are one of the biggest growth areas in publishing. Hooliganism inside the grounds has been almost totally eradicated. Everywhere the teeming terraces have been replaced by all-seater stadiums. Greasy burgers have been replaced by salmon bagels and *al fresco* meat dishes. But the soul of the game is still defiantly working class and a large part of that culture is a belief in the manly virtues; *ergo* – you can't let people take diabolical liberties with you.

I had arranged to meet McDonough in King's nightclub, located at King's Holiday Park on Canvey Island. The club and the sprawling estate of holiday homes are both owned by Jeff

King, a large, genial businessman who also owns and manages Canvey Island Football Club.

At lunchtime on a winter Saturday the club is full of men who either look very fat or very fit. In a world where football dominates the culture, the community is divided into those who play and those who stand and watch. McDonough walks into the bar amid much back-slapping and laughter, clearly relishing the camaraderie, the banter, all the sweet fraternal rituals of football. It is difficult to imagine him causing any blood-letting off the pitch.

'If someone walked up to you in a bar, Tony, and punched you straight in the mouth – what would your reaction be?' asks McDonough. 'Would you roll on the floor? Or would you punch him back? That's the way I've always been. You see some players who are very good at taking a little knock and rolling around and getting people sent off. I've never been like that. I've been a nightclubber and a party animal for twenty years and I've had one fight. And that was only because some bloke chinned my mate.'

So where does this fearsome reputation come from? 'I had a bad run six, seven years ago. I remember playing for Southend one Boxing Day and I got sent off against Northampton. I did punch the centre-half. Because I thought he took a liberty – the referee didn't do anything – and I punched him. I apologized to the lad in the bar afterwards. Then my first comeback game after suspension – Swansea away – and the ball came in to me at waist height. I volleyed it as a lay-off and the midfield player came through me kung-fu style. And he hurt me. He flattened me. And as he fell – and it's that split second – I had a couple of digs at him while he was on the floor. The linesman flagged up and got me sent off. And the manager, David [Webb], put me on the transfer list saying he couldn't trust me.

'I've never walked on to a pitch deciding I was going to beat someone up or elbow them or nut them. It's never premeditated. When people have – in the old-fashioned way of saying – done me, I've never rolled around on the floor. I will react the other way. I will get up and take the law into my own hands, because if the referees are not protecting me, then I have to protect myself. It only takes one bad challenge to end your career. I've been nutted, I've been elbowed, I've been punched off-the-ball.

If they are trying to win the ball in an honest fashion and they hit me full in the face – I don't even think twice about it. But if they are not trying to win the ball fairly, and deliberately trying to inflict damage on me, then I will start taking liberties with them.'

Although McDonough never quite made it in the First Division, he did achieve a considerable double as player-manager at Colchester, winning the GM Vauxhall Conference and the FA Trophy in the 1991–92 season, all with a team that cost £740, a figure that would not cover Paul Gascoigne's hair-dressing expenses. It was the proudest moment of his career. 'We were so poor we didn't even have a shoestring. The budget was that tight. What upsets me is that nobody ever talks about what this so-called raving lunatic has actually done.'

When Perry Groves, the former Arsenal player, was a sixteen-year-old apprentice at Colchester, he cleaned McDonough's boots. 'He's a pussycat,' says Groves, 'but at the same time he is a Charles Bronson figure. Most of the times he has been sent off it's because someone is trying to sort him out and the referee has not given him any protection. He doesn't like anyone taking liberties. He was only twenty-three or twenty-four and one of the stars at the club,' says Groves. 'Unlike other senior players, he would always talk to you. Most of them just did their training and left. No one dislikes him. Off the field he has a very placid demeanour.'

Groves was forced to give up top-flight football after snapping his Achilles tendon twice, an injury that robbed him of the pace that got him into the Arsenal side. Such is his regard for McDonough that he has followed him from Dagenham, down a league to Canvey Island in the ICIS Football League – the top end of non-league football. McDonough had to leave Dagenham after being sent off for foul and abusive language. Roy was miffed that the referee wouldn't allow what he called 'effing stitches' in his gashed ankle and head (Roy wanted medical attention – the ref wanted to play on).

In May 1994, after four successful years at Colchester, he was fired by chairman Gordon Parker, father of his wife, Jackie. The marriage ended when he fell in love with Liz Blacknall, wife of the club's groundsman. 'I'd always suspected he had affairs and then I discovered he was sleeping with Liz,' Jackie confided to the *Sun*. 'I saw Liz following Roy's car at 1 a.m. I chased her, forced her off the road then screamed at her. Then I went home and shouted at him and he admitted it. After this, I just want a divorce. But I still love Roy. I have done since I was eighteen.'

After his marriage broke up last summer, the *Sun* anointed him a football love rat. 'Soccer Boss Runs Off With His Wife's Lookalike Best Pal' screamed the headline. 'I played here recently,' says McDonough, 'and the young centre-half had seen the thing in the *Sun* about me and the wife and the girl and the divorce. Two minutes into my first game here and he's goading me about my wife, birds and all this stuff. And I said. "Behave yourself. If you behave yourself we'll be fine, because I just want to enjoy my football. But if you want to have a fight, we'll have a fight and rest assured you'll get hurt." From then on he was good as gold.'

McDonough has nothing but sympathy for Eric Cantona, Manchester United's flamboyant Frenchman who was suspended for eight months after drop-kicking an abusive Crystal Palace fan. 'He's a great player. He's a big, strong boy. But if someone takes a liberty with him – bang. Why should any man have the right to verbally abuse him, his wife and his family because he plays football? If someone verbally abused you, your wife and family in a bar, you would sort them out. A lot of people act at football matches in a way they wouldn't dream of acting in a pub. Because they know they'd get a right-hander.'

Football is full of bitter twists of fate: the injury that suddenly ends a career; the transfer that takes you to the wrong club at the wrong time; the yard of pace or ounce of luck that deems one man makes millions while another makes only a living. 'The dividing line is so narrow,' McDonough says. 'Stan Collymore [Liverpool's £8.5 million man whom McDonough played with at Southend] will not have to work another day in his life. Neither will Paul Gascoigne. I hope they know how lucky they are. It is a hard, hard level in the lower leagues. You are under pressure to win games and you've got your bills to pay.'

McDonough's day job is as a rep for a friend's food company, travelling the country selling snack foods and mineral waters. It must be a strange change of pace after being a full-time profes- sional for more than twenty years. Going from pro to semi-pro, McDonough went from a curiously childlike existence of having nothing to think about apart from football to a life that was torn between football, training and the job that pays the mortgage. 'It's tough. As a professional, your life was total football. The whole week, Monday to Saturday afternoon, was football. You'd get drunk Saturday night and get it out of your system. Sunday afternoon you might have a couple of beers and a bit of lunch. Then you would be thinking about Monday and the games you had that week. But now I work Monday to Friday.'

He says that football is not as much fun as it once was. Some central defenders would no doubt suggest that playing against Roy McDonough has never been a laugh a minute. But football's blackest sheep believes that the will to win has been overwhelmed by the terror of defeat. 'Bobby Moore was my manager at Southend. Lovely, lovely man. I had the utmost respect for Bobby. He had done everything. We were playing Rochdale away – of all people – in the middle of winter. And Bobby said to our full-back, "Watch so-and-so, he's quite useful, let him know he's in the game." In other words – kick him so he doesn't fancy it. Now for a man like Bobby Moore to say that to a player in his team – I thought hold on a minute. Bob had to win games to keep his job as a manager. But that's what runs through the whole of football these days. The fear factor.'

The fear factor seems light years away as we get a lift to the game from Jeff King in the back of his open-top van. Canvey Island FC play at a small, well-maintained ground where the stewards have to leave the ground to claim the ball from suburban gardens and small boys wear West Ham shirts, a reminder that Canvey's misty swampland is part of the Cockney diaspora. Canvey are playing Witham Town. McDonough, the big number nine, displays lots of surprisingly delicate touches, setting up his team-mates with a series of lay-offs, headers and flicks. Pushing forty, he still wins most of his tackles and, although be fails to score in his side's 2–0 win, all his shots are on target. As his career winds down, perhaps he is mellowing, for there are few signs of the temperament that has landed him in so much trouble. A believer in the beautiful game, he doesn't stop talking and is always appreciative of flashes of skill in younger players. 'Quality, son,' he tells them. 'Unlucky.'

For all the effing and blinding, for all the crunching tackles and elbows in the cakehole, there is something almost heartbreakingly pure about football played at non-league level. This is where they play the game not for glory and riches beyond all imagination, but for love and beer money. 'People can never take the memories away from you,' says McDonough. 'I've got videos of the double-winning year at Colchester. We scored 129 goals that season and set a record for the least number of defeats. The best day of my football career was when I led my team out at Wembley, going on for thirty-four years of age. I've enjoyed life, Tony. I would do my work. And then I would drink as much lager as I possibly could.'

When his legs finally go, McDonough wants to stay in the game as a manager. And he deserves the chance. Like Eric Cantona, he is not the sort of man who is destroying football, but the kind who keeps it alive. And if football in the nineties has no place for Roy McDonough, then it is nothing less than a diabolical liberty.

Nick Hornby

***Daily Telegraph*, 5 September 1993**

At the start of Nick Hornby's novel *High Fidelity*, the love-starved hero recalls all the people he had seen kissing by 1972 (year zero for his own snogging career), a list that includes such evocative names as Elsie Tanner, Barbara Windsor, Sid James, Jim Dale and Simon Templar.

This kind of eye for cultural detail is very Nick Hornby – it has made bestsellers of both *High Fidelity*, the tale of a north London record shop owner's search for love, and Hornby's previous book, *Fever Pitch*, the story of the author's *amour fou* for Arsenal. Few writers get under the skin of British life like Nick Hornby. But the qualities that make him a compelling read at home make him a baffling proposition on the other side of the Atlantic.

'*Fever Pitch* bombed in America,' says Hornby. 'They didn't know what to do with it. It had "Get World Cup Fever" on the cover and if it got reviewed at all it was in a round-up of books on how to play "soccer".'

But this month Hornby has a second crack at the American market, when *High Fidelity* is published there by Riverhead. Staff are enthusiastic about the story of sex, lies and vinyl, although they frequently do not have a clue what he is going on about (Elsie Tanner? Barbara Windsor? Sid James?). 'You only realize how English you are when an American's marked up your typescript,' Hornby says. 'They would ask me who's Bernard Manning? What's *Songs of Praise*? I said, it's this religious programme – your mum and dad have it on in the background on Sundays. And she said [Hornby does his very bad American accent]: "We have Channel 8, which is the evangelists' channel." But presumably you if have an evangelist channel cabled into your house then you're committed in a way that people who have *Songs of Praise* on never ever are. And *Songs of Praise* always got on my nerves because it meant you were going back to school the next morning – there's all that kind of feel to it.'

Hornby has a relaxed approach to what he calls 'the translation process'. There have been thousands of transatlantic queries and scores of changes. Yes, he would change the Tom Robinson Band to Television. No, he didn't fancy changing Clive James to David Letterman 'Because we don't *get* David Letterman here,' says Hornby. 'The book is set in North London, not the Bronx. It was a struggle making that clear.'

Was M & S a reference to sado-masochism? Was *Man About the House* the same as *Archie Bunker*? Tattoos turned out to be another problem. In a typical Hornby reverie, he reflects on all the respectable middle-aged men who had tattoos done when they were teenagers and now set off to the office every morning with 'M.U.F.C. KICK TO KILL' branded on their bodies.

'The difficulty was finding references that meant the same on both sides of the Atlantic. You can't change Manchester United to the Chicago Bulls unless you are going to move his record shop to Queens.'

It's a thought – and one that has already occurred to the American film industry. Disney and *Four Weddings and a Funeral* director Mike Newell have just bought the film rights for a co-production of *High Fidelity*, and currently the word is that the action will be relocated from Camden Town to either Seattle or Boston.

It is easy to work out why so many Brits love Nick Hornby's work. He writes about parts of British life – curry houses and pubs, suburban childhoods and London love affairs – that nobody else addresses with quite the same warmth and humour. But what do the Americans see in him? Is he an exotic figure to them? Is the Seven Sisters Road as mythical to them as Route 66 is to us?

'I don't think so. But one of the heartening things about the American response is that it doesn't come with the same baggage as the British response – they don't know anything about Lads, Laddishness, New Lad and all that. In America they don't even know I wrote a football book. So you're onto a real winner there.'

Whatever changes Hornby makes – Sid James metamorphosing into Sergeant Bilko, Elsie Tanner becoming Lucille Ball – it is not as much of a compromise as other British novelists make to break into the American market. Hornby doesn't set his work in America. But although his landscape is forever England, he points out that his literary hero is the American novelist Anne Tyler.

'A lot of the impetus for the book in the first place was American – I wanted character-based comedy with some pathos, which is not what the English are good at. We usually write either satire or slapstick. So Americans recognize the basic schtick even if they don't get the references.

'And I think you can be too precious about making changes: "I *said* Bernard Manning and I *meant* Bernard Manning! If you get me to change it then I'm going to flounce out!" I don't feel like that. But there's this whole riff in the book about Kate Adie and her record collection and there's just no way you can change it. That's when I think, well, I've read enough American novels containing baseball conversations. They can put up with Kate Adie for a paragraph.'

Father's Day

This is an expanded version of the essay that first appeared in the anthology Fatherhood, *edited by Peter Howarth.*

A son is always growing away from you. It doesn't quite happen on the day he is born, but by the time he can write his own name he is well on the way to becoming his own man. Every day of his life your boy is inventing an ever more elaborate private world where you are an outsider. A loving and supportive outsider, perhaps. But an outsider all the same.

By the time your son is in his early teens, you are sometimes aware that your child is now another country – with loves, fears, dreams, achievements and misdemeanours that you can only guess at. But if our sons grow further away from us as the summers die one by one, our fathers grow ever closer.

The morning after Oasis played Earl's Court, I discovered an empty bottle of bourbon and a gigantic poster ripped from the side of the venue on my son's bedroom floor. He was fifteen at the time – although it seems like only the day before yesterday that I sat up with him in the wee small hours as his milk teeth pushed through his gums and he screamed the roof off our little flat – and I wondered what I should tell him.

Son, you don't need hard liquor to be a man? Son, you take this poster right back where you found it? Son, when you are intoxicated, don't do anything that you will regret for more than a day? I knew exactly what my dad would have told me. Because he must have told me the same thing ten thousand times.

'Moderation in all things,' my father always told me. It was one of his recurring themes. Boy, did it recur. And when I was a roaring Essex teenager and the lager was flowing like tap water or when I was a speeding *NME* hack and the amphetamine sulphate was twelve quid a gram, his message went in one cloth ear and swiftly out the other. But with a son of my own – a smart, tough kid but one who wants to be Liam Gallagher when he grows up – the message finally made a lot of sense. As I stared at that empty bottle of bourbon, at last I understood. When it comes to drink and drugs, we walk a fine line between having fun and fucking up our lives. Moderation in all things. Of course. Almost ten years after my father's death, I finally believe him.

Even though I didn't always listen to my dad – at least not in my late teens and early twenties – I always thought that he was brilliant at being a father. He was so *good* at it. He was the toughest man I ever knew but he never hit me in his life and I respected him more than anyone in the world. I thought that was some feat. I still do.

'Moderation in all things,' wasn't the only homily. But life had a way of ramming home some of his other lessons a bit earlier than the one about knowing when to say no more.

'There's always someone tougher than you are,' he said, and had the decency not to gloat when I took my first serious beating (a torn black eye and a lot of badly bruised pride).

'Any mug can spend it but it takes a smart man to earn it,' he said, and after I had quickly blown my first serious cheque from my first successful book, he gave me a loan without making me beg. And, now I think of it, without ever asking for the money back.

I see now that the things he tried to tell me were the fragments of truth that he had learned over the course of a lifetime. He knew what he was talking about but for a long time I was too young and too dumb to listen. And now I wish my own son would take on board the few things I know to be true. Yet I know he has to learn them the hard way.

My father was good at being a father. Perhaps it was because, coming from one of those huge, sprawling, old-fashioned East End families, he had grown up taking care of younger siblings. Family legend recounted how my father went out to work so that his academically brilliant brother could go to Cambridge, an almost unimaginable destination in that neighbourhood at that time.

But, as good as he was at parenting, my father didn't have

any secret knowledge about bringing up a son, there was no master plan to follow or strict guildlines to adhere to. When I had a son of my own I discovered how much improvisation there is to being a father. That trusting face thinks you can do anything. But all the while you are winging it.

Although I ignored all his home truths as so much party-pooping (why believe in moderation when the night is young and the girls are pretty and you are sporting a new pair of Gatsby trousers?), I still believed that my dad had a genius for doing the right thing. I didn't realize that there are no rules to bringing up children. If only it were that easy.

What does the good father do when an eleven-year-old decides to stop doing his homework? Do you rant and rave? Or gently persuade? Is it best to quietly talk about the future or to wave a big stick? Who really knows? Who's to say?

And when a teenage boy brings home a girl who would be desperately inappropriate as a wife – or, far worse, a girl who would be all too appropriate as a wife – should a father quietly have a word in his boy's ear? Or should he keep his own counsel and hope it fizzles out of its own accord? Give the boy a packet of condoms or show the babe the door? Who knows?

Well, I always thought my father knew. But now I increasingly suspect that he was doing what every father does – making it up as he goes along. And doing a fair bit of praying.

Only now, with a son of my own, do I see the agonies I must have caused him. He was so proud of me going to a grammar school and must have been devastated when I left for a dead-end job as soon as I possibly could. But he told me he thought I was making a mistake and then let me get on with it. The serious business of screwing up my life.

Then there was sex and drugs and rock and roll, there was freelance poverty, there was divorce, there was another baby boy to bring up – but this one wouldn't have the priceless shelter of a nuclear family. Looking back, I feel like not so much a son, more a soap opera. It was a good job he loved me so much.

And I loved him. The problems we had – and he must have profoundly disapproved of most of the moves I made – were softened by the fact that the love he felt was unconditional. Dropped out, dead broke, strung out, knocked up or loaded – I was still his son. And he was still my hero.

Perhaps every father is a hero to his son. But my father was also the real thing. He really was a hero. In the cupboard of our living room in our suburban semi there was the Distinguished Service Medal that he had won as a Royal Naval Commando in World War Two. The DSM (officers are awarded the DSO) is the second highest honour in the armed forces. Only the Victoria Cross is higher – a fact that I knew by heart while my contemporaries were trying to remember that C is for cat.

But we were all children of the war. It filled our games and our dreams. If you were a little English boy growing up in the fifties and early sixties, you grew up steeped in World War Two. Spitfire, Stuka, Hurricane, Lancaster bomber and Bren gun – these names were as familiar as John, Paul, George and Ringo would be very soon. Unvisited places like Normandy, Dunkirk, Anzio and Hiroshima sounded as familiar as Clacton, Yarmouth, Frinton and Brighton.

And Elba – the island where Napoleon was exiled – that was the most resonant name of all. Because that was where my father's Commando unit – his 'mob', he called them – went on their last raid. That was where dozens of his friends were killed. That was where he won his DSM. That was where his war ended.

He never talked about the war – often he seemed like the only person in the England of the fifties and early sixties who didn't talk about it. Everyone in the family was intensely proud of him and friends and relations were always reminding me that he was someone special. He rarely mentioned it, and then only to talk about one day visiting the graves of his friends who had died (eighteen, nineteen they had been – not old enough to vote). But when he took off his shirt, you were reminded of his past because you could see that one side of his upper torso was a mass of scar tissue. The white skin was pulled tight and lined to the epicentre of the wound, like a star burst of flesh and blood. And there were the black nuggets of shrapnel that slowly pushed their way from his body for all his adult life. And of course there was the medal.

He had stopped being a Commando years before I was born, but that was the experience that defined him. All the young men he had seen killed and maimed and burnt – and the lives he had taken – did something to his heart. It didn't warp it, or make it cruel and empty. It made him impossibly gentle. He wasn't the hardened war veteran of popular fiction and the movies. He quite literally would not hurt a fly. If some wasp or bee or spider strayed into the Parsons home, my father would gently pick it up and carry it to the garden, where it would be set free. It used to drive me and my mum crazy.

His temper could erupt. And when it did, hard men folded, their legs turned to jelly, their bottle suddenly gone. I saw it a few times – with some cocky swimming-pool attendant in the sixties when I was learning to swim, and earlier, with some surly boss who refused to let my mother take a personal call when her father was dying from cancer in the late fifties. His temper always had a good and righteous reason to explode. But when it did he was uncontrollable, terrifying. And yet he never laid a finger on my mother or me. That would have been unthinkable for him. He was a violent man who learned to be gentle. A hard man who was sickened by violence.

I didn't understand the love he felt for me and the pride he took in my childish achievements until I had a son of my own. And then I looked at that tiny baby and there was some kind of chemical reaction inside me – here was the most precious and beautiful thing I had ever seen. Here was the best thing that had ever happened to me. And suddenly life had me as its hostage. Forever.

As my son grew, I could understand my father's frustrations. Not having enough time free from the tyranny of work. The disappointment he felt when I turned my back on a good education. And I could understand how he felt to be getting older, to live with that gnawing sense that time is running out. Because until you have a child and see how quickly it grows, you can kid yourself that time will never run out.

Our lives were very different. And in many ways they were the differences of the generation who came of age in the forties and the generation who came of age in the seventies. He had the war and rationing. I had peace and affluence. He was born into a depression. I was born into an era of entitlement. For me, there was no doubt that life would go on getting more free, more rich, more satisfying. I can see with my son and his friends that those certainties now seem as ancient as the workhouse and the soup kitchen seemed to me.

But unlike my father and my son, I came of age at a time when anything seemed possible, where everything was there for the taking. When I was twenty I packed my bags and set off round Europe for a few months. And other fathers might have objected but he thought it would do me good. He thought a boy should see the world. 'That's what I did,' he said. 'Except of course someone was always shooting at me.'

He was a good enough father not to tell me every time he thought I was making a mistake. I know he didn't like my taste in girls and, later, women. Or rather, he didn't like it when I brought home some sweet-natured nest-builder in a tank top who he adored and then dumped her for some painted Whore of Babylon who he didn't like at all. And I did that all the time.

What did he want for me? He wanted stability. He wanted me to find a job that I loved. He didn't want me to throw my life away on the wrong girl, the wrong career, the wrong choices that are so sickeningly easy to make. And now, as my son brings girls home and considers his career options and looks forward to his life as a man, I find that I want the same things for him. They seem like such pathetically modest ambitions. But as the son becomes the father, you realize how carefully these dreams have to be nurtured.

I don't want my son to knock anyone up. I don't want him to get a dose of the clap – or worse. I don't want him to fall in love with someone who isn't worthy of his love. I don't want him to be stuck in a job he despises. I don't want him to take bad drugs. I don't want him to be fat, forty and marooned in a loveless, joyless marriage. I want what my father wanted for me. And I managed to find some of that buried treasure. But not all of it. Who does, dad?

It broke my father's heart when I divorced. Not for my sake – I think after a while the father has to resign himself to the life his adult son creates for himself – but because he knew what it would mean for my son. That he would grow up in a messy tangle of hurt feelings, distance and bitterness – like every other child of divorced parents. It broke my father's heart because he knew what I didn't stop to think about until much later – that my divorce meant that my son would not enjoy the same kind of home that I had known. Different worlds, of course. Growing up, I had one friend whose parents were divorced. But very few of my son's school friends are growing up with both their parents. My dad would not have found that fact reassuring. He would have found it . . . 'disgusting', is probably the word he would have chosen. As a teenager – or even older – I would have argued with the blinkered certainty of youth about personal freedom and our inalienable right to constantly try, try again. But I wouldn't argue with him now. Not now.

My dad's generation grew up believing that nothing was more important than your responsibilities. My generation grew up believing that nothing was more important than your personal freedom. As I watch what seems like an entire generation of children growing up in families that have been shattered by divorce, wrecked by grown adults who will be forever stunted by their belief in instant gratification, I know which one of us was right. And it sure as hell wasn't me.

My father was only with a handful of women in his life. There was the East End beauty queen that my mum displaced. A farmer's daughter in Italy during the war that he sometimes alluded to (when I was about thirteen, my jaw dropped when my dad started babbling to a waiter in fluent Italian). And then monogamy with my mother. Almost fifty years of contentment, staying home and early nights.

My life wasn't like that. I had been with more women than that before I even had a vague idea of what I was doing. And I used to think that he was the one who had missed out. I used to think that I was the lucky one – what with my rock chicks and foreign babes and older women and younger women and all the rest. I thought that I was the one who got the sweet deal while dad stayed home with mum. But increasingly, I am not so sure.

We were different men. And I have sometimes thought of myself as an inadequate father – because surely I failed the fundamental test of fatherhood when I chose a woman that I couldn't and wouldn't grow old with. But I always thought of my dad as a great father. He was protective, strong and I could fall asleep knowing that I would wake up safe and sound. One of the enduring memories of my childhood is sleeping on the back seat of the family car, the lights of East End streets and Essex A-roads blurring high above (had we been to see my grandmother? Or to a pantomime at the Palladium?), then being swaddled in a tartan blanket and carried upstairs to bed. Did my son ever feel that secure? I would like to think so.

My son and I have travelled to New York, Thailand, North Africa and most places in between. We have had adventures. We have had a laugh. But surely being a father is about more than sharing good times. Surely being a father is about giving your son a foundation on which to build a life. I know my father did that. I am not so sure about myself. But then of course, my job isn't over yet. I suppose it's never really over. Certainly up until my thirtieth birthday I was often a source of worry and anxiety to my father. And I am sure it would have gone on for longer than that, if he had lived.

But we could always talk. Unlike mothers and daughters, fathers and sons can always find something to talk about. There is always football. As a boy, my dad had been a goalkeeper in Dagenham, playing in the same school side as a right back called Alf Ramsey. This was the same neighbourhood that spawned Terry Venables and Jimmy Greaves – and they boast about the North-East!

But the early sixties was too soon for a working-class boy to ascend to the heights of his profession while also keeping his East End vowels. My dad's childhood pal had to lose his Dagenham accent when he started to climb the ladder. And when my father bumped into Alf Ramsey (Sir Alf? perhaps not yet) over Romford dog track he found a changed man. After elocution lessons, Ramsey had been transformed into a ludicrous, coached 'oo-more-tea-vicar' mock toff. My father came home full of scorn and amusement. And I never forgot it, especially when there were attempts to change my accent. We moved from Romford – emotionally, still part of the East End – to rural Essex, the first of what would later become a tidal wave of the Cockney diaspora. But this was the early sxties, and my little country school was shocked to have a genuine, gor-blimey-guvnor Artful Dodger in their midst. My teachers seriously suggested elocution lessons for little Tony. And it was the biggest laugh my dad had enjoyed since he bumped into Alf Ramsey over the dogs. He was all for self-made men. But you should never forget where you came from. And you should always be proud of it.

Later I met plenty of people – journalists, lawyers, broadcasters – who had modified or changed their accents. Geordies,

Scots, Irish, New Zealanders, Scousers, Londoners. And I didn't think it was a disgraceful thing to do. Not at all. If you have a strong regional accent, it is perfectly natural for it to be softened when you leave the region. But it was never a possibility for me. My dad wouldn't have allowed it.

I passed my eleven plus. But it didn't mean I was better than him. Unlike some working-class parents whose kids make it to university, he never felt left behind. Far from it.

But he was upset when I left that school. He was proud of me and finally I understand that pride, the ferocity of it. I understand that the achievements of our children can mean more to us than our own. We want them *to get it right* as we suspect that we never did. And when they do, it is a victory over time, a triumph over the mortality of all flesh.

The father and the son are different men. I pride myself in being able to go anywhere, meet anyone, feel at home everywhere (which is of course the same as feeling at home nowhere). But my father didn't want to belong. He despised the establishment. He loathed authority all his life. He was, for example, a cop hater. The police made his blood boil. When they put on their sirens he insisted they were just 'going home for their bloody tea'. And if he ever got pulled over to the side of the road, he always made it worse by getting lippy. He wasn't one of these good citizens whose legs turn to mush at the sight of a blue uniform. He had a burning hatred of the law whom he accused of being venal, cruel and corrupt. As a child, I found it embarrassing. Later, I felt he was just making life unnecessarily hard for himself. And me. But by then it was too late to change. And I didn't really want him to change. I liked him the way he was.

But I grew up wondering how I could ever fill his shoes. I grew up in the shadow of his medal. How could I ever compete with that heroism? How could I ever experience anything that intense? How could I ever achieve anything that would be so worthy of respect? I still don't know.

And yet my father lived a very quiet, peaceful life. After the war – which was over by the time he was twenty – he worked on a stall and as a lorry driver. By the time I was born he was a greengrocer and by my teens he was working as a produce manager for a chain of supermarkets, driving around and making sure their stock was good. He had a company car, annual dinners at the Hilton (he was just under six feet tall, but well built, and he looked good in black tie) and he was full of complaints about the unions.

When I was growing up, the great debate in the house was if my dad should start his own business. His 'boys' – the fifteen- and sixteen-year-old lads who worked as his minions in the greengrocer's – would frequently go off to try running their own shops. And sometimes they would turn up years later with the Mercedes and the glam wife and the big house with the bar and the pool. And they would grin and slip me a ten shilling note and say they owed it all to my dad.

Yet just as he had resisted attempts to get him to become an officer in the forces, so he resisted efforts to get him to become a businessman in civvy street. But I think he sometimes wished he had. He didn't envy his boys their ulcers or their brushes with the taxman or even their glam wives. But he had a highly devel- oped sense of pride and I think he sometimes regretted not having greater material success. 'We could have been million- aires by now, Em,' he would sometimes wistfully tell my mum. And I remember that wistfulness as I dream of bigger contracts, more money and greater success. I don't ever want to be wistful about missed chances. Perhaps that is my way of living with the medal.

We were a working-class family. For the first five years of my life we lived above a greengrocer's shop in Harold Hill, Essex. Opposite was a patch of wasteland where they later built a bubble gum factory. We continued to live there even when my dad went off to work at a shop in Tottenham.

My father worked long days and he also worked Saturdays. My mum's brothers took me to Upton Park on Saturdays and my dad took me to the occasional mid-week game at White Hart Lane (watching Arsenal is my way of not betraying either my uncles or my dad). I don't think I ever saw a football match with him on a Saturday. My two memories of the 1966 World Cup Final are saying '*Fuck*' in front of my mother when the Germans equalized. And the other is that my dad had to work that day, that special day, just like every other Saturday.

He worked hard. Far harder than me. Yet I often feel like my father must have felt. I wonder what exactly I am working for, I wonder what I am missing, I wonder if it is worth it. And I see in myself his tendency to pull up the drawbridge, to shut out the world, to make his family the centre of the universe.

There was a mystery about him. Once, between greengrocer jobs, he worked in a warehouse that was held up by armed men. And one night, a bit later, I discovered two handguns on the back seat of his car. I never mentioned them to him but I strongly suspected that the old Commando was ready to shoot back if they came again. An unlucky yob had once walked into his greengrocer's shop in Barking asking for protection money. My father made sure that he never asked again. There was always something dangerous about him. None of the parents of my friends – those stolid home brewers and golfers and car washers – had fathers who sometimes left handguns on the back seat or who could toss would-be wideboys into the gutter. My dad was very hard. And I was very proud of him.

We were an ordinary working-class family but we felt special. We felt superior, even, not because of money or accents or social graces or education or any of that. We felt special because of my dad. Because of what he had done. Because of who he was. And because of the medal.

His great love was the sea. Even in his sixties, he was still the sailor he had been when he entered the armed forces in his mid-teens, and once a year he would go off alone to Cowes for the sailing. That was the extent of his social life, apart from gatherings with the regiments of brothers, sisters, in-laws and children (who eventually all moved out to our neck of the woods). After his annual escape to Cowes, for the rest of the year he would stay home with me and my mum, tending his garden, laughing at *Morecambe and Wise*, shaking his head at the footage from Vietnam where frightened GIs huddled together in the jungle. 'You should never stand together like that,' said my dad. 'Because all it takes is just one grenade to take out the lot of you.'

He loved his home but he could be very impatient with the trappings of domesticity. I remember one Boxing Day his sister turned the hoover on in her home and my father swore we would go somewhere else next year. And like him I find myself treating every vacuum cleaner I hear as a personal affront. You can love your home without wanting to hear vacuum cleaners after work. That's how my dad felt. And I agree with him.

He has been dead for ten years now. Lung cancer. I didn't cry at his funeral but I cried when I heard he had a tumour and that it was terminal. But then I had to be strong because I am an only child and it wouldn't have been right to fall to pieces. It is okay to cry, he had taught me. And it is okay to be afraid – only a fool is never afraid. But being a man also carries certain obligations, certain duties, certain responsibilities. He drummed that into me and I am glad that he did.

He had known about the cancer for a year or so, I reckon. But he kept it to himself. So when he collapsed and was rushed to hospital, God yes, it was a shock. But it was all over in a few weeks, which made it a lot easier for me and my mother than if it had dragged on for a year or more. Which of course is exactly how the old boy had planned it.

He faced up to the knowledge of what was growing inside him, the thing that would kill him at sixty-two, and he kept it to himself to protect those around him. He was still heroic, and he was still my hero. In the hospital, full of morphine, I could see he was frightened – of course he was frightened – but he was still the bravest man I had ever known. I spent my childhood games pretending to be a hero. My father was the real thing.

They say that headstones need special cleaning every ten years or so. And recently my mother went into the undertakers to enquire about having the headstone cleaned.

'Name of the deceased?' the undertaker asked her.

'Victor William Robert Parsons,' said my mother. 'DSM.'

'That shouldn't be hard to find,' the undertaker said. 'I shouldn't think there are too many DSMs over there.'

'No,' said my mother. 'I shouldn't think so.'

My father's life was always unimaginable to me. I couldn't imagine those war experiences. I couldn't imagine what it was like to love one woman for a lifetime. And I couldn't imagine what it was like to be him.

Yet I look at my son's uncharted future with my father's eyes. What if you can't get a job? What if she gets pregnant? What if you stop loving her? What if she stops loving you? What if you're not happy?

The son laughs with his friends and watches the girls go by while the father's lot is pride, fear, frustration, protectiveness and a profound love for someone who is both an extension of himself and yet very much his own person. The father and the son. One flesh. Two lives. And the son has absolutely no idea of what the father is going through until he becomes a father himself. Finally you see with the eyes of the ages.

My father taught me how to be a man and he taught me how to love. And I think that if I can leave my son an inheritance like that, then I will have done my job as a father.

My father died ten years ago but increasingly I find myself trying to come to some accommodation with what he believed and what I grew up believing.

My dad's generation was probably *too* concerned with responsibility – how many people of that generation spent a lifetime in a loveless, miserable, even brutal marriage? – but now I see that my own generation was far too obsessed with personal freedom – if you are in a bad marriage, you break it up at the earliest possible opportunity and worry about the children later. For my generation, nothing was deemed more important than your own personal gratification. Getting laid, getting smashed – this is what we had instead of washing the car on Sunday morning. Our major responsibility in life was to our own happiness. Pathetic, when you stop and think about it. There has to be another way. I hope my son can find it.

I see him learning, I see him growing. There was a time – when he was fourteen, fifteen – when he believed that a drop of the hard stuff was just what he needed to grease the transition to manhood. It didn't last long – how many times can you puke up your guts before you realize you can't look cool in a pool of vomit? But I later realized that my son had learned this fundamental lesson about alcohol far quicker than I did. I was still getting stupidly rat-faced when I was thirty.

It is never easy being the parent of a teenager. The teenage years are very different from the rest of childhood. The sweetness, the innocence, the heartbreaking trust – all those things you really, really loved about your child when he was growing up are pretty well buried when they hit their teens. Instead of this little blond angel with huge blue eyes there is a hulking brute with a baritone who looks suspiciously like another guy. And yet you are never free from someone who you first loved as a baby.

As I say, something chemical happens to you when you

become a parent. I looked at my son when he was born – and when he was a toddler, when he was five, when he was nine years old, when he was eleven – and I can honestly say that he looked like the most beautiful thing that I have ever seen. Was he really that beautiful? Or was it just my parental gene kicking in? God only knows.

But the curious thing is that I still feel exactly the same way today. I look at him now, towering above me, and I still feel like protecting him, I still feel like telling him everything I have learned, and he still looks beautiful to me – like God's second attempt at David Beckham. Could he really pull a Spice Girl? Or am I just looking through the adoring eyes of a father? I really don't know.

I know that I am not too worried about him. There may be mistakes along the way – about women, about work, about drugs – but with luck he will learn from all of them and be destroyed by none of them. I am not letting go or giving up but he is nearly eighteen and in the end you learn that, no matter how much you love them, you can't protect your child from life.

He knows what love is. He knows what bad drugs are. He knows that you get nothing without working for it. More and more, I know that I am starting to sound like my old man. But that's okay. My son is doing all right. I think his grandfather would have been proud of him.

Part Three
East

Introduction

Like a lot of little English boys, I grew up dreaming of America. New York, New York – that was the dream ticket in my youth. And then I went to Asia.

My first trip to Hong Kong was more intoxicating, more exciting, more bewildering than any drug I ever took in my life. Nowhere I had ever been offered such opportunities for romance, friendship and trouble. Asia felt like the last place in the world where you could go and find some honest, old-fashioned adventure.

I saw the bay of Yokohama, the geishas in Kyoto and the A-bomb dome in Hiroshima. I went down the Yangtze river and up the Great Wall in China. I crawled in the old VC tunnels of Vietnam. I drank a few beers in Manila. I was smiled at in Bali, ripped off in Bangkok, went dancing in Jakarta. I ate a hell of a lot of rice. And I fell in love.

Asia covers an awful lot of ground and there are greater contrasts, more impossible differences between these nations than anywhere else on earth. Vietnam and Japan hardly feel like they are on the same planet, let alone the same continent and the same is true of China and the Philippines, or Indonesia and Taiwan. I will never know it all and I will never get tired of it – which sounds like a definition of true love to me.

In the end I can only concur with Rudyard Kipling, who got it just right when he said, 'If you have heard the East a-calling, you will never heed anything else.'

Goodbye Hong Kong

Arena, **April 1997**

With the clock ticking closer to midnight, we took our drinks up on the roof of the China Club, Hong Kong's members-only bastion of feudal luxury. And what we saw up there took our breath away.

If you want to know why men love Hong Kong, then look at its skyline. This is the one place on earth with a skyline that makes Manhattan's towering vista look like an ugly sister. Nowhere else is so clearly full of money and sex and all your wildest dreams.

Up on the roof of the China Club you don't so much gaze on Hong Kong's glittering skyline as find yourself surrounded by it. A thousand feet above you is I.M. Pei's Bank of China, seventy storeys of insane parallelograms. Way down below, the Star Ferry chugs across to Kowloon just as it did in the days when Suzie Wong found her true love. And all around there are the city lights, the undying neon glow of this city in the South China Sea.

Hong Kong is not a sentimental place. If you are poor or stupid or lazy, Hong Kong will eat you up. If you have more money than sense, you can be certain of waking up with a sore head and an empty wallet (many of Hong Kong's watering holes were originally built to separate sailors from their shore pay). And yet gazing on Babylon's endless beauty, and breathing the humid air of a summer night in the tropics, you can't help loving Hong Kong.

There are far prettier places in the East. There are towns where it is easier to have a good time without detonating your credit limit. And although the hospitality of the non-Chinese population is legendary, the Chinese themselves are a cold, spitting, crotch-scratching breed. And yet Hong Kong pulls at my heart because I know that there is nowhere on the planet quite like it for being able to guarantee a young man all the exotic adventure he can handle.

When *Arena* sent me to Hong Kong to write a travel story more than six years ago, I had never been in the Far East. Since that first taste of south-east Asia, I head East as soon as someone leaves my front door slightly ajar. Hong Kong overwhelmed me then. And it overwhelms me still. What I found in Hong Kong was the most modern city in the world co-exisiting with one of the most ancient cultures.

If it wasn't for the British, Hong Kong would still be a clump of rocks. Yet although it is a British invention, it has an Asian heart and an Asian face. White boys are in the minority here. And they always were.

Jan Morris composed a list of modern, non-communist chinoiserie, a litany of Hong Kong's strangeness that included, *'the garish merry signs, the clamorous shop fronts, the thickets of TV aerials, the banners, the rows of shiny hanging ducks, the washing on its poles, the wavering bicyles, the potted plants massed on balconies, the canvas-canopied stalls selling herbs, the bubbling cauldrons of crab-claw soup boiling at eating stalls'.* Hong Kong has all the features of your home town. But it always lets you know that you are a long way from home.

The archetypal postcard image of Hong Kong – the orange-sailed wooden junk sailing blithely in front of the gleaming, hi-tech Central skyline – contains a core of truth. This is where all worlds meet – old and new, East and West, spiritual and profane, the next century and the last.

The last time I was in Wanchai it was the Festival of the Hungry Ghosts. As I and a lawyer friend made our way through the streets to a Vietnamese restaurant called Saigon Beach, bar girls and wise guys burnt fake money in the gutter to appease their heathen gods. Held every year in late August ('the fifteenth day of the seventh moon', Hong Kong time), the Festival of the Hungry Ghosts is evidence of a culture that is independent of both British capitalism and Chinese communism. And is likely to outlast them both.

The six million population of Hong Kong is almost totally Chinese, from the glossy office girls in Central with their mobile phones and mini-skirts, to the plump, round-faced babies who look like Buddha with an Elvis haircut, to toothless old grannies and of course the bespectacled businessmen in their salaryman uniforms, everywhere the businessmen.

The colours red and gold are everywhere in Hong Kong – in temples, restaurants, wedding ceremonies – red and gold, symbolizing wealth and power. The Chinese religion is a strange brew of ancestor worship, Taoism and Mahayana Buddhism. But mostly they worship hard cash.

And if Hong Kong is a place for business, it is also a place for men. Hong Kong is a place where expatriate wives and girl-friends can feel left out. This is where old attitudes endure. Every white woman I ever saw in Hong Kong looked like they had piles. They are uncomfortable here.

In Hong Kong the boys have something called the Kai Tak agreement. This means that when you leave the airport on some short jaunt – to the dark streets and bright lights of Jakarta, Saigon or Manila – you do not talk about it when you get back home. You do not gossip to wives or girlfriends. The Kai Tak agreement is both an affirmation of true friendship and a licence for debauchery. As with so many things in Hong Kong, the noble and the corrupt walk hand in hand.

Hong Kong takes your breath away before you even land. Even this late in the century, only a year away from the People's Liberation Army taking over from Marlboro Man, you fly into Hong Kong with an overture of excitement ringing in your head. Even now, your 747 still comes screaming into the very heart of God's Chinatown, through a jungle of billboards and skycrapers where washing dries on a million verandas crowded with green-ery. You fall in love with Hong Kong before you have even retrieved your suitcase.

You need money here and if you do not inherit it then you have to earn it or marry it. There are more Rolls-Royces on Victoria Peak, Hong Kong's highest point, than anywhere in the world. And when one primary school teacher asked her class of five year olds where leather comes from she was told, 'Gucci'. But most Chinese are not rich. And in a place of few laws, no welfare state and no safety net, life can be very hard indeed.

That New York vibe surfaces again and again – it's tough here, the locals smile. Hong Kong residents boast about costs the way New Yorkers boast about the crime rate. And it's true –

you have to be smart and you have to work hard. Once upon a time it might have been a place for idiot sons, slackers and the like, but those days are long gone. Hong Kong has not carried passengers for years. Those who come expecting an easy ride are soon found out.

The old cliché about Hong Kong was that it was populated by losers, the FILTH (Failed In London, Tried Hong Kong). And while there are certainly still a few white parasites out here, desperately clinging on to a big-cock status they would never enjoy at home, if you can make it in Hong Kong, you can make it anywhere.

They work six days a week minimum in Hong Kong. The rewards are enormous. What some London executive would take in a year, thinking he is doing pretty good because he is 'earning his age', the movers and shakers out in Hong Kong will make in a *month*. And they are the most generous people in the world.

The legendary hospitality of Hong Kong was built on junk culture – one of those shiny motorized launches staffed by a Chinese crew that every major company once had in Hong Kong for entertaining clients and themselves.

Junks were the last manifestation of colonial opulence. When Nick Leeson lost his Barings in Singapore, initial reports suggested he had his own yacht. But of course what he had was access to the company junk. And nowhere understood junk culture better than Hong Kong.

On a junk (which bears no resemblance to the bowed, wooden junks in the postcards), your two-man Chinese crew sails you to idyllic islands that look like something up river in *Apocalypse Now*, all ramshackle shacks, rancid dogs and old men in flip-flops. In these secret places they serve you cold beer and the best fish in the world. You sail back at midnight, the harbour glittering like a dream of heaven. And you understand that in this place the sons of Empire lived like kings.

'Off they go, one after another, towing speed boats some-times, with laughter ringing out across the water,' wrote Jan Morris of the junks in the eighties. But the laughter has died now. Junk culture is winding down. Last summer my closest Hong Kong mate and I tooled around in his company junk for a day. But sightings of similiar vessels were few and far between.

Now the boys tell wistful tales of how just a few years ago they would take a junk out full of Cathay Pacific stewardesses and water-ski in secluded harbours until the sun set in the South China Sea. As the changeover approaches, companies are cutting back on the junks. Floating around on a junk was once a standard leisure activity in Hong Kong. Now it truly is a privilege.

If you make a friend in Hong Kong he will be your friend for life. Perhaps it is because you are all so very far from your blood relatives. 'Out here, your friends *become* your family,' one short-haired lawyer from Liverpool told me.

But there is another side to Hong Kong – mean, grasping, ready to rob you blind. Hong Kong can be unforgiving if you are poor or you are stupid. Or just young, which is often the same thing. Almost everyone has a tale of being ripped off early on in their days in Hong Kong. And I mean ripped off big time, ripped off so that you nurse a hangover that cost you several thousands of pounds, ripped off by experts.

The tabs are expensive in the Wanch – £35 for a thirsty girl's tequila – but an old trick is to get you to pay the same tab twice, or get different members of your party to pay for the same bill. It easily happens when you are fresh off the Jumbo and being given a thorough medical examination by some willowy beauty of the night.

But this is in keeping with Hong Kong's ignoble tradition. Wanchai was built to roll sailors on shore leave. Later it was where the Americans on 'r and r' from Vietnam were separated from their money. The beautiful old tart has separated me from my pocket money once or twice. It is part of the Hong Kong experience.

But we never loved Hong Kong because it was cosy. We never loved it because it was familiar. We loved it because it was strange, wild, because it was at the end of the world. And perhaps we also loved it because we knew that we could not keep it.

Hong Kong is 235 islands, most of them uninhabited little rocks, plus a rugged tip of the Chinese mainland. Most of Hong Kong is rural China. But when we speak of Hong Kong we speak of Hong Kong Island and the tip of the Chinese peninsula, Kowloon. Beyond Kowloon are the New Territories, containing ninety per cent of Hong Kong's land mass, and beyond that is the future. China. And what else?

I know British people in Hong Kong who have made their home here. They are hardly 'expatriates' any more. They speak Cantonese, study Mandarin and will not be leaving after the changeover. They will stay in Hong Kong until someone starts shooting at them. Because it is home.

And there is another reason they will stay, the reason that Hong Kong has a special place in the hearts of many British men. When the flag finally comes down next year it will signal the end of Britain's greatest adventure. Hong Kong represents the century or two when the sap was rising in this country. When Hong Kong goes, so does any pretence of national potency. What red-blooded male animal could fail to be moved by that bleak day?

Life still feels untamed in Hong Kong. You can leave the moneyed offices of Central, jump the subway and a few minutes later be in streets black as the grave where toothless men gamble over fighting cockroaches.

And they tell you wonderful stories in Hong Kong – fantastic stories of extravagance, danger and good men brought low by bad women, respectable men who drifted into a world of gangsters and gamblers, pimps and prostitutes, the guys like you and me who fell foul of Triads in Hong Kong or the ex-KGB Russians who infest Macau.

Over cold Tsing Tao beers they tell stories of hostess bars and high stakes mah-jong parlours, stories where the protagonists end up dead or in prison or being blown by every woman in the room.

There was the parable of the civil servant who married a Wanchai hostess. She was addicted to gambling and he ended up sentenced to two years for corruption after his wife disappeared, believed murdered – but then he was dramatically released on appeal. Or the New Zealand QC who was shot in the eye when he tried to buy his Russian working girl out of the game. Or the smiling *gweilo* who slapped his credit card on the bar of some Wanchai haunt, got them to lock the door and was then entertained by every girl in the joint. Fantastic, incredible stories! And after you have spent a little time in Hong Kong, it doesn't surprise you that the stories are all absolutely true.

'The kingdoms of the world lay before us,' wrote Jan Morris in her classic 1974 piece on Hong Kong, 'Anglo-China', 'The skyscrapers of Victoria, jam-packed at the foot of the hill, seem to vibrate with pride, greed, energy and success, and all among them the traffic swirled, and the crowds milled, and the shops glittered, and the money rang.'

What will it be like after 1997? What will Hong Kong be like after the Union Jack comes down for the last time on 30 June next year? Nobody knows. The Chinese reluctance to kill the glorious cash cow must be balanced against the fact that they are handling something that is beyond their comprehension, beyond anything in the imaginations of Marx or Mao, a place of avarice and industry and fun. God, don't forget the fun.

Hong Kong has changed since I first rode the Star Ferry. It is not the same place. Already British Hong Kong has been consigned to history. When I ride through Central with my friend in his Porsche, we attract stares – but not for the reason we would have attracted stares six years ago. Now they are wondering – where did a white boy get the money for a Porsche? These days the screaming red Ferraris on the Peak are all driven by Chinese.

In the past being a westerner in Hong Kong was enough. You got deference. You got respect. You got a good bang for your buck. Not any more. Economic superiority has gone. *Gweilos* are leaving the good apartments on the Mid Levels and being replaced by Chinese.

Now white kids with British passports are pouring in to wait tables. There are stories of rich Chinese from up on the Peak (where once they were not allowed to live) learning English just so the *gweilo* waiters can take their order. And in Hong Kong the stories are always true. The white man's burden is no longer bringing civilization to untamed climes. These days the white man's burden is paying the rent.

But love is not rational, is it? And I love Hong Kong even if I know that it is not the Hong Kong that I fell in love with. Hong Kong still holds my heart. I feel it when I see the green and white Star Ferry, where William Holden met his true love, or when I see the tropical clouds hanging low over the silver and golden skyscrapers, or when the lights are coming on in old Wanchai. And I feel it when I see the rattling trams, the withered rickshaw boys, and Sunday in Central when Hong Kong's army of Filipinas take over the business district for a mass picnic. Because of the great impossible adventure that Hong Kong represents both to me and to my country, it moves me like no other place on earth.

And then there is the view of Central from Victoria Peak, the view of Hong Kong harbour from the Regent Hotel, the view of the exotic dancers when you have got a couple of Tsing Taos inside you and you are with some men who you know will be your friends for life, co-signatories of a dozen Kai Tak agreements.

There are no sights in Hong Kong. No world class museums or palaces or castles. Only the glorious sight of Hong Kong itself. Which, for many of us, will always be the greatest sight in the world. The opening paragraph of Richard Mason's novel *The World Of Suzie Wong* still captures the feeling you never escape in Hong Kong, that on this patch of land men witnessed the most beautiful culture clash in human history.

'She came through the turnstile and joined the crowd waiting for the ferry: the women in cotton pyjama suits, the men with felt slippers and gold teeth. Her hair was tied behind her head in a pony-tail, and she wore jeans – green knee-length denim jeans. That's odd, I thought. A Chinese girl in jeans. How do you explain that?'

It will not be easy to explain Hong Kong to those who never saw it. There are mean, dissenting voices who will tell you that the Chinese takeover of Hong Kong signals the end of British colonial pretensions, the final sinking of the sun on the very last outpost of Empire, and that we should be glad.

But not me. The British can feel proud of what they achieved in Hong Kong. Yes, it was stolen from the Chinese. But if it weren't for the British, Hong Kong would still be a fishing village. There is no shame for the British in Hong Kong.

And if there was ever a place in your heart for a little exotic adventure, then there was a place in Hong Kong for you. For that reason alone, Hong Kong was worthy of our love. It breaks my heart that it proved impossible for the British to keep Hong Kong forever. But then I guess that is true of all the things we love.

Kenzaburo Oe

Daily Telegraph, **19 May 1995**

Last December the King of Sweden presented the Japanese novelist, Kenzaburo Oe (pronounced Oh-A), with the Nobel Prize for Literature. The Swedish Academy announced that they were giving Oe the award – and the $930,000 that goes with it – because his writing is 'where life and myth condense to form a disconcerting picture of the human predicament today'. They could have added that no Japanese novelist has ever written more brilliantly than Oe about the division that exists in the soul of his country. For Oe, who is sixty, is a writer who has been formed by two very different nations – Japan before and after Hiroshima.

'During the war the teacher always asked – if the Emperor asks you to die, what would you do?' says Oe in his heavily accented but near perfect English. 'And the answer is – "Yes, I'd die! I'll die by *seppaku*! [ritual suicide]." '

Following his Nobel Prize, Oe is on a whirlwind tour of the West to promote the first English translation of his novel *Nip the Buds, Shoot the Kids*. Originally published in 1958 when Oe was twenty-three the book tells the story of fifteen boys who are evacuated from a reformatory to a small village that is abandoned by peasants afraid of an outbreak of the plague.

The influences are western – there are echoes of everything from *Lord of the Flies* to *The Adventures of Huckleberry Finn* – but Oe's obsessions are specifically Japanese. The Nobel Prize has given him a global audience but in his London hotel Oe says that he writes for his own generation of Japanese who grew up believing that the Emperor was a living god and then were abruptly converted to democracy. Oe vividly remembers when Emperor Hirohito addressed the Japanese people for the first

162

time telling them that they had to 'endure the unendurable' – surrender – after nuclear bombs were dropped on Hiroshima and Nagasaki.

'There were only two or three radios in our small village,' says Oe, whose father died in combat in 1944. 'So we assembled in a very rich man's house and we listened to the speech. I couldn't believe that the *Tenno* [Emperor] spoke in the voice of a human being! We thought he was God. I was ten years old. A very simple, naive boy. I believed that because he was God, a Japanese victory would somehow come at the end of the war. But when *Tenno* spoke in a human voice, I felt that we were abandoned.'

Almost overnight teachers who had been lecturing Oe and his classmates on the virtues of ritual suicide began steeping them in the ways of the West.

'The teacher said that American soldiers would be coming to the village by so-called jeep. He said – you can look at the jeep, you can look at Americans and you must greet them. I'll teach you the orthodox English greeting – hello! Everyone practised shouting – hello! And the teacher said – when American young men love American girls they make a kiss. The new Japanese young man must also study about kiss. I went to the forest and practised on a beautiful young oak tree. That was the first kiss of my life.'

Oe's two most famous books are *Hiroshima Notes* and *A Personal Matter*, published when he was twenty-nine and thirty. The former deals with national catastrophe, the latter with personal tragedy. In 1963 Oe's wife Yukari gave birth to their first child, Hikari. The baby was born with a cerebral hernia, a lesion of the skull through which a red growth of brain tissue protruded. Oe had to either agree to surgery which would close the lesion but cause severe brain damage or let the child die. Overwhelmed by the decision he had to make, Oe fled to Hiroshima.

'I escaped from my son to write a story on an anti-nuclear conference. But the conference was boring so I went to the atomic bomb's survivors hospital. There I met the doctor who was working with the survivors. He had many problems trying the relieve their suffering. But I saw that I must live with my son as that doctor tried to live with the victims of the bomb. So I returned to Tokyo and asked the doctors to perform the

163

operation on my son. We named him Hikari, which means "Light", and I prayed for him.'

The operation left Hikari with terrible brain damage. He couldn't speak and didn't respond to voices. 'But one day on the radio there was the sound of birds and the expression on his face became very vivid,' says Oe.

Oe bought a tape of birdsong and played it to Hikari twenty-four hours a day. The recording included a Japanese woman dully intoning the names of the birds.

'The young announcer was bored with this work so the voice is very flat and inhuman. But we continued to listen to the tape for three or four years. Then I was walking in the forest with my son on my shoulder and in the distance a water rail sang. And my son said very quietly in an inhuman voice, "This is a water rail." At first I thought I had imagined it. But then the bird sang again and my son said again, "This is a water rail." And after that he began to communicate with me.'

Oe and his wife discovered that Hikari knew the sounds of seventy birds. They began playing him classical music. He loved Bach, Mozart and Handel and started learning piano until medicine prescribed to control his epilepsy caused his eyesight to fail.

'If he missed a note he became very angry against the piano. So he gave up playing the piano and started writing down music. At first I thought that he was copying from memory. And then we discovered that he was creating original music.'

Thirty-two next month, Hikari requires constant care and still has only limited speech. But he is now one of Japan's most successful young composers and his two bestselling records have sold more than 100,000 copies. 'Like dew glittering on grass leaves,' is how Kenzaburo Oe describes his son's music.

Although only sixty, Oe says he is now retiring from fiction. He plans to study for five years and then write what he calls 'my last work', his life story.

'For many years I felt that I had to give my son a voice,' says Oe. 'But now when I listen to his music I know that he can communicate in his own voice. I was the champion of my young boy. But now I feel he doesn't need a champion. He can express himself.'

Let's Wedding

Guardian, **14 February 1992**

I had a futon in a guest room in the suburbs of Yokohama. In many ways the home of my girlfriend's parents could have been anywhere in the developed world. But the dining room looked a dream of Japan. The floor was covered with sweet-smelling *tatami* mats, the walls were made of creamy *shoji* paper screens, there was a small Buddhist family altar in the corner. It was a room untouched by the twentieth century.

On the first night of our trip to introduce me to honorable respected mother and father, the four of us sat on *Xaisu* (legless chairs) at the legless dining table and contemplated two huge lacquered bowls of *nigiri sushi*. The supply of Asahi Super Dry was endless. It was like dying, going to heaven and finding that God has a Japanese passport.

'*Itadakimas*' we cried ('I will begin!') and then Yuriko's father froze. Something wasn't right.

'*Misoshiru ga naizo!*' he said. 'There is no Miso soup! Why don't you make some!'

He was addressing his wife. And instead of telling him to get his own soup – or stuffed – Kyoko, Yuriko's mother, got up and went to the kitchen without a murmur. I had never seen anything like it. What was stunning was the way she did it without any sign of resentment. Welcome to Japan.

It is always a mistake for a *gaijin* ('outside person' – a foreigner) to think they know Japan. Before this trip, for example, I had never noticed that the Japanese don't kiss. That is, they regard kissing as sexual foreplay.

The thing about tradition in Japan is that it is unassailable. Inviolate. It always got a big laugh from honorable respected mother and father when I tried to help Kyoko with the dishes. They genuinely thought it was funny.

We were here to discuss marriage plans. It may be a dying institution in the West but in Japan ads for bridal gowns and Hawaiian honeymoons abound. 'Let's wedding,' suggest the signs.

In Japan they say a girl is like a *Kurisumas Keiki* – a Christmas cake. At twenty-two and twenty-three she is perfect, at twenty-four close to her prime but after twenty-five, it is all downhill. Sexist rubbish, of course. Yuriko? She's twenty-three as you're asking, but she has a cousin in her early thirties who has invested a lot of time in her career. In a country in which the average age of brides truly is twenty-five, it's middle-aged. Despite those bi-annual bonuses, desperation starts to bite and the corporate world becomes a dating agency. One afternoon we spent a happy hour laughing at pictures of possible suitors, nervously smiling salarymen who had made it past thirty without meeting the Office Lady of their dreams.

It is tough to be a career woman in Japan. Those I met seemed embittered and marginalized. Women are forced to choose between family and career. Having it all is a Western concept.

Yuriko's parents treated me to typical Japanese hospitality, limitless warmth and kindness behind a veil of formality and modesty. I soon felt like one of the family.

Japan is changing but in a country that was closed to the outside world for centuries, it changes more slowly than one would hope. Kyoko told us that even ten years ago, a salaryman would sweep his dinner to the floor if he considered it was not up to scratch, then watch the woman clear up the mess.

Not many salarymen would try it with a modern Japanese girl but you still see the old Japan everywhere. At family gatherings, the women pour the drinks.

You see more tradition in Japan than change. Women nurture. Men provide. It's a man's world. But it wouldn't be anything without an Office Lady or *Oku-san* ('Mrs Interior' – a housewife). In the home, Japanese men have everything done for them. Yet, curiously, it is the women who seem happy with their lot. One afternoon, Yuriko's dad found me admiring his expensive golf clubs.

'You enjoy golf?' I said.

'Not at all,' he said sadly. 'They are for business.'

Pity the poor salaryman. The company steals him from his family and takes the best years of his life. When he should be loving his wife or watching his children grow, he is drunk in some Ginza bar, boring some Filipino hostess with tales of office politics. What with all the corporate revelry, the average salary-man gets home drunk and exhausted at midnight, his children asleep, his wife a stranger.

Yuriko rarely saw her father when she was growing up. Weekdays he was out every night on company drinking duty (an obligation, not an option) and at the weekends he slept.

Even now, when he is senior enough not to have to go drink-ing every night, he sometimes has to play golf with clients and colleagues when he would be infinitely happier walking his dog or listening to his Mozart CDs. Or even spending time with Kyoko, his wife, the woman he loves.

It is true that women are under the thumb in Japan. But men are somewhere worse. *Otoko wa taihen desu*, as they say in Yokohama. It's hard being a man.

Trouble in Paradise – Manila

Arena, **May/June 1991**

Why are these people smiling? Despite the earthquakes, insurrection and poverty, the Filipinos remain the most sunny-faced, sweet-tempered people in the world. 'Where Asia wears a smile,' runs the legend, and for once the ad man's hyperbole is justified.

The Philippines are Spanish islands – more than seven thousand of them – set in the South China Sea. The Spanish were here for more than three thousand years and their influence will be stamped forever on the islands (named after Spain's King Philip II). Names, food, religion – all of them seem imported direct from the Mediterranean. This is a profoundly Catholic country where every Easter there are ritual scourgings and crucifixions, with men nailed to crosses as a testimony to their faith. Once a Filipino told me of a recent dream where the sky was full of angels and the Virgin Mary was weeping, and perhaps it's this unshakeable belief in the next world that keeps Filipinos smiling.

The Philippines are a place of exceptional beauty, full of exotic lagoons, endless beaches, and more coral reefs than you can shake a stick at. There are sugarcane fields, rice terraces, tropical vistas galore. Manila, the capital, has none of these things, but it is a fantastically vibrant city and a wonderful introduction to the country. Shockingly friendly, very noisy, very crowded – eight million people and counting – Manila is the Philippines on steroids, a dangerous paradise where bombs explode with alarming regularity and everybody smiles at strangers.

There have been a lot of explosions recently (President Cory Aquino just hasn't come through with economic change quick enough for the people, especially the military). But Manila is not the Beirut of the East. It is true that there are the blackened pock marks of shelling from a recent coup attempt in Manila and there are a lot of men in the streets with guns. But for all the noise, bluster and rumour, there have been surprisingly few casualties. In the six coup attempts against Cory Aquino over the last four years, only 168 people have been killed (more than ten times that number died in the summer's earthquake).

It's true that some establishments are very heavily protected – going into Café de Melati, a bar made in heaven, is like strolling through Dodge City on a Saturday night. But though there are an awful lot of men with guns in Manila – soldiers, cops, smiling private armies like the one watching over the millionaires' ghetto of Forbes Park – they hardly ever fire their weapons. I was in Manila for two weeks and never once felt remotely threatened. Who could feel threatened among such warm, beautiful people? Who could feel threatened in a city where they smile at strangers?

'Hey Joe,' smile the older Filipinos, always assuming that any westerner is a GI. If the NPA (New People's Army) take you for a GI then they will probably shoot you, though you are highly unlikely to encounter any of these communist guerrillas in Manila. All the action here comes from feuding army factions. The NPA stay down on Negros, kidnapping missionaries and teaching them to play basketball (the number one Filipino sport, despite their height). The Filipinos' sweet nature shines through even when they are taking you hostage. They don't chain you to a radiator in a basement for years. They play basketball with you for a few months and then let you go.

'NPA,' muses a philosophical bar girl. 'Nice People Around. No Permanent Address.'

An interesting day trip from Manila is an hour's drive north to Angeles (with a hard 'g'), the service town for USAF Clark air base. Being a service town means providing the Americans with whatever they need – and apparently what they need most are beer, broads and burgers. Angeles has the only McDonald's I ever saw with a doorman who carries a machine gun.

Fear of the NPA is real enough up here for the Americans to

169

impose a nine o'clock curfew on their boys, when they all have to be out of Angeles and safely back at base (did nobody warn them that soldiers sometimes get shot at?). Before the town gets an early night, though, you watch giant, crewcut nineteen-year-old GIs driving their Harleys through the shabby neon glow with their Oriental girlfriends clinging to their backs, and you feel like you have walked into a Vietnam movie. This is the closest you will ever get to Saigon in 1969.

Catch Angeles – or Olongapo, a little futher north, which services the US Navy – while you can. The Americans have an uncertain future in the Philippines, and now the arguments centre on when, not if, they will leave. But then, come to think of it, everyone – expatriate, communist guerrilla, Cory Aquino – has an uncertain future in the Philippines.

Manila is one of those cities where if you get bored, someone should put a pair of coins over your eyes. There are as many Thai and Chinese restaurants as Filipino in town, but go down to M.H. Del Pilar Street in Ermita, Manila's Soho, for some good home cooking. Filipino food is a hot, winning combination of Spanish and Asian food and you eat it with your fingers. It's messy but great. Try *Adobo* (chicken, port, octopus and garlic) and be warned that *Aso*, a very popular dish, is dog in spicy sauce. Check out *Asado* (smoked meat and papaya), *Ampalaya con Carne* (beef with melon) and *Adobong Pusit* (cuttlefish in coconut milk). But hold the stray mongrel, waiter.

One of the legendary bars of the East, the Firehouse, is also in Ermita, but I prefer the clubs, pubs and bars in the business district of Makati. This is a tourist-free zone, frequented by the expatriate community and funky locals. Makati is a sight for sore eyes. 'Nothing beats the Orient for grand vistas,' wrote P.J. O'Rourke, 'particularly of go-go girls. And they come and sit on your lap between sets, something the girls at the Crazy Horse never do.'

It is true that a lot of these places are girl-orientated – clubs where Asia wears a smile but not much else – but Manila has none of Bangkok's hard sell, and if you just want to drink a beer and shake your booty to Janet Jackson, then that is quite okay. It is all very relaxed, but Manila is capable of getting as wild as you can handle. Most of Manila's bar girls have a small baby back in their village, and they have been forced into an old profession in a new town by economic necessity. I would certainly consider their morals to be at least the equal of people in the West working in, say, journalism.

Manila is a huge, sprawling city with no fixed centre – it was once seventeen different towns – but it is easy to get around. The locals ride jeepneys (converted US Army trucks) and tricycles (motorbikes with covered sidecar), but most visitors take taxis. The taxis, like life itself for the visitor, are cheap and good.

Certain sights can't be missed. The Chinese Cemetery is like Père-Lachaise designed by Terence Conran. It is full of tombs that are like cosy mansions, full of furniture, air conditioning and coffee tables laden with Tsing Tao beer. The Chinese community believes in taking care of its relatives even in the afterlife. On Sunday – the great Chinese day out, from Gerrard Street to Manila – relatives pour into the cemetery to replenish the fridges in the tombs and to play mah-jong. One seat is always left empty for the deceased.

It is best to see the Chinese Cemetery in the company of one of the part-time guides who you will find lurking in the shade of a mango tree. They will happily tramp around with you for hours, pointing out the sights. Our guide cheerfully led us to stacks of exhumed bones, the remains of some unfortunates whose relatives had failed to keep up the payments on their tomb. Like sentimental bar girls, these guides will never ask you for money. You have to offer it to them, force it on them, stuff it in their pockets. Despite living in a country that totters on Third World poverty (at night you see people with torches searching rubbish tips for something they can use) the Filipinos hate to hassle anyone for money. Really, these people are too sweet for this world.

It is easy to forget how little the Filipino has when you are in Manila. The expatriate community – brokers, lawyers, businessmen of every hue – live like kings in sprawling colonial mansions with small armies of dedicated staff and big blue swimming pools in back gardens shaded by coconut trees. Copious parties are the order of the day – and great parties they are too, thrown by the most generous hedonists in the world – and when the Pacific moon is shining in a starry sky and the alcohol is flowing like lager, it is difficult to remember that you are only a few miles from Smokey Mountain, where a thousand or so Filipinos live on a massive steaming, rotting rubbish tip, scratching what passes for life out of what is literally a mountain of garbage.

There is much to outrage the liberal heart in Manila – cock-fighting, for example, is still very big and regarded with the equanimity of bingo – but the Malacanang Palace takes the fortune cookie. Malacanang is derived from the Tagalog 'May Lakan Diya' ('here lives a nobleman'), a reference to a Spanish toff called Luis Rocha who built it in the eighteenth century. This is where Ferdinand and Imelda Marcos lived during their reign of shopping and, though now designated a museum devoted to 'historical, art and heritage values', what it really seems like is the Imelda Marcos frock, shoe and accessory theme park.

The palace has been kept exactly as Mr and Mrs Marcos left it when their profligate reign ended so abruptly in 1986. There are warehouses of Louis Vuitton, entire basements full of haute couture, more shoes than one woman could wear in ten life-times. The sense of squandered riches is mind-boggling. The evidence of wasted millions is obscene. We were shown around the Malacanang in the company of Filipinos and they laughed.

They laughed at the degree of stupidity, greed and waste. They laughed at all those shoes. They laughed at silly old Imelda. It was probably the healthiest reaction. 'Imelda,' they chuckled with amused contempt, shaking their heads, and when we left all that absurd opulence behind us and stepped back out into the warm Filipino sun, they were still smiling.

Manila is a place of great parties and terrible poverty, of boys with guns and girls in high heels, a dangerous paradise where the next loud bang you hear could be either a champagne cork or small-arms fire. Nobody knows what is going to happen next in the Philippines. Nobody has a clue. Manila is not exactly the cosiest destination in the world and, as tension in the Philippines increases, it is becoming more dangerous daily. But what makes it worth all the risks are these fabulous people, who deserve a lot better than the lives they have at the moment.

Bengino Aquino, Cory's late husband, murdered by a Marcos nut when he returned from exile to the Philippines in 1983, described them best. 'The Filipino is worth dying for,' he said.

Ryuichi Sakamoto

***Daily Telegraph*, 29 May 1992**

They used to call him the most beautiful man in the world. That was when he was Japan's biggest pop star, driving the girls crazy with his band, the Yellow Magic Orchestra, back in the seventies. Since then he has been called many things including Japan's David Bowie (his glittering career is forever changing direction), a Renaissance man (he is a rock musician, a film composer and occasional actor) and 'still stunning at thirty-something'.

Ryuichi Sakamoto doesn't mind what you call him. So long as it is not Japanese. Constantly being identified as a Japanese artist is about the only thing that ruffles Sakamoto's scrupulously polite manner.

'I want to be recognied just as Sakamoto and not as the Japanese whatever,' he says. 'It is my life's goal. Nobody calls Peter Gabriel a British artist or David Byrne an American artist. Some people still think my music sounds Japanese but that's not true. I grew up with a very European musical tradition, playing Debussy and Ravel as a child, and post-war Japan was very Americanized.'

It would be hard to envisage a more international career. Sakamoto's music does not so much push back barriers as ignore them completely. There are half a dozen languages on his superb new album, *Heartbeat*, and a flotilla of different musical styles. It is truly and gloriously stateless. There's Russian rap, African rhythms, New York dance, French funk – even a sentimental love song, 'Sayonara', which sounds like someone pretending to be Japanese.

'After the war was the most free time in Japanese history,' says Sakamoto. 'People were enjoying their democracy, a totally new thing in Japanese history. The people were poor but very positive about the future, the future of their children. 'Sayonara' is my nostalgia for that Japan.'

Sakamoto will be Mr Music in Spain this summer. He is conducting his thirty-minute composition *El Mediterraneon* at the Olympics opening ceremony on 25 July in Barcelona, composing something else for the World Paralympics in Barcelona this September, and giving a concert at the World Expo in Seville on 20 July.

Right now Sakamoto is possibly the hottest composer of film soundtracks in the world. He composed (in tandem with David Byrne) the Oscar-winning score for Bertolucci's *The Last Emperor*, Pedro Almodovar's *High Heels* and coming soon, Peter Kominsky's *Wuthering Heights*. His film scores are suffused with a kind of melancholy beauty, gorgeous aching melodies that make only brief appearances on his own albums.

'Writing for films,' he says, 'you have to combine your musical imagination with all the mathematical adjustments you have to make. Sometimes the tempo has to change from frame to frame. Film projects come with so many business and psychological conditions. Time limit. Budget limit. The story itself. The visual language of the film. You have to have a lot of musical imagination.' He smiles shyly. 'I really enjoy it.'

Sakamoto has also composed the score for Nagisa Oshima's *Hollywood Zen*, in which he also acts. It was Oshima (director of the notorious *In the Realm of the Senses*) who directed Sakamoto in the role which introduced him to many people in the West: the prison camp commandant he played in *Merry Christmas Mr Lawrence*. In this film his camp (and I do mean camp) commandant was forever on the verge of hysterical rage. In the flesh, however, Sakamoto is a charming, sleepy and infinitely gentle man.

'That's why I don't want to act so much,' he says. 'In the international film scene the only parts for a Japanese man are as a Second World War soldier or a modern businessman involved in conflicts between the States and Japan. And I don't want to get a bad image.'

Sakamoto, thirty-eight now, was part of the first generation in Japan to rebel against their elders. Though he parted company with radical politics when student protest became increasingly violent, he has retained some of the trappings of his hippy idealism.

'To me internationalism doesn't go far enough – I believe in Outernationalism. Internationalism sounds like some kind of a deal – people still remain within their nationalities while sharing something beyond their borders. My concept of outernationalism is: just forget about our nationalities. We can live together without that. New York, where I live now, is like that. There are a lot of racial problems. But there are still five million people from everywhere on one rock, a tiny island. And you share parts of all those other people. Which is beautiful. Fantastic. I want to make my music like that.'

The inspiration for two songs on *Heartbeat*, the title track and 'Heartbeat – Tainai Kaiki II' came from New York (he lives with his wife Akiko Yano, also a musician, and their two adolescent children). The heartbeat is the sound of the city, the eternal boom of house and rap music constantly pouring from ghetto-blasters and car radios. It is also something more ancient. Sakamoto says this music is popular because the relentless beat reminds the listener of the first sounds he ever heard.

'Kids like listening to dance music because it sounds like the heartbeat of their mother. They want to hear that heartbeat so bad because they want to go back to their mother's wombs. Life is tough. The economy is tough. We hide in headphones yearning for the heartbeat we heard for nine months in the womb. It's not a short time.'

Like many Japanese children growing up in the affluence and aspiration of the post-war period, Sakamoto started playing piano at three. Perhaps he longs for the womb, I suggest, because it was the only time he did not have to practise his piano scales. 'I didn't practise so much,' he smiles. 'Mostly just before I went to see my teacher. But only for a few hours.'

Will he stay in New York? 'It's not an easy place to live. Violent. Rude. People aggressive. Gun shooting. A difficult place to bring up kids. Japan is very safe. Japanese children get a good education apart from not being taught about what Japan has done in the past. I really admire the Germans because they teach their kids what their country did.'

I tell Sakamoto that Japan always seems more like a family than a nation to me. Everybody has their role, everybody has their place. The Japanese all have a tremendous sense of belonging.

'Families can be good or bad,' says Sakamoto. 'They can be too close sometimes. When I was a kid I wanted to be foreign. That never left me. I still want to be a stranger in my own country.'

Japanese Tourists

Daily Telegraph, **7 August 1993**

Deep in the gloaming of Southwark Cathedral, a dozen pairs of Japanese eyes contemplated the reclining figure of the Bard. Their guide, a young woman called Atsuko, was quietly explaining in Japanese that the nave has a Shakespeare monument because when the cathedral was a parish church and Southwark was the home of Elizabethan drama, this was where he worshipped.

'Is this where he's buried, then?' demanded a young Irishman, strolling up to the statue. The Japanese looked mildly shocked. Shakespeare buried in London?

'Is he in there, then?' asked the young man, peering at Shakespeare's inscrutable visage. I realized he was talking to me.

'He's buried at Stratford, isn't he?' I said, 'I think he just worked around here. The Globe was just round the corner.'

So the young man left us, presumably for Stratford and, no doubt, taking the Central Line. No, not *that* Stratford – too late. He was gone.

'All Japanese people know Dickens and Shakespeare, Arthur Conan Doyle and Agatha Christie,' my wife Yuriko had told me. 'We grow up reading them. So the Japanese are always surprised to learn that British people know nothing about our great Japanese writers like Soseki Natsume and Basho.'

The Japanese would be even more surprised if they knew how little British people know about their own heritage. All morning we had wandered the gloomy backstreets of south-east London with this group of cultural wayfarers, while the indigenous population stared at us with question marks hovering above their heads. Borough High Street? Nothing down there mate.

But, as the traffic roared across London Bridge, we stood on the site of the White Hart Inn – 'immortalized by Shakespeare in *Henry VI* and Dickens in *Pickwick Papers*', Atsuko said; and the George – 'As featured in *Little Dorrit*' – while tattooed locals who couldn't tell *Little Dorrit* from Little Jimmy Osmond frowned with confusion at tourists gazing with wonder on these nondescript alleyways. But, ironically, the Japanese think the British have rich cultural lives.

'People are living with art here,' said a woman in her sixties, the wife of a professor of economics. 'I was amazed at the free-admission system of museums and galleries.'

'If you go to see a play or a musical in Japan, it is very expensive and you have to book months in advance,' said Chiharu, a sound engineer in her mid-twenties. 'Here there are lots of ticket agencies and you can go on the spur of the moment. The British have a more relaxed attitude to art.'

This is a good time for the Japanese to visit Britain. The yen is strong with an exchange rate of around Y160 to £1, compared with Y240 only a year ago. Air fares from Tokyo to London have been more than halved. But the Japanese are not coming here just because it is cheap. They are coming because they are mad about the place.

'There is history on every street,' said Chiharu. 'London hasn't changed that much down the years. Tokyo has been completely rebuilt twice this century.'

In Japan, a country where nature and the divine are inseparable, Shinto, the state religion, emphasizes man's oneness with natural forces. In the greenery of England, many Japanese seem to see a glimpse of heaven.

'I came to see the beautiful roses,' said one woman. 'I love the wonderful, beautiful parks,' said another. 'There's a feeling of freedom in London that you don't get in Tokyo.'

But while it is touching to be around foreigners who love your country as much as the Japanese love Britain, I never escaped the feeling that they only know or only want to know half the story. The Britain that the Japanese know and love is the one of great literature, civilized people and beautiful parks. They ignore the modern Britain of belligerent beggars, reeling drunks and dogs called Rambo, although they see it all around them. For most Japanese, Britain is a place of cultural pilgrimage.

'At school I studied Dickens and Shakespeare,' said one doe-eyed young woman, 'but my favourite book is *Alice's Adventures in Wonderland* by Lewis Carroll. I wanted to see the country where my favourite authors were born.' She was on her honeymoon.

It is time to revise the images that are conjured up by the term 'Japanese tourist'. The expression is bandied about as a byword for gawping, camera-happy boobies. The reality could not be more different.

'The recent trend is for Japanese tourists to avoid package tours,' says Mieko Tarumoto-Snell, who, with her English husband John, runs a company called London (Japanese) Walking Tours. 'We are finding there are many "repeaters" – Japanese who have been here before and are coming back to discover the country for themselves. They know their way around. They know what they are interested in. And they are much bolder than they used to be.'

It was to cater for this sophisticated new breed of Japanese traveller that the Tarumoto-Snells set up their company three years ago. It was one of their guides who led us through the nooks and crannies of Shakespeare's and Dickens's London. Other treks include the City's 2,000-Year History, Royal and Aristocratic London, and Sherlock Holmes's Casebook.

In addition to the regular walks (twice a day, seven days a week), there are special programmes including Roast Beef and Table Manners at an English Home, Scone Making for Afternoon Tea at an English Home, and English Flower Arranging at an English Home. And I thought you just stuffed them in a vase.

These special programmes might sound a little dry, but they are wonderful glimpses into the English way of life – even for a *gaijin*. In the company of two Japanese guests, I attended afternoon tea at the beautiful Kensington home of Kitty Black, who spent fifty years working in the London theatre.

Between anecdotes about Binkie Beaumont and other giants of Shaftesbury Avenue, Kitty instructed us on the ritual of afternoon tea. 'You eat the scones first and then the sandwiches to take away the sweet taste,' she said.

'Is that the way to do it?' I asked. 'Scones first, sandwiches last?'

'Well, you can do what you like,' said Kitty. 'But if you don't do it in that order, the scones get *cold*.' We were instructed to put butter, jam and cream on our scones, which must have been quite a culture shock for digestive systems accustomed to delicate slivers of fish, though everyone pronounced the scones *oishi* (delicious).

As we sipped tea from bone-china cups and admired the paintings of Black's ancestors, the thought crossed my mind that the Japanese might think we all live like this. Did they realize that the average Englishman's home has nothing older than a piece picked up at Habitat in the mid-eighties? You can never tell with the Japanese.

I had imagined that the most popular walk would be Royal and Aristocratic London. But the Japanese are far more interested in Holmes and Watson than in Diana and the Windsors. Perhaps it is because they already have a monarchy and one that's in good working order.

'Our most popular walks are Sherlock Holmes's Casebook and the Haunted Pub walk,' says Mieko, who came to England in 1966 to go to Exeter University and never went home.

On Saturday afternoon, about sixteen Japanese men and women congregate at Embankment tube station, their ages ranging from late teens to early sixties. The guide, Iliroko, has brought along photographs of Conan Doyle and Sherlock Holmes in his various cinematic incarnations and, as she leads the way down the Strand, the Japanese do more than take photographs. They actually take notes. 'For my information, for my knowledge,' explained one young woman. 'To get the most from my trip.'

After two hours of wandering through the great sleuth's London, we stand outside the approximate location of 221b Baker Street. Holmes's fictional home is now part of the Abbey National Building Society which straddles 215–229 Baker Street, but the Japanese pose for pictures next to a small brass plate bearing a quote from Sir Arthur Conan Doyle's *A Study in Scarlet*: 'We met next day at 221b Baker Street and at once entered into possession.'

Not one of the Japanese expresses surprise or disappointment that the historic address has been plastered over by the passage of time. With the exception of ancient Kyoto, which the Americans did not bomb, the cities of Japan have been totally rebuilt over the past fifty years. Compared with Tokyo or

Hiroshima or Nagasaki, the streets of London still look positively quaint.

Meanwhile, strapping young beggars sway uneasily by, demanding a contribution towards their next can of Special Brew. It is not a sight you would see on the streets of a Japanese city, but the Japanese in London put up with behaviour they would find outrageous at home. And despite all the evidence to the contrary, they retain a touching faith in British civilization.

'I still believe in the existence of the English gentleman,' said one young woman, lapsing into that casual racism that so often gets the Japanese into hot water in the world of international diplomacy. 'I think that the bad manners and bad service are mostly the fault of the foreigners and immigrants.'

But despite their *amour fou* for Britain, all the Japanese I have met have complained about how terrible the service is in Britain. Japan is a country where people are scrupulously polite. No doubt the by-product of having 120 million people (half the population of America) crammed into an area the size of Montana. Our brusque, uncaring attitude to service is the one thing they can neither forgive nor overlook.

Coming from a country where even the cheapest purchase is lovingly gift-wrapped and presented with a respectful bow, the Japanese are stunned by our nation of surly, lethargic shopkeepers. 'Even if a shop is very crowded, the staff still go for their lunch!' exclaimed one lady.

Japan is clean, efficient and polite. Britain is none of these things. But it has many attractions. Remarkably, it is seen as safe. Not compared to Japan where tiny children go to school alone and women can walk unmolested anywhere at any time, but compared to America, where last year a Japanese boy died on Hallowe'en because he knocked on the wrong door and didn't know the meaning of the word 'freeze'.

'It's not as dangerous as we expected,' said a Holmes-loving honeymoon couple. 'We had heard we had to be careful but people are mostly friendly. Apart from waiters. They look down on you if you don't speak English very well.'

Said one woman: 'People are mostly very kind, but at the Tower of London I didn't know how to use the toilet – the door shut automatically – and the woman working there became very angry. It was scary.'

Like all the other Japanese searching London for literary ghosts, this woman also loves great British institutions like Fortnum & Mason, Liberty and rock 'n' roll.

'I am a big fan of Def Leppard, the heavy-metal group,' she said. 'I heard one of them died recently and wanted to visit his grave.'

I had imagined that this combination of the old and the modern – so redolent of what I love about Japan – must be one of Britain's major attractions. But while all Japanese have a deep reverence for their country's traditions, many of the younger ones are contemptuous of Japan's contemporary culture.

'The modern culture in Japan is just a copy of the West,' said Kazue, a young woman in a Donna Karan T-shirt. 'Here the modern culture is *original*.'

What young women like Kazue love most about England is that it is not Japan. It has been said that the Japanese are more like a family than a nation and life there really is as comforting and as claustrophobic as that. We look at that land of industry, intelligence and grace and say to ourselves: 'Damn, damn, damn. Why can't Britain be more like Japan?' But it is some solace to learn that the Japanese yearn for the wayward individualism that is sanctioned here.

'People, neighbours, family are *nosey* in Japan,' said one young woman. 'They always want to know what you are doing. Why you are not like everybody else.'

'I like the freedom you get here,' said another. 'There's more individualism. In Japan everybody conforms. Here nobody does.'

Thursday night was the Haunted Pubs walk. Hiroko led a group of us around some of London's gorier landmarks. We were shown the Rising Sun pub, the meeting place of grave-robbers who kept the physicians of Bart's supplied with fresh bodies for their anatomical studies; then we strolled around Charterhouse Square, burial place of plague victims – even the ones who were still alive.

Where Newgate prison once stood, Hiroko led us through a pub and down into a black cellar where a thin shaft of daylight broke through a hole in the ceiling. She explained that this is where prisoners were kept before they were hanged.

'Some kind people put food and water through the hole,' said

Hiroko, 'but some people put waste,' she said delicately, 'because they knew the people kept here were prisoners.'

As we trooped into the Blackfriar pub, a tall, spotty young barman leered stupidly at our group. 'Aren't they cute?' he said to no one in particular. 'Don't you want to just take them home?'

Personally, I could have cheerfully stuffed a kendo stick down his throat, but the Japanese were so engrossed in what Hiroko was telling them about the pub's history that they didn't even notice him.

Japan Revisited

Sunday Times, 18 October 1992

The Japanese don't kiss. That is, they kiss people they are romantically involved with, but nobody else. They certainly don't go in for the wanton kissing of friends, family and business associates that we constantly indulge in.

So, when my wife and I flew in to Tokyo to visit her parents, Narita airport witnessed the bizarre sight of Yuriko and her father smiling politely at each other – they hadn't seen each other for a year – while I rashly attempted to kiss the man.

It caused a few double-takes among the hordes of Japanese returning home, up to their necks in Louis Vuitton, but the *gaijin* has to work hard to be exotic in Japan these days.

A few years ago a gawky, big-nosed foreigner might have attracted flocks of dumbfounded Japanese, but no longer; planeloads of foreigners are pouring into Japan. *'Gaijin da!'* ('Foreigner there!') is not a cry you hear much any more.

Just over one million foreigners are legal residents of Japan now, with somewhere between 100,000 and 200,000 illegals – that's one per cent of the population. On western maps, Japan is shoved off to the right-hand side of the planet. On Japanese maps, it is the very centre of the world. And in Tokyo, where you are surrounded by the languages of twenty nations, that's exactly the way it seems.

Japan is where people come to make their money and make their mark. One of the hippest spots in Tokyo is Caffe Bongo, the creation of the brilliant young British architect Nigel Coates. Caffe Bongo looks like a jet plane that has crashed into a forum in ancient Rome. And as you watch the young Tokyojin in their

Issey Miyake, Comme des Garçons and Yohji Yamamoto sip espresso and murmur, 'Cakey-taberu?' ('Want some cake?'), you are left wondering why nobody ever asked Nigel Coates to build a place like Caffe Bongo in the West.

Western celebrities, such as Sinatra, Schwarzenegger, Michael J Fox and Jimmy Connors, are all over Japanese TV, smilingly endorsing the local products. Japan offers freedom for creatives such as Coates and easy money for celebs such as Frank and Arnold. Limitless horizons, endless cash – these were once the two best reasons for going to America.

But, despite reports that the Japanese economy is not as immune to recession as it once was, it is Tokyo that feels like the capital of the world now. In Shibuya, a wonderland of bars, cafés and *depato* (department stores), and the only place I have ever seen that actually throbs with neon, there are Russian seamen who have jumped ship peddling junk jewellery, there are Filipino men who work (illegally) on construction sites and Filipina women who work (legally) as hostesses in the labyrinth of 'salarymen' bars. There are Turks, Pakistanis and Indians who have flocked to this land of abundance and opportunity to do the 'three Ks' – *kitanai* (dirty), *kitsui* (hard) and *kirawareru* (disliked) – the jobs that the indigenous population doesn't want to do.

Like any mature economy, the Japanese like having cheap labour but are not so keen on seeing their homogeny threatened. Stories of *gaijin* crime abound in the headlines, as Korean thieves and Nigerian credit card fraudsters head to this previously crime-free country for rich pickings.

And it is not all fun and *sake* for the visiting *gaijin*: Japan is not the easiest place to visit. Earthquake and war has meant Tokyo being rebuilt twice this century, but they have still not got around to naming the streets. You can't go anywhere without a little map and a lot of optimism, and the average Japanese speaks about as much English as a New York taxi driver (all Japanese are taught at least three years of English but they dislike doing anything they can't do perfectly).

You do see English all over Japan, but it is a peculiarly warped version of the language, known as Janglish. This enchanting version of English, also known as Anglo Ornamental, is sometimes meaningless, often grammatically

185

insane, but always has a life-affirming breeziness about it that makes it hard to resist.

LET'S MAKE A FUSS TONIGHT, urges a sign in a Tokyo *depato*. O HENRY EXCITING FOOTBALL BACK TO CAMPUS, raves the back of a teenager's jacket, while STYLISH AMUSEMENT is the credo displayed on a middle-aged man's sweatshirt. DRINK UP! ENJOY REFRESHING TIME! commands one of the ubiquitous vending machines.

The vending machines sell *sake*, whisky, chocolate, underpants, you name it. Although it is a very convenient way to pick up ice cold Sapporo and Kirin beer (especially if you are staying in a modest business hotel where they don't have room service), you never see drunken schoolkids rolling around, only sloshed salarymen. In Japan, everybody does what is expected of them.

That celebrated homogeny of the Japanese can be alienating. Everybody seems to be in uniform – the grey-flannelled salarymen, the blue-suited high school kids (sailor suits for the girls, Prussian uniforms for the boys), the white-gloved taxi drivers, the girls murmuring sweet nothings at the bottom of lifts in the glittering *depato*, the flock of joggers skirting the walls of the Imperial Palace.

Just crossing the road can make you feel as if you don't belong. The Japanese stand placidly waiting for the light giving them permission to cross, whether or not there is a car in sight. Even Japanese rebellion is regimented. Every Sunday in Tokyo's Yoyogi Park, rock bands dressed like the young Leo Sayer scream things like, 'DO YOU RIKE WATCHING TV? DO YOU RIKE WATCHING TV? I RIKE WATCHING TV!' while girls in their early teens dance in perfect unison.

In Japan everyone has their role to play. It feels more like a family than a nation. You can get very lonely there. Happily this time I was with my wife Yuriko and staying with her parents. But the more the *gaijin* sees of Japan, the more foreign it seems.

The family home turned out to be infinitely more traditional than I had expected. Naturally there were Mozart CDs, Fortnum & Mason tea, and Liberty prints – plus two corgis – but there were also features that you would have seen hundreds of years ago: futon (no plurals in Japan), a 4ft-deep bath (for soaking, not washing) and a small, Buddhist family altar. One room was like a westerner's dream of Japan. There were *tatami* mats, *shoji* paper screens, sliding doors, *zaisu* (legless chairs), a *kotatsu* (a fire burning behind a wooden frame in the well underneath the legless dining table – essential in homes without central heating) and an endless supply of Asahi Super Dry beer with our sushi, sukiyaki and tempura.

It's a man's world. 'There's nothing hot on the table,' said Yuriko's father one night, as we surveyed a feast of sushi, and her mother went off without a flicker of resentment to prepare miso soup. They were both sweet, decent, intelligent people but you are never left in any doubt in Japan that the man rules. The man provides. The woman nurtures.

The thing about tradition in Japan is that it is unassailable, inviolate, irrefutable. We went to a party at an uncle's house and the women poured drinks. Even a liberated, Western educated young woman pours her man's beer without qualms. 'It doesn't mean anything,' Yuriko told me, probably worried that I would expect the same treatment back in London. 'The beer-pouring is just to be polite. The bowing is just a greeting. It's tradition. The tradition ends at Narita airport.'

One of her uncles admired my use of chopsticks. 'Nice hand control,' he said in his perfect English.

Yuriko's parents treated me to typical Japanese hospitality – which is a limitless warmth and kindness behind a veil of formality and modesty. I soon felt like one of the family. In fact, I became so accustomed to our lifestyle (we had ham and eggs for breakfast but ate them with chopsticks) that I began to forget I was a *gaijin*. One day we were coming back from walking the dogs under the park's bare cherry trees when we were alarmed to see a lone *gaijin* walking down the street, curiously eyeing up the houses.

'You would never have seen a *gaijin* in a neighbourhood like this a few years ago,' said Yuriko, and we all glared at the man with open hostility and suspicion, afraid that he might be one of those bad foreigners we had been reading about.

Tokyo's blood pressure is always dangerously high. The Impermanent City, someone called it, and it always seems like the most modern metropolis in the world. But Tokyo is a city low on sights – the Tokyo Tower, for example, is a dreadful orange-coloured rip-off of the Eiffel Tower – other than the awesome sight of Tokyo itself, ten million people on the edge of the

187

twenty-first century, endlessly balancing business and pleasure. You take Tokyo by neighbourhoods – Aoyama, Roppongi, Akasaka, Shibuya, Ginza and Shinjuku will cater for every taste, fulfil every need. What they all have in common is sex, money and raw fish.

Tokyo can be hideously expensive – one Shinjuku bar charged £5 for a bowl of nuts – but today it feels as New York felt when I first went there in the seventies. Always, Tokyo makes you understand why those Russian seamen jumped ship.

One night, I was staring at the stars from the very top of a Tokyo hotel when, suddenly, they turned on the city lights. All of them. All at once downtown Tokyo erupted with pulsating primary colours, a riot of neon shimmering in the Asian night. It looked like all the promise of the West, fulfilled here at the other end of the planet, at the start of the world, and it made at least one *gaijin* catch his breath at this glimpse of the unforgiving beauty of tomorrow.

Evelyn Lau

Daily Telegraph, **17 November 1994**

On Tuesday night Evelyn Lau, Canada's leading young writer, got up at a reception in her honour at her country's High Commission in London and – fortified by the miniature bottle of vodka she had bought for the occasion – read a story that began with the words, 'It is your wife's fortieth birthday, and I am torturing you to the sounds of a tape of Dylan Thomas.'

The response of the assembled diplomats, dignitaries and journalists is not recorded. But whatever their reaction to 'Mercy', one of a dazzling collection of short stories that Lau published this week under the title *Fresh Girls*, it is unlikely to have been the toughest reading of her young life. Because when the twenty-three year old author gives readings in her home town of Vancouver, it is not unknown for former clients from her days as a prostitute to appear in the audience.

'They don't say anything,' laughs Lau, who laughs a lot. 'They just sit there and stare at me. And sometimes I give the best reading ever. Because I am determined that they are not going to see me waver. I will not give them the satisfaction of showing I'm anxious or flustered. But the past is inescapable.'

Between the ages of fourteen and sixteen Evelyn Lau lived on the streets of Vancouver, lost in a fog of drugs and selling herself on a street called Broadway. But she never gave up on her dream of being a writer. At seventeen, she quit the street and devoted herself full-time to writing. She produced a 900-page manuscript that, after many rejections, was eventually accepted by a publisher. *Runaway – Diary of a Street Kid* was an immediate hit and remained on the Canadian bestseller list for thirty-two weeks. She was eighteen.

The 'ex-hooker turned writer' tag has been a gift to a hundred headline writers and will no doubt serve a thousand more. If Lau, who has won more than a dozen awards for her writing, resents the handle then it is because she has always been a writer – before, during and after her years on the street.

She published her first poetry at the age of twelve, but her writing was always a source of bitter conflict with her parents, ferociously ambitious Chinese immigrants who wanted their academically brilliant daughter to become a doctor. When she was nine, Lau received psychiatric counselling for becoming suicidal after receiving what were seen in her home as low exam marks. Incredibly, the mark she received was 89 per cent.

'I never felt like I was loved or that I could ever satisfy them or anyone else in the world,' she wrote of her parents in *Runaway*.

Lau was only allowed out of the house to attend school and take piano lessons. Mercilessly bullied at school for wearing her mother's cast-offs (the memory of a pair of green trousers still stings), her life revolved around the mailman, who brought her rejection slips from literary magazines, a few acceptance letters and the occasional small cheque.

An essay competition in the *Vancouver Sun* won her a prize to meet the Pope, but her writing infuriated her parents, who felt it showed she was not concentrating on her homework. Lau was forced to write in secret, hiding her writing under her school books. At fourteen the fights became unbearable and she ran away with a change of clothes, a few poems and $10. The most shocking thing about *Runaway* is that Lau maintains that her life on the street was an improvement on what went on before.

'That was not hell,' she said of her time served on Broadway. 'The acts were comparable to housework. Even simpler than that . . . Although it may sound hard to believe, all the events that took place during these two years were easier on me emotionally than living at home, which is why I have never gone back.'

Despite its sensational packaging – the teenage Lau glowers moodily from the cover – *Runaway* is a remarkable book full of

EVELYN LAU ·

truly moving passages, such as when the under-age prostitute fantasizes that the middle-aged client buying her dinner is a publisher.

Lau demurs. 'I hate that book!' she says. 'I didn't know enough not to bare everything. It has been so hard for me to be taken seriously as a writer. But the book was necessary. I wouldn't have gotten away from that life without the writing. One of the things that concerns me about the book now is that teenagers might think, oh, if I want to be a successful writer I should run away from home. And that's horribly mistaken. The writers I admire – John Updike, John Cheever – tend to come from solid, middle-class backgrounds.'

Fresh Girls is told in cool gleaming prose that echoes her hero Updike, although the subject matter could hardly be more different. Lau's short, sharp stories about the wilder shores of lust feature whips, clamps and even a special guest appearance by a carrot. But curiously there is little sexual charge in the book.

'I don't think I've ever written a word that was erotic. Erotica would have to do with the the the enjoyment of sex. In my work sex is a way of abusing someone, a way of asserting your power over someone. Or a way of hurting yourself.'

I had read that Lau seems older than twenty-three – she says she has no friends her own age – but in fact she seems ageless, at once impossibly mature yet also very young, like someone who went straight from being a child to being an adult. I ask her why the men in *Fresh Girls* are all middle-aged professionals, with psychiatrists and doctors a speciality.

'That's because a lot of the men I saw, men who were in a position to have a woman come up to their hotel room, were professionals,' says Lau. 'But also writing about them was a way of getting back at my parents. Because they had always wanted me to be a doctor, I almost sought out men who were doctors. I was saying to my parents if you could only see these people from these exalted professions, crawling around on the floor.' She laughs. 'Completely futile!'

Lau is in buoyant mood because she has just sold her next book to an American publisher. *Other Women* expands on her great theme of always feeling like an outsider. Lau admits she is sometimes uncomfortable, even in Vancouver.

'I am well-known there as a writer and that's where all my

friends are. But also my parents are there. And although I never run into them, I would like to be further away.' She is no longer laughing. 'Because I still feel that they can hurt me,' says Evelyn Lau.

Part Four
Our Britain

Introduction

Journalists always get sent on the road in the run-up to a general election. But in the spring of 1997, rather than put me on a campaign bus with a bunch of smooth-talking, spin-doctoring politicians, the editor of the Mirror *sent me to some of the places that the campaign trail would never reach.*

I went to Knowle West in Bristol, the heroin estate that proves no teenage junkie ever looked like Ewan McGregor in Trainspotting; *St Mellons in Cardiff, the estate with the greatest concentration of single mothers in the country. I talked to pensioners in Birmingham, unemployed teenagers in Liverpool and a doctor in Newcastle who told me that the poverty in his city – recently voted one of the grooviest destinations in the world – meant that tuberculosis was making a comeback.*

The five features were printed in the Mirror *on five consecutive days just before Tony Blair's election. I wouldn't be so bold or so stupid as to claim any credit for that. But it was certainly good to get out of the office, good to get out of London. Much more than this, it was an education. Tuberculosis? I didn't even know that TB still existed.*

The three remaining stories are about the death of Princess Diana, her funeral and its aftermath. They are emotional pieces, and if I was writing them today they would probably be different. But that was exactly how I felt at the time. And so did the rest of the country.

Liverpool

***Daily Mirror*, 7 April 1997**

'I am waiting for my life to start,' says Mike Jones, sixteen, of Kirkby in Liverpool. 'I want to work. I want to pay my mum some money for my keep. I don't want to have to ask her for everything. But there's nothing out there. Just nothing.'

There was a time when further education was a passport to a better life. But in the nineties staying on at school is more likely to be regarded as a last resort or an act of desperation.

In 1979, one in eight young people went into further education after they turned sixteen. Now the number has shot up to one in three. We are a nation with a massive student population of 1.7 million – many of them very reluctant students who are only sitting in a classroom so that they are not standing in a dole queue. Mike Jones is one of them.

'I didn't realize how tough it was out there,' he says ruefully. 'It's a big job finding even a little job. There's nothing at the Job Centre – not even packing things on the back of trucks or stacking shelves. I have done a bit of that myself – but you can't do a temporary job stacking shelves forever, can you? All the jobs are part-time. Or else employers want experience. But how can you ever get experience if you can never get a job in the first place?'

'The only jobs around are stupid jobs, hardly real jobs at all,' says Mike's mother, Sue, an attractive 43-year-old brunette. 'They pay £1.50 an hour, £2 an hour – grown men are being asked to support families on that kind of money! Kirkby Industrial Estate is like a ghost town. Factories there once employed entire families. And now those entire families are out of work.'

There was a time when we believed that life would be a little bit sweeter for our children. What else does a parent work for? We assumed that each new generation of British children would inherit a better, more prosperous country. But the Tories have proved us wrong.

'In my day you could always leave a job and get another,' says Sue. 'That seems a long time ago now.'

Now even people who are only in their thirties or early forties can look back on the good old days when the working man and woman had a degree of freedom that is unimaginable today. There was a time in this country when, if you were ready to graft, you could always pay your way. That's all changed.

'I would hate to be his age now,' says Sue. 'And who thought there would ever be a time when we didn't envy someone for being sixteen years old?'

Liverpool has an unemployment rate of 16.9 per cent. Confronted by what this statistic means down at the Job Centre, Mike stayed on at school. He is taking a multi-mechanics course at Knowsley Community College in Kirkby. But it feels like a waste of time.

Sometimes teachers don't turn up. Other times Mike and his fellow students are given three-hour lunch breaks because nobody knows what to do with them. Sometimes they are sent home early. It would be fine if he felt like he was actually learning something. But this isn't further education. This is a farce.

'I don't think I am going to be a bad mechanic,' Mike says. 'I don't think I am going to be any kind of mechanic at all.'

Once upon a time a boy of Mike's age would be learning a trade that would last him – and this country – a lifetime. Now they are shoved on some meaningless course that teaches them nothing, just so that the government can crow about declining unemployment. The very concept of further education is debased by these toytown training schemes.

The Tories are getting a bargain with young Mike Jones. He gets a grant so small that it is almost invisible to the human eye – £86 a term. So for just £258 a year, this boy who can't find work is kept off the unemployment register. Which seems like a good deal for Honest John.

'They just drift these days, don't they?' says Sue. 'My eldest boy is in the army and my daughter is in college. They come out of school at sixteen and don't get dole money at that age. They just stick them on these stupid little schemes. But there's this big grey area between the employed and unemployed. Mike's not working. Mike can't find work. And yet he is not classed as unemployed.'

It's not even as though Mike Jones has ever had any interest in mechanics – although perhaps he could work up some enthusiasm for the subject if someone could work up enough enthusiasm to actually teach him. But there is something that he has always wanted to do, something that he is good at, something that he will continue to do even if nobody ever pays him to do it.

'I was always good at art,' he says. 'Painting. Drawing. Cartoons. It's what I was good at and it's what I love. I still draw every day, every chance I get. And I will keep drawing even if nobody ever wants my pictures. I wanted to study animation. But I was told to forget it by my teachers and the careers officer. They said there's no jobs in it and no future in it. There's an animation course I could have gone on but it costs £500 for twelve weeks. Who has got that kind of money?'

There was a time when the talents of bright working-class kids were nurtured and encouraged. Now those talents are left to wither and die in laughable little training schemes that lead to nowhere but a sense of hopelessness.

Mike Jones doesn't expect the world to bend over backwards to help him become an animator – or indeed to find some other use for his talent. But it would be encouraging if he could find some work – and he is not fussy – to tide him over until his dream has a chance to come true. Instead this gifted boy is packed off to play at being a mechanic. How many more intelligent, talented working-class kids like Mike Jones are seeing their life drift by in phoney training schemes?

'I know what I want to do with my life,' says Mike. 'And I know it's not going to be easy. But right now I would be more than happy to settle for a job – any kind of real job – so I can pay my mum for my keep, so I don't have to ask her for everything and so I have a chance to watch Liverpool play every once in a while.'

'My son is being sold short,' says Sue. 'And that's not just a mother talking. All of his generation are being sold short.'

In Liverpool they hate scabs, Tories and Manchester United –

although not necessarily in that order. In this age of moderation and restraint, when so much effort goes into soothing the fears of Middle England, feelings still run high in Liverpool.

'There is still a sense of community here,' a local told me. 'You saw it most clearly in the response to Hillsborough. Cut one and we all bleed.'

There is a warmth, humanity and fighting spirit about the people of Liverpool that embodies all that is best about the old working class. And yet there is an air of desperation here too.

'Did you notice that there are shops advertising sales everywhere?' one Scouser asked me. 'We have sales all year round in Liverpool.'

Over the last twenty years 75,000 manufacturing jobs have disappeared in Liverpool. So many people have left the city in search of work that the population is now well under 500,000. Those that are left behind are often the most vulnerable – one third of the population is either unemployed, sick or retired.

'Ninety-five per cent of my patients don't pay for their prescriptions,' says Dr Rob Barnett, a local GP who was born and bred in the city. 'This city has an ageing population, which will cause many problems in years to come. The number of hospital beds for geriatrics has been reduced while the number of pensioners has increased. Patients are sleeping in the corridor of the Royal Liverpool. Since the last election the Government has been telling us that they are pumping money into the NHS – but the money goes to marginal seats. It goes to the leafy shires rather than the inner city'.

Seen from the ferry on the Mersey, Liverpool is a strikingly beautiful city. And as you would expect in a place so famous for the sporting and musical heroes it has produced, there are plenty of tourists around – Norwegian lads in town for the big match at Anfield, American girls in the Cavern on Mathew Street to see where the Beatles first shook their fringes. But Liverpool is not ready to be turned into a tourist attraction.

They still dream of social justice here. They don't accept that Maggie Thatcher changed the political map forever. On the waterfront, a world away from the gleaming development of Albert Dock, five hundred dockers have been on strike since 1995, some of them sacked for questioning overtime rates, the rest for refusing to cross a picket line. It is difficult to think of anywhere else in the country where a strike would have held for so long.

Even the pensioners in Liverpool are not averse to a bit of direct action. I met Ron and Rose Sandford, who have a combined age of 160, the day before they set off to a pensioners' march and rally in Manchester.

'Politicians are not listening to old people,' says Ron, eighty-four. 'Neither are the media. They don't consider us newsworthy. Murder comes first. But what the Tories are doing to old people must come close to murder. Some pensioners are not heating their homes properly simply because they can't afford to.'

'Tomorrow is a Pensioners Action Day,' says Rose, seventy-six, offering me a digestive biscuit. 'We are marching through the streets. There are eleven million pensioners in this country and we need to be respected as a voting block. If they think the old people are going to keep quiet, they've got another think coming.'

'This is a city with a lot of fight,' reflects Ron. 'Too much sometimes. Must be all the Irish blood.'

Liverpool's waterfront has never looked lovelier yet at the end of the twentieth century it faces empty seas.

But not every son of Liverpool seeks his fortune elsewhere. Some stay – like Ted Spencer, a builder and developer whose projects include Lime Street station.

Ted is a local working-class boy made very good indeed and he has clear ideas of what Liverpool needs.

'We need a training system to teach real crafts,' he says. 'If you have those kind of hand skills then they last you a lifetime. You can teach a cabinet maker to do a lot of things. And you can teach an engineer to do anything. We need jobs where lads get dirty and go home tired. You don't get real jobs without first having real training.'

Ted has put his money where his mouth is – we are talking in Gostin's, his busy workshop on Hanover Street where young men are making fine English furniture to be sold all over the world. The activity and noise feel light years away from the wasted, empty days of young Mike Jones and all the reluctant students like him.

'The people of Liverpool don't want much,' says Ted

Spencer. 'Good schools for our children. Real jobs when they leave school. Decent care for the old and sick. That's not too much to ask. Is it?'

Birmingham

***Daily Mirror*, 9 April 1997**

Savraj Bains has nine O Levels, three A Levels, a BA and an MA – and yet for a year he still couldn't find a j-o-b.

'I want to be a lecturer in economics but colleges are just not taking people on,' says Savraj, twenty-five. 'So instead, when I finally found a job, I worked in a petrol station. That didn't last long. Now I work at a Sikh community centre in Birmingham.'

In John Major's Britain, qualifications are frequently not worth the paper they are printed on. What is perhaps even more depressing is that someone with two very good degrees is not in the least surprised when the country can't find a use for his talents.

'I'm a realist,' says Savraj. 'I've studied politics and economics and I know something about them. Graduates don't have very high expectations now.'

Savraj Bains is British – born and bred in Wolverhampton, where he still lives with his family. He is also a Sikh. And like any child of immigrants, he is the product of two cultures without belonging totally to either of them.

'My generation has problems of roots and identity,' he says in an accent that is pure Black Country. 'We haven't got a country. I was born in England. I could never leave Blighty. And there are very British qualities that I can see in myself – a reserve, the stiff upper lip. But there are barriers that stop me completely belonging – barriers on both sides.'

Savraj Bains was educated in state schools, yet he has the kind of qualifications that many people who send their little darlings to private schools would die for. Like many Asian families, the Bains family has an unshakeable belief in the value of hard work, discipline and education.

'Even when I was very little, before homework was being set in school, my dad made me do a couple of hours every night,' smiles Savraj. 'And I did it because I was scared of him!'

Avtar Bains, Savraj's father, arrived in this country from the Punjab in 1965. He worked in the foundries of the Black Country, later becoming a bus driver. Later still he set up his own business driving partly finished garments between Wolverhampton and London. From the age of thirteen, Savraj helped his dad at night and at weekends, still managing to get good grades at school. During the recession Avtar's business went bust and now he is back on the buses.

'It's wrong to think that Asian values equal Tory values,' says Savraj. 'When people like my father came to this country, they came with nothing and worked alongside the British working man in the factories. Of course there was some racism in the workplace but the ordinary working-class person was mostly warm towards them. They might have a go at them but they didn't smash their faces in. They were honest towards the immigrants. The Tories say one thing and do another.'

Savraj is anxious to point out that the life of the British-born Asian is not an endless round of racism, setting up your own business and arranged marriage. In many ways he had a typical British childhood in the eighties. For a start he loved Paul Weller and The Jam, a taste that owes more to punk rock than the Punjab.

'I am conscious of the fact that I'm different,' he says. 'But that's not because I really *am* different – it's because people think I am. When I meet white people – when I went to college, say – the first topic of conversation is always arranged marriages. And I get bored explaining it. Yes, couples are introduced to each other in the Sikh community. But there is always the power of veto. You can always say no. Nobody has to marry anyone they don't want to.'

The place where Savraj works is the Sikh Community and Youth Service in Handsworth, helping Sikhs of all ages with the problems that come with 33 per cent unemployment, more than double the rate in the rest of Birmingham. Doesn't he feel that someone with his qualifications should be working in a job that pays better than a community centre ever could?

'No, because Sikhs are expected to do work for their community,' he says. 'If we don't help ourselves, nobody will.'

Handsworth has all the problems of any inner city area in Britain and some of its own – drugs, gangs and criminals who know their acts of violence and violation will go unpunished. Shops are closing down as trade declines due to the menace in the streets. Business is bad for everyone except the mugger and the burglar. Perhaps worst of all, there is racial tension in Handsworth – though it is not between white and black, but black and brown. 'A lot of ladies get their jewellery snatched in Handsworth,' says Savraj. 'Asian ladies. The aggressors are often black Afro-Caribbean. And of course this causes tension. There is no love lost between the two communities, although Sikhs believe the human race is one.'

But believing the human race is one is not always a piece of cake. Britain has only been a multi-racial, multi-cultural country for a tiny fraction of the country's history and it would be naive to expect there to be no tensions. Yet there is one thing that Savraj Bains can say with certainty about Britain. It's his home.

'Ultimately, this country has been good for my family,' says Savraj. 'There is a level of tolerance here. A respect for individual freedom. I don't think that I have to work harder than a white person to succeed – at least not in the field of education, where I want to work. But I still notice that white people lock their car doors when they drive through Handsworth. They think we're different. But we're not.'

A Brummie called James Dobbs once wrote a song called, 'I Can't Find Brummagem' about a native son returning to the city and not recognizing the place. That was in 1828. 169 years later, they are still developing Birmingham.

One look at the Gravelly Hill Interchange – better known as Spaghetti Junction – and you might think that Birmingham is massively over-developed, like a weight lifter who has ingested too many steroids. Yet the real surprise in Birmingham is not that the city is so built up but that, among all the shopping precincts and motorways, you can find pockets of great beauty and calm.

And in one important respect, Birmingham hasn't changed at all. The city was once the cradle of the Industrial Revolution and almost half of Birmingham's employees still work in manufacturing.

There are around five thousand factories and works in the area covering one thousand different trades. Even this late in the twentieth century, they still make things in Birmingham.

Industry and business have always flocked to the Birmingham area, attracted by a large pool of skilled labour and plenty of land for expansion. And as you wander the gigantic shopping malls of Birmingham, it certainly feels like a prosperous place. But there are two groups who are excluded from the city's prosperity – the very young and the very old.

Harry Rees and Florence Creen – better known as Ciss – have both just turned eighty years old. They are part of the best generation that this country ever produced – the generation that fought World War Two and then built the welfare state, the men and women who fought for Churchill and voted for Attlee. And how does the country repay them? On their eightieth birthday, Harry and Ciss were rewarded with an extra 25p a week. It's called the 80-plus Age Allowance, awarded to provide extra warmth and nourishment – although it will not buy you a first class postage stamp.

'This government have whipped pensioners,' says Harry in his small, neat flat in Harborne. 'We have had nothing but lies, deceit and hypocrisy from them. If the 25p allowance had increased with inflation since it was introduced in 1971, it would now be worth £1.50. That isn't a fortune. But it's a great deal better than 25p.'

Harry shows me a letter from Peter Lilley, the Social Services Secretary, agreeing with these calculations, although not promising to do anything about it.

'The Tories broke the link between pensions and average earnings and said they were linking pensions to the cost of living – but they haven't done it,' says Harry. 'They broke their promises to the people who built this country. I pray to God that this is the last month of Tory rule.'

Harry moved to Birmingham from South Wales sixty years ago and spent a lifetime working on the railways. Ciss brought up a family and spent years working in a car factory, wrapping bumpers. Despite failing health – Harry is going blind with glaucoma and Ciss had a triple by-pass operation on her seventy-fifth birthday – neither of them is content to suffer in silence.

'We're *militant* pensioners,' Ciss tells me proudly. 'And we're militant because we gave so much and get so little. The state pension is £61.15. But nobody *gives* it to us – we worked damned hard for it. I never say thank you for my pension. I don't want a pat on the back and to be told I'm a clever little woman. Because I earned that pension.'

Harry was a founder member of the West Midlands Pensioners Convention. Ciss is a former chairman of the same organization. Both of them have had heart surgery and are not as active as they once were. And yet they will fight for the rights of pensioners until their last breath.

Not much frightens this generation. They were children during the Depression and young adults when the Luftwaffe's bombs were falling. They spent the best years of their lives fighting poverty and the Nazis. But you sense that what does cause them endless distress is what they see as Tory plans to privatize old age.

'*The Financial Times* advised its readers to invest in old people's homes – they said, *invest in granny farms,*' says Harry. 'God help old people if this government wins the election. Now they're talking about getting us to take out private health policies. Where are we supposed to get the money from? 'Why should we pay into private health care?' Ciss demands. 'We built the NHS!'

'There are 2.6 million pensioners on income support,' Harry says. 'But if they gave us a decent pension, we wouldn't have to ask for anything. These last eighteen years have been devastating. Since 1979 this government has failed to provide adequate services for the elderly. Pensioners who should be wearing glasses can't afford to – free eyesight tests ended in 1989. They put VAT on heating – so now many pensioners have to choose between staying warm or eating properly. That's not a choice that a pensioner should have to make.'

Most galling of all, pensioners are told to tighten their belts while MPs are dipping their snouts in the trough.

'MPs gave themselves a 26 per cent pay rise. We get 2.1 per cent. They give themselves more in one go than they have given pensioners in eighteen years. Why the hell are old people treated like this?'

Harry and Ciss embody all that is best in this country – courage, humour, a distrust of authority, a generosity of spirit, a humanity that can't be crushed by adversity. This country would not exist without them. They don't want hand-outs. They just want dignity in their twilight years.

'We've lived too long,' says Ciss. 'We've committed no crime. We've just grown old.'

'Fifty years ago we fought against greed and injustice,' Harry Rees tells me, the valleys still in his voice sixty years after leaving Wales. 'And we are still fighting it in this Tory government.' Harry shakes his head sadly. 'Don't grow old in Britain,' he says.

Newcastle

Daily Mirror, **8 April 1997**

They have got it all in Newcastle – crowded pubs, busy restaurants, gleaming new hotels and the worst rate of tuberculosis in the country.

Incredibly, as the country prepares to elect the government that will take it into the twenty-first century, some people in Britain are still suffering from a nineteenth-century disease.

'TB is a disease associated with poverty,' says Dr Colin Bradshaw, a GP in South Shields. 'It results from overcrowding and malnourishment. One hundred years ago it was almost wiped out. But at the end of the twentieth century, TB is making a comeback in Newcastle.'

Last year Newcastle was voted one of the party cities of the world, along with Rio de Janeiro and New York. And when you see the underdressed lads and lasses come roaring through Bigg Market on a Saturday night, the reputation seems deserved. They know how to have a good time here.

But beyond the bright lights and laughter, there is another Newcastle, the capital of a region where around 100,000 jobs have vanished in just twenty years.

Geordies tell you that the skyline has changed in these parts. The pit-heads have gone. The cranes of the shipyards have disappeared into the history books. The yards that once built a quarter of the world's ships – including the world's first oil tanker at Jarrow – are now almost silent apart from some modest resurgence of ship repair work on the Tyne. The Newcastle that made a living by getting its hands dirty has been allowed to die.

In 1979, when Margaret Thatcher stood outside her new home in 10 Downing Street quoting St Francis of Assisi, the region's shipyards employed 30,000 men. Now they employ 2,000. At the start of the eighties the iron and steel industry provided work for 19,000. Now the figure is closer to 6,000.

South Tyneside is the blackest unemployment spot in the country. The official count puts unemployment at around 20 per cent but even this figure is ludicrously optimistic. It doesn't include under-eighteens who are on toytown training schemes that are not designed to find them a job but merely to keep them off the unemployment figures. And no matter how they cook the books, nothing can disguise the fact that Newcastle has lost its historic role and has yet to find another. We hear a lot about the decline of our traditional industries. In Newcastle they understand the despair, misery and frustration that can't be measured by all the statistics.

'The biggest growth industry in Newcastle is bloody wine bars,' one local told me. If Newcastle has a lesson for our political leaders, it's that you can't replace jobs with wine bars.

'We had a young man come in here with a knife,' says Pat Buttle of the Newcastle and Gateshead Centre of Unemployment, shaking her head. 'He wasn't going to hurt anyone except himself. But it took two hours to get the knife from him. He was at his wits' end. And the unemployed do commit suicide. They suffer endless rejection, they're told to get on their bike – but what can they do when companies don't even send a rejection letter to their job applications?'

Pat and her colleagues help the unemployed in every way they can – with benefit claims, health problems, writing CVs, anything. The one thing they can't do is find them jobs. Because with one in five skilled men standing in the dole queue, there are no jobs. In Newcastle it often feels that the most acute gap in the country is not between rich and poor but between those in work and the unemployed.

'We had another man in here who had just lost his job after being employed for thirty years,' she says. 'He thought that people who are unemployed don't want jobs. After he had applied for fifteen jobs without even receiving a reply from one of the companies, he realized that he had been wrong. So there are misconceptions even among the working class. It's not until they suffer unemployment themselves that they appreciate what it means.'

Ironically, the centre where Pat works is located right next door to Bigg Market, the strip of pubs, clubs and restaurants – but mostly pubs – that is largely responsible for Newcastle's reputation as a party town. But unless they can scrape some crumbs from the black economy, the unemployed are excluded from the 'toon's' good times.

'The results of unemployment turn up in the doctor's waiting room,' Dr Bradshaw says. 'Ill health, both mental and physical, has increased phenomenally as unemployment has got worse. If you're unemployed, there's more chance of you having heart disease, more chance of you being depressed, more chance of you committing suicide. But I can't prescribe jobs – only pills. What we do is not a health service any more, it's a sickness service.'

Newcastle is changing from a place where people made things to a place where people provide services. Down by the Tyne shining modern hotels and restaurants are replacing abandoned warehouses. Sometimes the new hotels and the blackened warehouses stand next to each other, like neighbours who don't talk, symbolic of the new and old Newcastle.

Tourism is booming here. Newcastle is now the thirteenth favourite destination in the UK – more popular than Canterbury and Stratford-upon-Avon. Alan Shearer, Bigg Market and 'The Blaydon Races' are now more appealing than Shakespeare's birth place.

And it's not difficult to see why – Newcastle is a strikingly beautiful place, full of elegant Victorian architecture that largely escaped the worst excesses of mindless modern planners and corrupt architects like John Poulson. 'People think it's going to be all kids with no shoes and men with dirty faces,' one Geordie told me.

The dirty faces have all gone. The North-East coalfield now has one privately owned pit employing just two hundred men. In 1970 there were 65,000 miners here. Now miners are an endangered species. And so are all those jobs where for generations sons followed their fathers and their grandfathers.

Exactly sixty years ago, in his book *The Road To Wigan Pier*, George Orwell bitterly complained about the living conditions of the working man in the north of England – the terrible housing, the filthy jobs, the long hours, the back-breaking work, the tough conditions.

What Orwell could never have imagined was what the world would be like when the slums were cleared, when the jobs had gone and the working man had outlived his usefulness, when he had endless idle hours to fill – when he had to look forward to an entire lifetime without work.

Orwell wrote about the drudgery of work. But it's unlikely that he would prefer the degradation, misery and misplaced shame brought by unemployment. It's a different and far more corrosive kind of despair.

There are now one million fewer men in work than when John Major came to power. In a place like Newcastle, one of the powerhouses of the Industrial Revolution, the jobs they worked in – skilled, physically demanding jobs building ships, mining coal and making steel – are gone forever. In many households, it's now the woman who is the breadwinner.

I spoke to one woman who had mixed feelings about the role reversal in Newcastle's work force. She had grown up in an age when women were encouraged to stake their claim in the workplace. But a world that had little use for men clearly didn't seem right.

'Women want to see an equal society,' she said. 'But we don't want a society that takes away the pride of our men.'

'It is very common in the North-East that the woman is the breadwinner,' says Pat Buttle. 'I'd say that's true of one in three households. The working woman in the North-East often has two, three or four jobs. Employers avoid paying tax and National Insurance. Workers rights? These women don't have any rights. And their quality of life is nil. I know a woman whose last cleaning job ends at midnight. And she'll be cleaning again at six the next morning.'

'The jobs have changed,' confirms Dr Bradshaw. 'It is often the woman who is working now – but in a low paid, low skilled, low status job. In South Shields the mining and ship building has gone. A few men have found jobs but they are less secure with less status and for less money.'

This is the reality of what the Tories call, 'a varied and vigorous' labour market. 'Varied and vigorous' means skilled men wasting their lives in the dole queue while their wives and partners do part-time or temporary work in shops, offices or cleaning – often combining two or three of these jobs to make up something approaching a living wage.

'A job for life has become a job for a week – or a day,' says Bob Howard, the Trade Union Congress's regional secretary.

Again and again, I heard the same refrain – 'Job security doesn't exist any more.' The real jobs that do exist are often provided by foreign companies, who seem to have more faith in the Geordies than British companies. But the likes of Nissan of Japan and Siemens of Germany are not in the region out of the goodness of their hearts. There has always been a large, highly motivated, highly skilled workforce in the area. One of the problems facing Newcastle is that the old skills are being left to wither and die.

'Foreign companies are attracted here because there is a large pool of skilled workers,' I was told. 'But for fifteen years there have been no apprenticeships. In the future there is going to be a massive skills shortage. It's the people in their fifties who have the skills – not the teenagers. They are not being trained. Once the older workers trained the next generation. Not any more.'

'We need genuine, job-related training,' says Bob Howard. 'Under the Tories, the training schemes offered to our youngsters are just a way to soak up the unemployment figures. They need to be preparing for work. The next government has to make sure that training is a passport to a job.'

Newcastle's story is not just one of gloom and despair. Even now, against all the odds, there is a community spirit. Newcastle's story is one of resilience, hope and humour as well as suffering. 'A Geordie,' I was proudly told, 'is a Scotsman with his brains kicked out.'

But they don't believe it for a minute. The people of Newcastle have a civic pride and a strong sense of identity. Good times, bad times, they love this place and they are right to love it.

And they are a hardy bunch – as you can see by the way they dress for the beach even when icy winter winds are whipping off the Tyne.

But the problems facing the area are deep rooted and will not be easily cured. Tuberculosis could turn out to be less harmful than long-term unemployment. This is an area where some families have not worked for generations.

Newcastle's problems are a measure of the challenge facing the next government of this country. This is not Middle England, that semi-mythical place that we hear so much about these days. This is the old industrial heartland. And it has been left to rot.

Sometimes it feels like Middle England is the only part of the country that matters now, that blessed land of designer lager, golf clubs and credit cards. Newcastle has got all of that – more of it than perhaps you would imagine – but there is an older, neglected Newcastle and the politicians should listen to what these people want too.

And what this forgotten Newcastle wants is what it wanted when the Jarrow marchers headed south, what it wanted when the shipyards were alive, the one thing that it has always wanted.

Newcastle wants to work.

Croydon

Daily Mirror, **10 April 1997**

'Jobs are not for life any more, are they?' says a fifteen-year-old girl. 'My dad was a mechanic with the Royal Mail for twenty-five years and then he was made redundant. In the middle of his life, he had to learn how to do something else. Now he teaches people with learning difficulties.'

Teenagers grow up fast these days. But growing up fast has less to do with all the clichés that are usually advanced – videos, drugs and declining moral standards – than their knowledge of the uncertain world that is waiting for them beyond the school gates. When I was a teenager, the adult world seemed like a secure, settled place. It's not like that any more.

'When my dad lost his job after twenty years, he went look-ing for another one,' says a fifteen-year-old boy. 'They asked him how many GCSEs he had. But he had left school at four-teen. He didn't have any GCSEs. He didn't have anything.'

'Work was more set in the past,' says a sixteen-year-old boy. 'Now everyone's swapping jobs. My dad was in his job for nine-teen years and then the place closed down.'

'My dad worked at the Prudential for twenty-five years,' says another sixteen-year-old boy. 'Then he was made redundant.'

What did he do?

'He found another job,' shrugs the boy. 'Just got on with it.'

These children have seen a lot of, 'just getting on with it'. Many of them – most of them, it seems to me – have fathers who suddenly found themselves on the dole after half a lifetime of working hard, believing they had a job for life. These fathers – and it's the fathers rather than the mothers who seem most vulnerable in the work place – are skilled, hard-grafting men in

214

their forties and fifties who had to forget their old careers and learn something new. The alternative was the DSS.

It happens everywhere, of course. But what's significant about these teenagers is that they do not live on some deprived inner-city estate or an abandoned industrial wasteland. They are all from Coulsdon in the Croydon area, where the outer fringes of London meet the leafy suburbs of Surrey. Every British child now lives in a home where job insecurity is a fact of life.

Coulsdon is a mixed area. There are big, expensive houses just down the road in Purley, and in the other direction the semis and council estates of Croydon. Most of the kids at Woodcote High School come from families whom the sociologists would classify as skilled working class and lower middle class. Their parents work in clerical jobs in Croydon and London, they run small businesses, work in shops and hospitals. It's a pleasant area, a place of modest affluence. And in the nineties it has felt the pinch.

Teenagers are frequently accused of being apathetic. But if the students at Woodcote High School are anything to go by, this is nonsense. They care desperately about social justice, job prospects and their education. It's not politics they are apathetic about but politicians. They have no tribal allegiance to any political party. Labour have lost too many elections in a row for that. Whoever wants their vote in the election after the next one is going to have to earn it.

'I was brought up in a Labour household,' says a self-possessed sixteen-year-old boy called Shamiul. 'But if I support Labour it will be because of what I decide myself, not what I'm told at home. I think that Labour are the better choice but I don't know – I've never lived under a Labour government. Britain is Conservative. We have lived all our lives under the Tories. We have been educated under the Tories. Perhaps we will take our GCSEs under a Labour government but this is still a Conservative country. Everything's privatized now.'

Today's teenager knows that it's tough out there. Having a job today doesn't mean you will have one this time next year – or even next week. Qualifications guarantee nothing. But instead of breeding cynicism and lethargy, at Woodcote High the cold climate seems to make them work even harder.

'Things aren't getting easier,' says Jag, sixteen. 'You are

either at the top or the bottom. People realize you have to work to get anything – you've got to go to university, got to get your degree. I want to teach PE. But even a degree doesn't guarantee a job. Things are much more competitive these days.'

'I know someone who has a law degree,' says Priya, also sixteen. 'And she's working as a waitress. The old days were better. My mum didn't go to college but she earned a good income. Now you get less reward for more qualifications. These days you are expected to do the same job for less pay.'

'But you still have to get your qualifications,' insists Jag. 'Because if you don't then all that's out there is some 50p job. It's quite sad. But nothing is going to fall into your lap.'

'You're afraid of getting qualifications and then they lead nowhere,' says sixteen-year-old Alan.

'It's very competitive out there,' says Shamiul. 'Most people our age are going to college. Only a minority aren't.'

'But it's not a job for life any more,' says Charlotte. 'My mum was a psychiatric nurse. She thought she had a job for life. But she didn't.'

'But you can't expect to leave school without GCSEs and find a job,' insists Shamiul. 'You have to look for it. You have to work for it.'

If they want to leave school armed with a fistful of GCSEs, then they are in the right place. Last year their school had the fourth most improved exam results in the Greater London area. With 59 per cent of students getting five or more GCSE passes at A to C grade, Woodcote High is a very successful comprehensive school.

And the successful comprehensive does exist – despite all the cuts to funding, despite the contempt that the Tories have for state schools, despite all the odds against them. The good comprehensive exists not because of the government but in spite of it.

We all know what the unsuccessful comprehensive school looks like – teachers on the verge of a nervous breakdown, anarchy in the classrooms and thirteen-year-old girls getting knocked up behind the bicycle sheds – or where the bicycle sheds would be if some of the little darlings hadn't burned them down.

But what does the successful comprehensive school look like? It might be politically incorrect to say so, but what Woodcote

High School looks like is an old grammar school from the sixties.

There are smart school uniforms. The headmaster takes assembly in his gown. The children stand up when he enters the room. Woodcote is clean, bright and disciplined. And they play games here – there is none of this ridiculous modern prejudice against competitive sports. At Woodcote they believe getting kicked in the goolies on the football field is as important to a child's development as learning to conjugate his French verbs.

Woodcote is the kind of comprehensive school that even the Labour front bench would be happy to send their children to. Not that everything is sweetness and light.

'I have had five years of funding cuts,' says Ian Wilson, the school's 46-year-old headmaster. 'Teachers have had a 2.7 per cent increase in pay while my budget has gone up by just 1.1 per cent. That's why five teachers have gone in just three years. We haven't had to sack anyone yet but when they have left they haven't been replaced. The result of the cuts is that teachers are taking lessons that are not their first subject – so you'll find a Geography teacher teaching English. Teachers are always reluctant to admit that things are getting bad or difficult. But there's no denying that the profession has taken a battering. We have been told so many times that we're not doing a good enough job that we feel we're failing the nation. When teachers are trained we're always told that there should be a praise-to-blame ratio of three to one with pupils. Apparently the same doesn't seem to apply to teachers.'

Woodcote is a success story on anyone's terms. It is massively oversubscribed. Last year 500 children applied for the 180 available places, including some who were attending local independent schools until their parents found they could no longer afford the fees.

What attracts them to Woodcote are exam results like the one the school enjoyed in GCSE Business Studies – a 100 per cent pass rate with grades A to C. But Ian Wilson feels that too much emphasis is placed on how many GCSEs a school can rack up.

'Of course schools need to be judged by results – but results are not the whole picture,' he says. 'Because leagues treat schools in middle-class areas and rural areas exactly the same as inner city schools. And the fact is they are not the same – exam results don't tell you that. Passing exams should not be the only criteria of success. We want to turn out kids who are respectful, polite, willing to learn, willing to work with other people, flexible. We are told that they are going to have portfolio careers – changing jobs probably more than once in a lifetime. And we need to prepare them for that.'

Like me, Mr Wilson went to one of the old grammar schools – those temples of excellence where children from working-class backgrounds could get a superb state education. But he is a passionate believer in comprehensive schools.

'Comprehensive schools work best when they are truly comprehensive,' he says. 'Not when some parents send their children out of the area to selective or grant-maintained schools.'

Although they look like a throwback to my schooldays, Mr Wilson believes that school uniforms are an important part of the comprehensive ideal.

'It creates a community, irons out differences. If we didn't have uniforms, some of them would be coming in their Armani jumpers. And some wouldn't.'

Perhaps surprisingly, all of the students I spoke to were in favour of uniforms because they encourage equality and discourage more well-heeled students strutting around in designer labels. There is a pride and self-respect at Woodcote. In the words of the school's youngest teacher, 23-year-old Tracey Archer, Woodcote High looks, 'respected, clean and loved'. She started teaching art at the school last September, her very first job.

'I am loving it,' she says. 'My mother and sister are both teachers and I never expected it to be a bed of roses. The reward is obviously not in the money. But if you love your subject and love working with kids, you are rewarded in other ways. I'm always busy, it's never boring and I love art. I always go home with a story to tell.'

The teaching profession may be haemorrhaging teachers, but Tracey is still full of enthusiasm, despite running out of paint and knowing that there is no money for new paint until next month.

'I feel sorry for teachers sometimes,' a sixteen-year-old girl tells me. 'They are expected to perform miracles.'

It is fashionable to wring our hands about teenagers but the ones I met at Woodcote High seemed a decent bunch – intelligent, sensitive, sceptical. And I suspect that they are fairly typical of their generation. In the next century this country will belong to them and they will probably do a good job with it – given the chance. But with their cash-strapped schools and underpaid teachers, all they are being given at the moment is half a chance.

'What education in this country desperately needs,' says the head of Woodcote High, 'is a declaration from the state that children matter.'

Bristol and Cardiff

Daily Mirror, **11 April 1997**

Mary Smith did not know her son Christian was a heroin addict until the night the police knocked on her front door.

'There were nine policemen in my front garden,' says Mary, a 47-year-old housewife from Knowle West in Bristol. 'They had a warrant for my son's arrest. He was fifteen years old.'

When Mary Smith learned her teenage son was a heroin addict, she discovered that the neighbourhood was full of teenagers just like him.

'The mother is always the last to know,' she says. 'I later found out that when my son was fifteen he shared a marijuana joint with seven friends at the local swimming baths. They all became heroin addicts. Every one of them. Eight years later, every one of those boys is either in jail or waiting to go in jail.'

To the visitor, Bristol looks like a place of beauty and affluence. There is some of the finest Georgian architecture in the country here. Whiteladies Road on the edge of Clifton is full of restaurants and pubs. On the stretch of Whiteladies Road that they call The Strip, there are almost fifty drinking joints in the space of a mile.

But leave the well-heeled students knocking them back among the bright lights of The Strip and look beyond the big white houses on Royal York Crescent, and you will find another Bristol where life is something to be endured, not enjoyed.

In St Paul's the site where there was once a bank is still boarded up after the riots of the eighties. In Hartcliffe there's the burned-out husk of a stolen car. And in Knowle West, in startling contrast to the fresh faces of the little children, there are an alarming number of teenagers who have the blurred eyes, rotting teeth and pale, yellow skin of heroin addicts.

Last year there was a record number of people who committed suicide by jumping off the Clifton Suspension Bridge, that nineteenth-century symbol of Bristol's ingenuity and grit. A former fisherman, his old fishing waters now turned over to Spanish nets, is paid to dig bodies out of the muddy banks of the Avon Gorge. Last summer he was busy – there were five suicides off the bridge in just three weeks. But in Knowle West they kill themselves more slowly.

'Oy was on the telly the other night,' says a thin lad in a fake Calvin Klein jumper. 'Chatting about drugs.'

Addiction is a way of life here. In an area of 45 per cent unemployment, an army of young people have attempted to fill the void with hard drugs. And junkies breed crime.

In a neighbourhood where everyone once left their doors unlocked, now only the foolish carry handbags after dark. Yet in Knowle West every heroin addict speaks in a voice that is full of the west country.

Even in the most deprived areas of Bristol – St Paul's, Filton, South Mead, Hartcliffe, Knowle – you are never far from the countryside. As you step over plastic lemonade bottles that have been used to smoke crack, you can glimpse fields in the distance, shining in the spring sunshine like a vision of a better world. The young junkies don't notice.

But to Mary Smith and the other mothers who form Knowle West Against Drugs (KWADS), these teenagers are not dangerous addicts to be avoided like lepers. They are their children.

'The night the police knocked on my door was the start of it,' she says. 'I had no idea that there were so many kids around here taking heroin. I set up a public meeting and I discovered there were lots of mothers like me. And hundreds of children like my Christian. There are around six hundred heroin addicts just in Bristol South. And they want help. They are desperate to get off heroin.'

The aims of KWADS are simple – to stop future generations going on hard drugs and to help young addicts come off the stuff.

'Some of the fathers act macho and want to kick them out,' says Mary. 'But the mothers are different. We will never give up on them.'

Mary Smith and her friends talk to schoolchildren about the reality of addiction. For the teenagers who are already hooked, they have arranged a needle exchange programme to prevent the spread of AIDS and hepatitis – and to prevent dirty needles being dumped in the neighbourhood's hedges, letter-boxes and drains.

There are countless horror stories in Knowle West like the woman who returned home and discovered her son had sold all her clothes. Or the family who found their Sunday joint had been sold to buy heroin. Or the girl who needed to shoplift £400 worth of goods every day to feed a £130 habit – the value of stolen goods dropping dramatically as soon as she was past the store detective. Or there was a boy who overdosed at sixteen whose brother recently hanged himself. The misery is endless.

'Eight months ago heroin was £90 a gram.' says Mary. 'Now it's £30 a gram. They get ten hits to a gram. And for the first six months they feel wonderful. They think they can fly! It's pure escapism. But they don't know what they are getting into. Heroin breaks up families, ruins health, ruins lives. And the tragedy is it wouldn't be happening if they had jobs. Because they would be too knackered for heroin. But this community is trying to save itself.'

Knowle West has received funding from the local business community. 'Expert scrounging,' smiles Mary. Soon a Drug Centre opens for the benefit of local addicts and their long-suffering families. It will have trained, professional counsellors and two doctors, two days a week.

Despite having a 23-year-old son who has been in jail seven times for drug-related crime, Mary Smith will not give up hope.

'If this neighbourhood didn't have a drug problem, it wouldn't have a crime problem,' she says. 'And if we didn't have such high unemployment, there wouldn't be a drug problem. Most of the kids on heroin around here are good kids. In their hearts, they are ordinary, decent kids. All they need is for somebody to give them a chance.'

*

Like Knowle West in Bristol, St Mellons in Cardiff is a community trying to claw back its future. St Mellons is the estate where John Redwood famously slagged off single parents.

'Who the hell does John Redwood think he is?' says Sue

Sheppard, forty-two. 'He came down here with his own agenda. He went on about teenage mothers with no morals who were having children out of wedlock and living on benefits. He tarred everyone with the same brush because he wants to become Tory leader.'

There are certainly single parents on St Mellons. But while some of them conform to the cliché of the teenage girl fresh from the bike sheds and desperate for something to cuddle, the vast majority of them are divorced women like Sue and her friends Roberta Williams and Angela Horton, both thirty-four.

'Nobody chooses to be a single parent,' says Roberta. 'I was married. My old man walked out on me. Now I am trying to bring up my children as decently as I can on the poverty line. I live on £84 a week income support. From that £84 I have to pay everything. I took out a loan to give my kids a Christmas. Around here you don't save for next Christmas. Because you are still paying for last Christmas.'

'I just took a computer course on Information Technology,' says Angela. 'Passed with flying colours. But there are no jobs. I don't want to be sitting on my backside. I don't want to be on income support. I want to work.'

'This country is divided into the haves and have-nots,' says Sue. 'If you've got an executive job, an executive house and an executive car – you're okay. But what about the rest of us?'

Twelve years ago St Mellons was countryside. Now it's a huge estate that is learning to become a close-knit community. After establishing links with local businesses, including a sympathetic pub, there are now community buses, workshops, an Education Centre and day trips for children who would otherwise not have a holiday.

The new estate still has problems – no work, no secondary school for miles, a notorious reputation – but it's a young, vibrant neighbourhood with lots of life, often visited by children from other parts of Cardiff, despite parental disapproval because of the bad publicity.

'I do unpaid work for the community,' says Roberta. 'I work with children and teenagers. After eighteen years of Tory rule, many of them are apathetic. They have low self-esteem, low expectations. We try to change that. There are enough adults around here on Prozac and anti-depressants.'

'Look at all we have achieved with nothing,' says Sue. 'We don't need people kicking us while we are down. We're not asking for freebies. Just a reasonable way of life. We need jobs. Schools where the funding is not cut every year. Enough to eat on the table, enough money in your purse so your kid can go to the swimming pool. And that's not just St Mellons. It's the whole country.'

As my train pulled out of Cardiff and the railway yards gave way to green rolling fields, I asked myself – what is the mood in Britain? And it seems to me to be one of wary optimism.

Nobody is expecting a change of government to turn this country into Camelot. Nobody is expecting all wrongs to be righted by kicking out the Tories. But what the people of this country do expect – what they believe and what they demand – is that Labour will make this country a better place.

We are sometimes told by jaded commentators that there is little difference between the two major parties these days. But that is not how it looks out in the real world, that is not what the view is like seen from the heart of Britain.

Labour and the Tories do not look the same if you are an unemployed teenager left to rot on some toytown training scheme. Or if you are a pensioner who is forced to choose between heating and eating. Or if you are a middle-aged man who is suddenly told that the skills that have earned you a living for twenty-five years are no longer required. Or if you are a doctor witnessing the devastating effects of long-term unemployment turn up in your surgery. Or if you are a headmaster told to produce better exam results with fewer teachers. If you are one of these people – or indeed even if you are someone who always voted Tory until the day you watched your business go under – then the choice between Labour and the Tories looks pretty stark.

You can cast your vote for progress, justice and hope. Or you can cast your vote for cynicism, stagnation and decay.

Things can only get better, says the song. But although there are deep wells of despair and bitterness in Britain, this is also a place of resilience, humour and hope. Despite the ravages of recent years, this is still a great country, and the greatest thing about it is still the people, still recognizably the same people who had the courage to beat Hitler and the compassion to build the welfare state.

Now it is time to vote again, in what will almost certainly be the last general election of the twentieth century. In all corners of the country, the consensus is that our Britain deserves more than it is getting at the moment.

And if our country finally decides to leave the Tories out for the dustbin men, then as a poet once said, we could be on the verge of a time when hope and history rhyme.

Diana

***Daily Mirror*, 5 September 1997**

In any bereavement, there comes a moment when the unimaginable becomes the unbearable, when you realize that your loved one is truly gone forever.

Despite the fields of flowers that have sprung up in memory of Diana, and despite the rivers of tears that have already been shed, we are not quite there yet.

We will only truly comprehend that she is gone when we see the faces of her sons on Saturday. Then we will really understand the extent of their loss. And of our loss too.

Why is it still so difficult to believe that Diana is dead? At first I thought it was because she was so famous, such a part of our emotional landscape that we thought she would always be there. But saying goodbye to her is not so impossibly difficult because she was so famous. It is because she was so alive.

Perhaps only someone who knows what it means to be deprived of love can have such a genius for giving it. Her hugs, her kisses, her compassion, the way she stood up for the forgotten, the sick, the outsider – all that has gone now, all that has been taken from the world.

And the world is a colder, darker place without her in it. She was more glamorous than any film star. But we do not mourn her because she was a superstar or a supermodel. We mourn Diana because she had a heart that was bigger than Buckingham Palace.

She championed the people who had nobody. Yet despite this national outpouring of real and bitter grief, we should not start believing she was a saint. She was gloriously human.

And how much we took for granted. We thought that we

knew what the future had in store for her – she would surely become our own Jackie Kennedy, the golden girl who ends up toasting herself on a rich man's yacht. Instead she is far closer to John F. Kennedy, an immortal symbol of youth and hope in a world that will be forever diminished by her passing.

Evita? Marilyn Monroe? Princess Grace? The cult of Diana is going to be far bigger than all of them. In life people could not get enough of Diana. God only knows how big she will become in death. She could yet outlive the royal family.

She was the best of the royal bunch. She made them seem human, she made them seem relevant and then they turned their backs on her. And if the people could love her so easily, why couldn't the man she married?

Beyond the bitter tears for Diana, there are other resentments. Of the media, of which I am a part, for constantly feeding the obsessional hunger of the public, of which I am also a part.

Of the evil little bullies who pursued her with their wretched cameras even as she lay dying. And of the Fayed family, who had the final, terrible responsibility for someone so precious and special.

I can't find tears for Dodi Fayed. No matter how I try, I can't help wishing that she had never laid eyes on him.

Diana dreamed of escaping this country for another life in another nation. The terrible irony is that if she had stayed here she would be alive today. This was her home. And although she suffered intrusions here, it was also where she was most loved. We miss her more than any words can say.

There is an aching sense of loss that nags like real, physical pain. This feeling is familiar to anyone who has ever lost a parent, a partner or a child. Yes, life will go on. But it will never be the same. It will never be so good or so sweet as it was when she was in the world.

It seems odd to feel this way about a stranger. But of course she was not a stranger to us. We knew her so well – in all her despair, in all her humanity, all her betrayals.

And Diana was betrayed again and again. There was the mother who walked out on her when she was six years old. There was the husband who always loved someone else. There was the fabulously rich family who were unable to protect her.

Let them all weep. She deserved better from all of them.

Her greatest love affair was with the people. And her memory will haunt this country. In the work she did, in the feelings she inspired, in the grief we will feel long after she is buried.

You can see her face every time you look at the handsome features of her oldest son, our future King. The destiny of the royal family will be decided by how William responds to his unenviable fate. But the future of the monarchy seems pathetically irrelevant on the eve of Diana's funeral. What really matters is that these two boys have been deprived of a mother's love.

And when the funeral is done, what will be the next chapter in Diana's never-ending story? There will be the trial of the paparazzi, of course, including the photographer whose surname is, appropriately enough, Rat. There will be, I believe, growing resentment that the Fayeds did not protect our Princess as she deserved to be protected. There will be discussions about what sort of royal family we want in the next century. And there will be a lot of talk about a memorial.

But Diana's memorial is out there already. Step into the streets of our country and you will see it. Whatever worthy charities or buildings spring up in her honour, Diana's true memorial is already staring us in the face.

We will remember her because of the love that she gave, the love that she inspired and the love that she leaves behind.

Westminster Abbey

***Daily Mirror*, 8 September 1997**

Being part of the congregation in Westminster Abbey was an experience that I will carry with me for the rest of my days.

It was an honour to be there. But was there ever an honour more heartbreaking? From my seat behind the Spencer family, I had a clear view of Princes William and Harry.

These boys carried themselves like men, only breaking down when Elton John sang of their mother, 'our nation's golden child'.

You knew that somewhere their mother was watching, and was very proud of them. But I pray to God that I never have to look upon the faces of two children so shattered by tragedy.

The funeral service for Diana, Princess of Wales, lasted just over an hour. Yet that time was so packed with raw emotion – some of those emotions completely unexpected – that even now I find it difficult to come to terms with everything I saw and felt.

There was the raw emotion of seeing her coffin. The searing, angry brilliance of her brother's speech. And of course those two boys – tall, handsome William so like his beautiful mother, little Harry looking far younger than his years – both carrying themselves with a dignity that grown men would be hard pressed to match.

Perhaps most surprising of all was to feel compassion for people that, in all honesty, I had felt little for over the harrowing week since Diana's death.

Before the service Mohamed Al Fayed walked into Westminster Abbey and the sight of the man truly stunned me. Supported by his blonde Scandinavian wife, he seemed almost sick with grief, quite literally reeling with anguish.

You realized that here was a man who had lost his son, lost his son's partner, and lost his own future. Golden years had suddenly turned to ashes in his hands. And the immeasurable, unthinkable cruelty of seeing such hope turn to such despair was written over every inch of his face.

You could not look at that man and fail to be moved. Consumed, like the rest of the country, with my feelings about Diana, I had not properly contemplated this man's own tragedy. How many times have I damned that drunken Ritz driver for hurtling Diana towards her death? How many times have I asked how anyone could employ such a maniac? Now I looked at the stricken features of Mr Al Fayed and saw only a man who had lost his cherished son.

And it was more than the sentiment of the moment. Too many of us have been too eager to place blame for Diana's untimely death. It is worth asking ourselves – how can we admire Diana's humanity while showing so little humanity ourselves? How can we applaud her compassion when all we do is spit bile?

It was the same with the royal family. Earlier in the week I had seen the empty flag pole above Buckingham Palace and flown into something approaching a rage. How could they stick to protocol at a time like this? How could they be so unfeeling?

Now I looked at the Queen enter the Abbey, grim-faced and almost paralysed with regret, and I felt that it had always been presumptuous to assume that no tears were being shed behind the walls of Balmoral. Although they would later be savaged by Earl Spencer, the royal family were clearly a family in mourning.

Very slowly, accompanied by her grandson Edward, the Queen Mother entered the Abbey, walking with a stick, her brave presence reminding us that there is no crueller destiny than being asked to bury our children, or the children of our children. She should never have had to endure such a bitter fate. If your heart didn't bleed for the royal family on a day like today, then it's unlikely you have one.

Who could fail to be moved to the edge of tears by the sight of William and Harry? But now, as Prince Charles slowly followed the coffin of his ex-wife into Westminster Abbey, it seemed time to feel some sympathy for our much maligned future King.

Regrets? Charles looked as though he had a million of them.

He seemed suddenly old, suddenly aware of the prize that had slipped through his hands, a treasure he would never know again. He had the hardest role of the day.

To mourn someone you love is the most natural thing in the world. But how do you mourn someone whom you have loved and lost? Whom you have married and divorced? His eyes searched the ancient corners of the Abbey for answers he knew would never come.

It was astonishing to be among that congregation in Westminster Abbey. The cast list was incredible, unrepeatable, awesome. Some of the biggest names in the world were there – Tom Cruise, Henry Kissinger, Steven Spielberg, Thatcher, Pavarotti and George Michael. And for this one special day they were all just extras.

Only Diana could have pulled a crowd like this. But there was none of the rubber-necking and excited gasps that you usually get when people are in the company of the famous. People hardly glanced at Hillary Clinton as she walked by. There was only one true star in Westminster Abbey. And the sight of her coffin garlanded with white flowers made you realize, for the very first time, that you would never see her laughing face again.

'I can't believe it,' millions have repeated since she died. As William hung his head and Harry held his head high, you believed it now.

Being a part of that congregation was like a dream because everywhere you looked there were faces you recognized. But most people in the thousand-year old Abbey were not rich or famous. For every celebrity like Cliff Richard or Richard Branson there were a hundred ordinary people, many of them charity workers who had joined forces with the greatest humanitarian of modern times.

Diana was truly the People's Princess. And the people were well represented in Westminster Abbey.

Through the brilliant sunshine and late morning shadows of Parliament Square, eight Welsh Guards carried Diana's coffin into Westminster Abbey. The red-jacketed Guards carried her to the altar slowly and gently and with infinite care, as if determined to keep her from all the suffering and anguish in the world she had left behind. To be so close to her coffin was profoundly shocking. To think of Diana inside that coffin –

beautiful, broken, lifeless Diana – was overwhelming.

The tears had flowed freely during the last seven days. But when the cortège arrived and you saw the faces of William and Harry standing behind their mother's coffin, not crying although their hearts were quite obviously shredded with misery, you knew that this was a day for keeping emotion under control. Or at least trying to. Because if the tears started, when would they ever stop?

They looked so blond, so brave, so young, so dignified and so completely and totally bereft. Their world had fallen apart and would never be put back together. Everyone in that Abbey must have felt like putting a comforting arm around their shoulders. God, they are children. Only children. At times Harry looks like a baby in an adult's suit.

The sight of those two fair-haired boys wrenched your heart and yet made you grit your teeth. If they were fighting back the tears, so should everyone else.

We sang Diana's favourite hymn. 'I Vow To Thee, My Country' is an old-fashioned hymn about patriotism and faith and yet it seemed curiously relevant. Like Diana herself, 'I Vow To Thee, My Country' is almost bursting with emotion. The first verse talks of a love of country so strong that it is prepared to 'pay the final sacrifice'. The second verse talks of another country with no armies and no King, a country built of love.

And this seems to be Diana's true legacy. In her life there was heartache and pain. But she rose above it and, in a world of cynicism and cruelty, she showed love and compassion for people that had precious little of it in their lives.

It seems to me that she showed us something real and valuable every time she embraced one of the sick and dying and the forgotten. She showed us how good we can be.

There were two short poems from Diana's sisters, Lady Sarah McCorquodale and Lady Jane Fellowes. 'For my sake, turn to life and smile,' said Sarah, and perhaps one day it will be possible. But not now. Not yet. There are still tears to be shed. And how they flowed when Elton John sang his reworking of 'Candle in the Wind', now called 'Goodbye, England's Rose'.

Elton had seemed close to breaking down when he entered the Abbey with George Michael. You felt deeply nervous for him. Surely he wouldn't be able to get through the song without cracking up? But all doubts vanished when Elton began to sing. He sang from the heart and, fighting to keep the tears at bay, he sang with real feeling.

Only near the end of his beautiful, moving tribute did his voice break. And when he sang of 'our nation's golden child', I also had to choke back the tears.

And this was the point that Diana's children seemed to lose control. We had heard classical music, hymns, the golden voices of the Abbey's choir. But this was a song written just for their mother, and every line echoed with a sense of love and loss. It seemed that nothing could be more moving than that song from Elton John. But then came Diana's brother.

It was not easy to be a member of the press and sit in Westminster Abbey listening to the words of Earl Spencer. His passionate, moving tribute was laced with much anger and bitterness towards the media and their treatment of his sister.

While respecting his view, I personally think he lays too much blame on our doorstep. The press and Diana worked in closer collaboration than Earl Spencer perhaps realizes. There were journalists and authors among her friends and allies. But I understand his sorrow and fury and his tribute will be the strongest memory I have of his sister's funeral service. It was wonderfully written, passionately delivered and it communicated both the magic of Diana and the sense of loss her brother will carry to his grave.

It was a brilliant, unforgettable tribute to a woman he called, 'the essence of compassion, style and beauty'. He spoke of her contradictions – the aristocrat who was ultimately classless, the very British girl who transcended all borders, the insecure woman who had a genius for making others feel loved, secure and wanted. He got her just right. He captured Diana's special spirit. For a few precious minutes, it was with us once more.

His voice finally cracked and broke at the climax of his speech, as he vowed to his dead sister to respect William and Harry's royal roles, while protecting them from the strait-jacket of duty and protocol.

It was incredible to share the same air as a man making such an astounding speech. He was on fire with anger and bitterness and yet his words were full of love. He poured bile over the media and the royal family and yet completely captured his sister's shining, vulnerable soul. I listened to Earl Spencer and I was filled with the overwhelming certainty that this man knew Diana better than anyone.

That is why his speech touched the hearts of even those of us who work for the media he despises. Even more than Elton's song, this was the moment I found myself holding back the tears.

And when he had finished there came a sound that Westminster Abbey had never heard in a thousand years. The applause for his speech began with an uncertain, stuttering ripple and then spread and swelled throughout the Abbey. Applause? At the funeral of the mother of our future king? Protocol changed forever during that ovation. It was the final reminder that Diana's death has shown us that we need to invent protocol and traditions that reflect the needs of our own age.

Did that funeral service really only last for an hour? It was so crammed with memorable emotion and unforgettable sights that it feels like a lifetime. At the end I looked away from William and Harry, their blond heads hanging, and stared at the grief-stricken face of Prince Charles. Will this man ever recover from this blackest of days? As they took Diana's coffin away, he couldn't tear his red-rimmed eyes from it.

It seemed like more than mere grief. He looked like a man who wished he could turn back time. To see their fairy tale end on such a note of regret was heartbreaking. Possibly Charles only learned what Diana really meant to him during that service. But it felt like we all learned a lot during that hour in Westminster Abbey.

The sight of those brave, beautiful boys showed us that there is a place for restraint as well as emotion. Elton John's emotional song showed us that keeping control and weeping bitter tears both have their place in life. And perhaps we also learned the depth of our sadness at losing Diana, our Princess. But as her brother unforgettably and movingly said, our grief is nothing next to that of her two boys.

'How great your suffering is,' Earl Spencer said, his voice finally breaking with sadness, which seemed to sanction our own tears, 'we cannot even imagine.'

Yet if we cannot imagine their suffering, that does not invalidate our own feelings for this special young woman. Diana loved people. And that is why the people loved her. It really is as simple as that. Diana's coffin – and at last you had no difficulty believing that she was truly gone – was carried to the Great West Door of Westminster Abbey. The guardsmen who carried her moved slowly, as if she had all the time in the world.

All that was left was the silence and the sound of muffled bells.

We had said all our goodbyes. And now she was going home. The two thousand of us who were in Westminster Abbey for her funeral service will never be the same again.

Wills and Harry

***Daily Mirror*, 15 September 1997**

There are two reasons why the Royal Family have come through the traumatic events of the last two weeks strengthened rather than weakened.

One is William. The other is Harry.

The unbearably moving sight of these two boys walking behind their mother's coffin has secured the Royal Family's future for the next hundred years. Their dignity and bravery in the face of such overwhelming grief wrenched the heart of a nation.

How could anyone talk about getting rid of the Royal Family when these two boys are its future? What president of a British republic could ever inspire the respect, love and affection that millions feel for Diana's sons?

In the dark, angry days before Diana's funeral, there was a lot of talk about the death of the monarchy. The Royals were said to be unfeeling dinosaurs, woefully out of touch with the mood of the nation.

Those commentators who predicted the end of the Windsors now seem like prophets on a par with Neville Chamberlain fresh from his talks with Herr Hitler and promising peace in our time.

As Diana would have wanted, the future of the Royal Family is secure. Yet it's important we do not deny the emotions that were abroad before the funeral. Some people have said to me over the last week that all that anti-royal sentiment was whipped up by the media. This is rubbish.

There was real anger in this country. And it was felt by millions. Nobody seriously believed that Prince Charles and his family were failing to comfort those two boys. And nobody could have believed that the public's anguish was anything like the agonies being suffered by William and Harry.

What upset people was that the Royal Family seemed blind to the country's sadness.

There were a million flowers outside the palaces of London, but heartless protocol decreed that the flagpole above Buckingham Palace remain bare. From Balmoral there was only silence.

At the eleventh hour the Royal Family eloquently showed that they acknowledged and appreciated the feelings of the ordinary people who mourned Diana.

Charles and the boys looked at floral tributes and graciously accepted condolences. Andrew and Edward appeared on the Mall. And the Queen made her speech on the night before Diana's funeral.

With a few sensitive words and gestures, anti-royal sentiment was neutralized. And when the boys took that long, slow walk to Westminster Abbey, all talk of this country ditching the Royal Family at any time over the next century was made redundant.

As someone who was in Westminster Abbey for Diana's funeral service, I had a close-up of the Royal Family's grief. I saw that they were devastated by her death. Then how could so many people come to suspect that they did not share the nation's sadness?

Because the Royal Family are part of old Britain – undemonstrative, buttoned up, reluctant to show their emotions in public – while the people who created that sea of flowers are very much a part of new Britain – emotional, passionate, willing to show their feelings. Just like Diana herself.

Old Britain and new Britain were always united by grief. What divided us so bitterly for a while was how we should express that grief.

At the funeral service it felt like old Britain and new Britain were at last trying to understand each other. They must continue to do so.

One day the two sides of our nation's character will be united when William ascends to the throne. But we should all pray that is not for thirty years or more.

Give the boy time. Give him years and years. And then

William – so much the son of both Charles and Diana, a child of both brave, dignified old Britain and passionate, caring new Britain – will be our tallest king.

In more ways than one.

Part Five
Backlash

Introduction

If you dish it out, then you also have to take it. But you don't have to take it lying down.

Above the Parapet

Arena, September 1996

Anthea Turner sent me a letter. In it she thanked me for some comments I had made about Chris Evans in a newspaper column after the albino-tinted shock jock had threatened to kick Anthea in the head, complaining that one of her light-hearted programmes was 'full of ugly people'. I had gently pointed out to Chris that, unlike *TFI Friday*, at least it wasn't presented by one. Anthea said it was the first time she had smiled in three days.

Now I happen to be an admirer of Anthea Turner. She gets called bland – and worse. Harry Eyres, the part-time TV critic of the *Spectator*, compared her to a glacé cherry and thought that made him Clive James. Actually what that made poor old Harry was an arsehole. Because anyone who can single-handedly front a live show like *The National Lottery* with an audience of 10 to 20 million without one bead of sweat ever breaking out on their upper lip is a broadcaster on a par with Des Lynam. Try it some-time, Harry. You will find the air is quite difficult to breathe up there. But Anthea's vastly underrated skills as a live broadcaster were not the reason I rushed to her defence against the ginger peril.

No, the reason I stuck up for Anthea Turner was because I could see how *The National Lottery* had raised her fair head way above the parapet of life in our time. On breakfast television she was part of the furniture. But on *The National Lottery*, she was in the firing line. With her face plastered so often over so many of our television screens, she had become far more than just another broadcaster. All of a sudden, she was discussed, disseminated and abused – especially abused – on a daily basis.

242

Some of the bile she inspired (especially from ageing female columnists) made the press look equivocal about Pol Pot. A lot of her publicity was, quite literally, hysterical and I sympathized with her because I felt that, in my own small way, I knew exactly what she was going through.

At the end of last year, I agreed to write and present a number of television programmes that were to be made in the first half of this year. There was a *Without Walls* documentary for Channel 4 about men and women called *Equal But Different*, a three-part series on the class system for BBC2 and a run of nine late-night cultural review programmes for Channel 4 called *Big Mouth*. I agreed to do a bit of telly, your honour, and suddenly the world was ready to slap me around like a red-headed stepchild.

At least that's how it felt. The programmes were shot back to back. But the broadcast dates actually overlapped – so *Equal But Different* appeared two days before the first part of *Parsons On Class*, while *Big Mouth* began two days before the last episode of *Parsons On Class*. For a while there, you couldn't miss me. For a few months I was the most overexposed man since Boy George was a size ten. Not to mention the most loathed. At least by my colleagues in the press. You get a curiously skewed view of the world when your head is that far above the parapet. No doubt there are members of the public who consider me an arrogant, pompous, ugly pencil dick. And who can blame them? But the great thing about the public is that if they don't like you, they will watch something else. Only television critics watch programmes they hate. And as my frequent broadcasts blurred into one another, beginning to resemble some ham-fisted bid for world domination, they hated mine with a vengeance.

Naturally I have no right to whine about getting called dirty names. Everybody who dishes it out should know how to take it. You can't play the acid-tongued iconoclast who makes a good living laying into all and sundry and then squeal like a stuck pig when it is your turn to take some stick. Otherwise, you turn into Chris Evans, the media's playground bully. And yet it is undeniably shocking to see just how much pure loathing you can inspire.

For every week that I dared to cavort all over the television schedules, there was a background noise of undiluted venom. If there is one thing that journalists hate then it is a journalist who appears on television. As a nation, we despise the tall poppy. And as a breed, hacks hate to see any of their number getting above himself.

Out of the avalanche of opprobrium I have inspired this year, one of my favourite criticisms came from Alix Sharkey who – wagging his finger at Miranda Sawyer, my *Big Mouth* sidekick, and myself – suggested that journalists should never appear on television. I relished his remarks because I knew that Sharkey had once put his name forward for a job on *The Word*. Did he decide that journalists shouldn't appear on the box before his job application belly-flopped? Or after?

But don't expect fairness when you lift your head above the parapet. Prepare to get stomped on. You should also expect to be vilified from dawn to dusk. And if you are going to avoid Anthea Turner's fate – unable to smile for three days, which is pretty depressed by any standards – it is important not to wallow in the ill-feeling you inspire.

It is television etiquette for press clippings of a show to be collected and sent, neatly bound, to the presenter. This means that every once in a while a fat wedge of toxic waste drops through your letterbox. Now you would have to be some kind of masochistic nut to pore over your hate mail. And yet you can never completely shut out the critics.

Time and again, I would find unfavourable mentions of myself in the press even *when they were reviewing someone else*. And you would not be human if you didn't find yourself wishing this carping chorus ill. Thus life above the parapet increases the store of hatred in the world. For example, the TV critic at *The Times* – a mutt-faced blonde, according to her little by-line picture – dismissed *Equal But Different* as 'a silly programme' and I found myself taking an interest in her career. Who exactly is Lynne Truss? I noted she later published a book about being single and living alone called *Making the Cat Laugh*. So that's Lynne Truss of *The Times*, I reflected – a woman who lives with a cat because she looks like a dog. Discussing my programme on men and women.

And who *is* this AA Gill wanker? Is that name meant to be classy? In the *Sunday Times* 'AA' dismissed *Big Mouth's* cultural agenda because we suggested that our very first musical guest – Burt Bacharach – was the coolest man on the planet. So AA wrote off a show that later had Tricky, Roy 'Chubby' Brown and Steven Berkoff all in the same studio – a line-up, I would suggest, that you could not find on any other show on British television. I didn't believe a word AA said. But I have certainly noted down his name. I see now that when you lift your head above the parapet, you eventually develop Italian Alzheimer's Disease. You forget everything except for your enemies.

There was also criticism that chose as its central theme the worldly lament – *he used to be good.* As they laid into my output this year, critics would shake their heads sadly and reminisce about the good old days of my participation on *The Late Review* and general cultural commentating. 'Now his weak one-liners prove Parsons just wants to be David Frost,' moaned the man at the *Daily Mail*. But these people never told me I was any good at the time. Where were they when I needed them? Where were they when I *was* good?

Yet you should not expect fairness when your head is above the parapet. And I actually came out of my few months in the spotlight with my faith restored in the British press. There were firm but fair, well-written profiles of me in the *Independent On Sunday*, the *Observer* and the *Guardian* – which was heartening in a medium where criticism is increasingly polarized between puff pieces generated by press officers and hatchet jobs fuelled by personal envy.

But if you want nothing but rational argument, and if you want justice, and if you want a good clean fight – then don't raise your head in the first place. And I would never ask for fair play. Let the dog-faced losers from Wapping to Northcliffe House do their worst. I would rather be on the receiving end of a thousand hatchet jobs than ever feel the need to write one. And while it might be awful to be on the receiving end of Victor Lewis-Smith, AA Gill or Lynne Truss – think how much worse it would be to actually *be* Victor, AA or Lynne. The flesh crawls.

The actual shows went well. I was proud of the work and the ratings were good – a million for *Equal But Different,* a total of 6.1 million for *Class* and around 800,000 every week for *Big Mouth* – with the bonus for Channel 4 that I come a lot cheaper than Gaby Roslin. But the value of the work was almost irrelevant: when you raise your ugly mug above the parapet, it is not the work that reaps the whirlwind of press cuttings. It is anything but the work.

As the world was going up in flames from Canary Wharf to Croatia, my affable bust-up with Melvyn Bragg on Radio Four's *Start The Week* inspired a leader in the *Daily Express* – a reflection on the decline of good manners, etc. *Parsons on Class* turned up as a cartoon in *Private Eye* (suddenly I was worthy of satire). And when Chris Evans started screaming about me being a punk has-been on Radio One (a bit rich coming from someone whose best lines are all written by Danny Baker), the *Guardian* called and read me a transcript of his rant as though I was the Foreign Secretary. But that's what it's like above the parapet, your importance is overestimated just as surely as your work is underestimated.

So what would I advise anyone considering such a venture? I would tell them that there is nothing you can't survive if you have thick skin and high ratings. And I would tell them what I told Anthea Turner: when you're breathing the air up there, you should always subscribe to Andy Warhol's dictum. Don't read your reviews. Weigh them.